7-95

G000320274

Hippocrene U.S.A. Guide to
EXPLORING FLORIDA

Hippocrene U.S.A. Guide to
EXPLORING FLORIDA

Anne Rankin

HIPPOCRENE BOOKS
New York

Copyright © 1992 by Anne Rankin
Photography © 1992 by Anne Rankin

All rights reserved.

For information, address:
HIPPOCRENE BOOKS, INC.
171 Madison Avenue
New York, NY 10016

ISBN 0-87052-029-6

Library of Congress Cataloging-in-Publication Data available

Printed in the United States of America

*In memory of my parents
Bill and Dean Rankin
who loved Florida.*

ACKNOWLEDGEMENTS

My parents first introduced me to Florida, and our explorations of it together are the source of some of my happiest family memories. A very special and affectionate thanks goes to my uncle, Mike Rankin, who has given me a Florida home in recent years and helped me understand our family's Florida connections. My cousins Tim and Judy Rankin planted the seeds of this book over ten years ago when they took me to Juniper Springs in Ocala National Forest. I thank them for introducing me to "the other Florida" and for their good friendship. My great aunt, June Rankin Brown, known to us all simply as "Aunt June" brought Florida to my Pennsylvania childhood with her Christmas oranges and summer visits. She had an important impact on my life for which I will always be appreciative.

My husband, Barry Mahoney, and our children, Katherine and Michael Mahoney, have been supportive and enthusiastic about this book, even in the face of regular "wish you could be here with me on this beautiful beach" phone conversations. All writers in their own right, their suggestions have been invaluable. I hope all three understand how much I have enjoyed our times together in Florida and their help on the book. To Barry, especially, goes a very deep appreciation for the support of the partnership we share, which underlies all my work.

CONTENTS

LIST OF MAPS

INTRODUCTION

SEARCH FOR THE OTHER FLORIDA

Floridians say that if you get sand in your shoes the first time you visit Florida, you will return. I carefully knocked sand into my shoes on my first trip and I did return — many times. But each trip left me feeling I was missing something. Something about Florida eluded me. I sensed a natural and historic drama — an untamed quality that belied its miles of neat housing developments and meticulously landscaped attractions. It came through in the violence of sudden downpours and palm-thrashing winds, in the pounding of the surf and the eerie stillness of prehistoric Indian burial mounds. The Florida I saw seemed too new, too tame.

Each time I visited Florida I wondered what was between "attractions," in the vastness of palmetto and pine scrub and along hidden waterways. What lay between Saint Augustine and Orlando, Disney World and the Everglades? Guidebooks didn't give much help. Where is the *real* Florida, I wondered. What was it like before the magic kingdoms...?

It was lunchtime on a mild November day and I was on my way from Orlando to Cape Coral. Eager to get off the highway, I took note of a state park marker along the road, stopped to pick up a sandwich at a local store, and followed the signs down a side road. In the park I found a piece of natural Florida which I shared that day with two women searching for orchids, an older couple strolling hand-in-hand, and a ranger emptying trash cans.

It wasn't an important landmark, just a small state park in central Florida. The historical event it commemorated was a minor skirmish in the long series of Seminole wars. But the place brought me closer to that other Florida that had previously eluded me. It gave me a sense of how old the area is in both natural and human time. The air smelled of pine. Rustling palmettos and occasional bird calls accentuated the stillness. A flock of robins, startled by my footsteps, noisily emerged from the underbrush, then sank back down again, out of sight.

Although I had to get to Cape Coral that afternoon, I tarried far longer than I had intended. As I walked each path, swayed across a rope bridge, and paused on a silent point where two rivers merged, I imagined Indians slipping through the undergrowth and felt the spirits of another era, of a wilderness men and women could not tame.

Reluctantly, I tossed the remnants of my lunch in the covered trash can and drove back to the main highway. I knew then what I had only sensed before. There was another Florida, in time and space. I vowed to find it.

The search took me on a longer journey than I had expected. Florida has over 100 state parks; several national forests, parks, and monuments; myriad local recreational areas; and hundreds of miles of extraordinary beaches. Its history of European conquest goes further back than anywhere else in America. Four nations tried to conquer Florida. Three failed. Florida's swamps and sharp-edged palmetto groves, its insects, alligators, and snakes, withstood onslaught after onslaught of exploration. In the past, Florida was an explorer's nightmare.

Today, Florida is an explorer's dream. It is a land of many moods with seasons of two kinds — natural and tourist. The peninsula boasts a rich variety of plants

from deciduous hardwoods in the north to lush tropi-
cals in the south. It is home to many birds and animals
found nowhere else in America. Clear springs bubble
up in its interior and dark rivers disappear in its sink
holes. The Everglades, at the southern tip, remain one
of the wildest parts of America. As I explored Florida
in different seasons, experiencing its range of moods
and climates, I came ever more under its spell.

This book is designed as a resource for others who
want to explore Florida within its larger context, who
want to go beyond the popular attractions to find out
about what lies between and what came before. The
purpose of *Exploring Florida* is to set individuals and
families on their own quest for Florida's historic, scenic, and recreational gold.

Exploring Florida is divided into four parts. Part I,
Advance Planning for Modern Explorers, gives some idea
of what to expect in different parts of Florida at different times of year, suggests what to take, how to get
around, how to locate lodgings, food, and fuel, and
what recreational facilities and creature comforts one
can expect to find at parks and other sites. A map at the
beginning of each chapter shows relevant locations
throughout the state. Part II, *Florida's Frontiers: From
Prehistoric Times to the Space Age* briefly outlines Florida's long history and for each era lists places where
visitors can learn about it at first hand.

Part III, *Florida's Wilderness: From Coast to Interior*,
describes springs, rivers, lakes, forests, wildlife and
bird refuges, and coral reefs where visitors can experience the rich natural and scenic resources of the state
in a full range of activities from primitive backcountry
canoeing or hiking to handicapped-accessible boardwalks and viewpoints. Part IV, *The Search for the Perfect
Beach*, gives a start toward one of the most delightful
of all Florida activities. It doesn't really matter if we

ever find the perfect beach, or if anyone else agrees with our choice. What matters is the search — the careful toe burrowing into the sand to find just the right consistency, the practiced eye scanning for the precise shade of blue, the perfect mix of sky and sea, the intact shell in the still wet band just where the tide turns.

Within each section, where appropriate, *Exploring Florida* is organized into the seven geographic areas used by the Florida Department of Commerce, Division of Tourism: Northwest, Northeast, Central East, Central, Central West, Southwest and Southeast. Thus it should be easy to use this book with the state's free annual *Florida Vacation Guide*, which gives a wealth of updated information on attractions, parks, and local contacts in each region. Maps at the beginning of each chapter show the location of tourist sites by geographic area.

This book does not include information on specific accommodations or restaurants, except for occasional references to places that are especially relevant to historic or natural sites. There are already many good guides to lodging and food, as well as regularly updated lists from local chambers of commerce. Any prices I quote are based on 1991 costs and should be used only as a guide. What I have tried to do here is give Florida visitors and residents some new ways of looking at and experiencing the state. First time travelers, repeat visitors, and residents can use the book to get an overview of the state's history and natural environment and to explore in depth and off the beaten track, both close to home and far afield.

Florida's beauty and mystery go deep into the interior, wind along the panhandle Gulf coast, and stretch all the way to its northernmost borders. The beauty is often quiet. The history may require imagination to put structures on sketchy foundations and people in empty buildings. But the effort brings a feeling of belonging, a sense of pride in the area's uniqueness and an awareness of its delicately balanced eco-system. The explorer who makes the journey into the other Florida will gain an appreciation and respect for a strong and beautiful land, with a heritage as rich and as long as any state in America.

FLORIDA'S SEVEN GEOGRAPHIC AREAS

PART I

ADVANCE PLANNING FOR THE MODERN EXPLORER

Today Florida is an easy place to travel. Almost anything a person could need is easily available and it is hard not to have a good time there, even if you go on the spur of the moment. You may not depend on advance planning for survival, as did the earliest European explorers, but planning ahead can enhance your Florida trip —help you squeeze every minute of pleasure out of your vacation hours and every penny out of your vacation budget. Prices and conditions in Florida fluctuate widely depending on the season. There are times when you can live better than an early Spanish nobleman for very little money and come close to feeling that you have the state all to yourself. Other times you may have to pay top-dollar for everything.

CHAPTER 1

GETTING THERE —
GETTING AROUND

The Best Time to Visit Florida

Florida is a good place to be any time of the year, which is why so many people retire there. However, different seasons offer different advantages. The "best" time for you depends on where you plan to go, what you want to do, whether you like quiet or prefer the whirl of high-season activity, and how concerned you are about keeping costs down.

Florida has two kinds of seasons — "natural" and "tourist." The natural seasons are wet and dry. The wet season, roughly from June through October, brings daily rains — sometimes torrential rains, usually in the afternoon. In late summer and fall the rains may take the form of severe tropical storms or hurricanes. Insects, especially mosquitoes, thrive during this period. The dry season, approximately from November to May, yields very little rain. Temperatures vary over the year, but the range is usually not extreme. It is warm all year round in southern Florida, with temperatures (in fahrenheit) ranging from the 70's to the 90's in the summer and the 50's to the 70's in the winter. In northern Florida temperatures range from the 70's to the 90's in the summer and from the mid-40's to mid-60's in the winter, with occasional dips to near or below freezing. Humidity tends to be high year-round, but soars during the rainy season.

The Everglades are particularly influenced by these natural cycles. The ideal time to visit them is in the winter, especially March and April just before the rainy season starts. Then the birdlife and wildlife are concentrated in the remaining wet areas and most easily seen. Then too, insects are least troublesome. However if you have a chance to see the Everglades during the wet season and don't know when you will get back, take it! They are unique and endangered. Visit them while you can!

Hurricanes and tropical storms get a lot of media attention in the late summer and fall and sometimes it seems like Florida is under constant threat of being blown away. That's really not the case. Severe storms are relatively infrequent and in these days of careful weather monitoring you will be given plenty of advance notice to get out of a threatened area.

Tourist season is summer in northern Florida and winter in southern Florida, so any time you visit you can enjoy it or avoid it, depending on your preference. It runs from mid-May through mid-September in the north and from late December through the end of April in the south. Around Orlando and Disney World there are two peaks: December through April and June through August. Tourist seasons in Florida seem to be influenced as much by weather elsewhere and by vacation and school schedules as by conditions in Florida itself. Thus travelers who can explore Florida during spring or fall often get the best of all worlds. If you can visit Florida during these months, do it! Florida's weather is at its best throughout the state and accommodations and car rental rates are at their lowest.

If you can't go then, there are still a lot of options. Florida is a big state and almost any month is low season one place and high season somewhere else. The summer traveler who wants to keep costs down can head south and have a choice of excellent, reasonably priced accommodations with amenities that may more than offset the inconvenience of summer heat. Everything is air-conditioned and most coastal areas have a good breeze. No matter where you are, you'll find that Florida summer mornings are usually lovely. You can get up and out for a full program of activities before the heat mounts and the clouds roll in. When the afternoon rains come you will be ready to settle down for some indoor, air-conditioned activities.

If you visit in the summer and want to avoid the tropical heat of southern Florida, prefer the conviviality of high season life, or simply want to enjoy the multitude of outdoor activities available in northern Florida, head toward the panhandle, the eastern beaches above Cape Canaveral, or the state forests and recreation areas of the northern interior. In winter you can choose your place as well — the tropical warmth of southern Florida during its most active time of year or the quiet of a cooler, but still moderate, off-season northern Florida. You can't go wrong in Florida, but the season and the part of Florida you choose will influence the atmosphere and cost of your trip.

Clothes and Gear

Florida is a casual place unless you plan to dine in ultra-deluxe restaurants. You won't need a lot of clothes and here, as elsewhere, the "layer principle" of packing will stand you in good stead no matter where or when you plan to explore. With the layer principle you have one outfit for the warmest possible weather and other clothes (which can be worn separately) that you can keep adding for cool weather or overly air-

conditioned spaces. Thus you can start with a sleeveless or short-sleeve shirt, then add a long-sleeve shirt,
light sweater, and a windbreaker.

Florida is humid and you'll find you want to change
clothes fairly frequently to let things dry out. You'll
probably want to have at least two pairs of shorts and
lightweight slacks, bathing suits, and sleeveless or
short-sleeve tops. Public self-service laundries are
easy to find, however, so you don't need to pack a lot
of extras. Comfortable walking shoes, as well as
sturdy sandals, are a must. For special occasions think
casual. Bring something that's fun and comfortable.

You'll also want an umbrella, good sunglasses, a
scarf or hat, insect repellent, and sunblock. A small
backpack or belt bag is handy for carrying valuables,
extra clothes, or picnics to the beach or on walks. You
may also want maps, a camera, notebook and pens,
and reading material. If you plan to picnic you may
want to include a few basics: knife, can-and bottle-
openers, corkscrew, water bottle. Car travelers may
want to carry an insulated bag with refreezable blue-
ice or an ice chest and ice to keep drinks and picnic
food cool.

Tourist Information Services

There is no lack of information on Florida. The especially helpful, annually updated *Florida Vacation Guide*
is available free from the Florida Division of Tourism
(Department of Commerce, Direct Mail, 126 West Van
Buren St., Tallahassee, FL 32399-2000; 904-487-1462).
This magazine-size booklet gives an overview of each
of the state's seven regions along with a description of
attractions, maps, information charts on state and national parks, and a list of local chambers of commerce
with addresses and phone numbers. It is designed to

help people plan their vacations and is well worth getting ahead of time.

An equally valuable tool for exploring Florida is the *Florida State Parks Guide* distributed by the Department of Natural Resources (Division of Recreation and Parks, 3900 Commonwealth Blvd., Tallahassee, FL 32399-3000). The format of this guide changed radically in 1990-91 and is now an information-packed magazine that includes descriptions of each park by region, a park locator map and index, and everything else you need to know to begin to enjoy this outstanding park system.

If you need to see a place before you can really decide where to go, you may want to get a copy of "The Perfect Place," a nine minute video that highlights Florida's many vacation alternatives. It is available from the Department of Commerce (attn: D. Burch, Room 410A, Collins Building, Tallahassee, Florida 32399-2000). Enclose a check payable to Florida Department of Commerce for $15.00 for VHS; $25 for 3/4 inch. You may also want to write for information from the Florida Attractions Association (P.O. Box 10295, Tallahassee, FL 32302; 904-222-2885). Visitors eager to explore the state's rich historical tradition can contact the Department of State, Bureau of Historic Preservation (R. A. Gray Bldg., 500 South Bronough St., Tallahassee, FL 32399-0250; 904-487-2333).

You can get information about specific communities by writing to the local chambers of commerce listed in the *Florida Vacation Guide*. Local tourist development councils often have information as well. Ask for the TDC Listing from the Florida Department of Commerce (Visitor Inquiry, 126 Van Buren St., Tallahassee, FL 32399-2000; 904-487-1462). When you are traveling in Florida be sure to stop in local Visitor Information Centers. They have racks of free leaflets on local attractions, state parks, accommodations, and restaurants, as well as helpful people who will be happy to answer your questions. One of the things you will notice early in your travels around Florida is that Floridians just love to talk about their state.

One of the best investments you can make if you plan to do much traveling off the major highways is the *Florida Atlas & Gazetteer*, available for $12.95 from bookstores throughout Florida or from Delorme Mapping Company (P.O. Box 298, Freeport, Maine 04032; 207-865-4171). This atlas shows all the roads in Florida in 100 large and detailed maps, along with a gazetteer listing parks, campgrounds, fishing spots, golf courses etc. The book is a rather awkward size, but the information it gives is worth the inconvenience of lugging it around. Not only is it invaluable when you find yourself on roads that don't show on a regular state map, but it is a wonderful resource for learning about the lay of the land in different parts of Florida.

Florida continues to improve its access to physically challenged visitors and now most state parks, beaches, and other public facilities have good accessibility. The state publishes a special guide, the *Physically Challenged Guide to Florida*, available from the Department of Commerce (Division of Tourism, 126 West Van Buren Street, Tallahassee, FL 32399-2000; 904-487-1462). It provides a listing of city and county contacts from which you may obtain the most up-to-date information on access.

Routes to the Sunshine State

The early European explorers had only one way to get to the Florida peninsula — by ship. Today, of course, the choice is much wider. Most people cross the state's borders in autos or drop down from the sky.

Others enter the state on trains and buses. Only a few of the state's millions of visitors still come by boat.

It is easy to get to Florida by air. Orlando and Miami are major air hubs; three other cities — Fort Lauderdale, Tampa, and West Palm Beach — have frequent service to most major American cities and some foreign countries. About a dozen more cities have several flights daily. Although you can get to almost any major city in Florida by air, it's important to keep in mind that the cost of flights between Florida cities can be more expensive than renting a car and driving, especially if you have several people in your party.

Air fares vary by season. Airlines flying out of Orlando, especially, often have tour packages that may include a free rental car or discounts on lodging. If you have any flexibility in arrival and return dates you may be able to take advantage of reduced fares. Your travel agent can help you, or you can call the airlines using the following toll-free numbers:

American Airlines — 1-800-433-7300
Continental Airlines — 1-800-525-0280
Delta Airlines — 1-800-221-1212
Midway Airlines, Inc. — 1-800-866-9000
Northwest Airlines — 1-800-225-2525
Pan American World Airways — 1-800-221-1111
Trans World Airlines, Inc. — 1-800-221-2000
United Airlines — 1-800-241-6522
USAir — 1-800-428-4322

Travelers who come to Florida by car have their transportation problem within Florida solved. Those who arrive in recreational vehicles have their accommodation problems eased as well. The motor route into the sunshine state has a lot to recommend it if you have the time to drive. If you do cross the border by car, be sure to stop and take an orange juice break at one of the state's Welcome Centers.

If you want your car in Florida but don't relish the long drive, inquire about the Amtrak's Florida Auto Train, which carries passengers and their cars from Lorton, Virginia (just south of Washington, D.C.) to Sanford, Florida. The train departs from each end daily at 4:30 p.m. and arrives at 9 a.m. the next morning. One way rates for a car are around $200. Adults ride for around $140; children age 2-11 go for half price. There are substantially lower rates during certain periods. Tickets include meals and a wide reclining seat. First-class passengers enjoy full-service dining in special two-level dome cars. Bedrooms or roomettes are available for an extra charge. For reservations and information contact Amtrak toll-free 1-800-872-7245.

If you want to go to Florida by train without your car, you can do that too. There is one route along the northeast corridor of the United States from New York to Miami and Tampa/St. Petersburg and another from the Midwest through Philadelphia or Washington D.C. Fares vary by season. Call Amtrak, 1-800-872-7245 for information. Jacksonville is a busy hub for both interstate and intrastate service by Amtrak (3570 Clifford Lane, Jacksonville, FL 32209 ; 904-768-1553).

If you are an overseas visitor and expect to visit other states in addition to Florida, you may want to get a National USA Rail Pass which provides 45 days of unlimited travel and unlimited stopovers anywhere in the U.S. for $299; or an Eastern Region Rail Pass which provides 45 days of unlimited travel on the east coast (including Florida) for $179. You can get the pass either from a travel agent overseas or at Amtrak Stations in major cities in the U.S. Before you purchase the pass you may want to compare its cost with Amtrak's regular fares. For information contact Amtrak Distribution Center (P.O. Box 770, 1549 W. Glen Lake Ave., Itasca, IL 60143) or call the toll-free number given above. If you plan to rely on trains for all your travel into and around Florida, study the map and timetables carefully to make sure the places you plan to visit have adequate train service. American trains do not provide the frequency and wide geographical coverage that European trains do. You can get an Amtrak timetable from 400 N. Capitol St. NW, Washington, D.C. 20001.

If you prefer to travel by bus, Greyhound/Trailways is the company. It has buses between most major American cities, and the Ameripass provides an inexpensive way to travel. The pass allows a rider to go anywhere for a flat fee of about $200 for 7 days, $261 for 15 days, and $380 for 30 days with extensions available for $10.60 a day. Children aged 5-11 pay half fare; one child of 4 or under can travel for 10% of the adult fare. A new moneysaver fare with a 30-day advance purchase enables travelers to travel between any two cities in the U.S. for $68 one way or $136 round trip. You can get information about fares and bus schedules from local bus stations.

Tour and charter companies run express buses to Florida also. Astro Tours (2923 Northwest 7th Street, Miami 33125; 305-643-6423) offers bus shuttles between New York and Miami leaving from each city at 10:00 a.m. daily in the winter, alternate days the rest of the year. Buses also stop at Hialeah and Miami Beach. Fares are $65.00 one way; $124 round trip. The trip takes 26 hours. Keep in mind that even express buses take time. The journey is about 72 hours from Los Angeles to Miami, 36 hours from Chicago, 28 hours from New York, and 24 hours from Washington. Buses are an inexpensive way to travel, but one has to weigh price against time and exhaustion.

Ways of Exploring Florida

Once you are in Florida, there are lots of options for exploration. Travel by auto is the most popular. Roads are good, car rentals are cheap, and many places aren't easily accessible by other means. But the traveler who habitually reaches for the car keys closes out some special experiences. There are many ways to explore Florida, each providing its own special perspective. Planes, trains, and buses criss-cross the state. Bicycle, boat, canoe, horseback, and hiking trails take travelers off the beaten track and into the state's most beautiful and pristine natural areas.

The Florida Recreational Trails Act of 1979 authorized the establishment of a network of recreational, scenic, and historic trails that provide a whole range of possibilities for people who like to spend time outdoors. Eventually this system will link state parks and forests with local and national parks and forests. It isn't all in place yet, but the network grows yearly.

Car

The quality-of-life costs for the popularity of the auto are very high in Florida and as you fight the traffic, especially in the south, you may wonder how Floridians ever allowed the auto to gain such supremacy. However, whether we like it or not, public transportation in most cities and between smaller communities in Florida is inadequate. If you want to explore off the beaten track and visit the places described in this book, you'll find it much easier to have a car.

Renting a car is possible almost anywhere if you have a major credit card and are over 21 years of age.

Often the best rates are at airports where the rental offices are either inside near the baggage claim area, or nearby and accessible via mini-vans that shuttle back and forth between office and airport. The toll-free numbers for reservations with the major companies are:

Airways — 1-800-952-9200
Alamo — 1-800-327-9633
American International — 1-800-527-0202
Avis — 1-800-331-1212
Budget — 1-800-527-0700
Dollar — 1-800-800-4000
Enterprise — 1-800-325-8007
Exchange — 1-800-777-2836
General — 1-800-327-7607
Hertz — 1-800-654-3131
Lindo's — 1-800-237-8396
National — 1-800-227-7368
Payless — 1-800-729-5377
Sears — 1-800-527-0770
Superior — 1-800-237-8106
Thrifty — 1-800-367-2277
USA — 1-800-592-7100
Value — 1-800-327-2501

Although sometimes you decide to rent a car on the spur of the moment and have to take what is available, the best way to get the lowest rate and avoid a nasty and expensive surprise at car return time is to do some advance planning. Decide ahead of time what size car you need — rates are lowest for subcompact cars and increase with the size of the car. Keep in mind that as car size goes up, gas costs usually go up as well. Second, decide how long you will need the car. Weekly rates (usually for 5-7 days) often give a cheaper per-day cost than daily rates. Thus the total cost of a five-day rental on the weekly rate actually may be less than a four-day rental on the daily rate. (Beware, however, if you keep the car for more than 7 days; you may be charged the daily rate for the extra days.)

Finally, estimate the total number of miles you expect to drive and divide by the number of days you will rent the car to get the average number of miles per day. Rates are quoted either for unlimited free miles (which means you pay a flat rate for the rental period whether you drive 50 miles or 2000) or for a specified number of free miles, after which rental is charged at a per-mile rate, such as 42 cents a mile. If you plan to do much more than let the car sit in the parking lot you are probably better off with the unlimited mileage rate. Distances in Florida are long and the daily cost of a car rental that ticks up at 42 cents a mile can rise rapidly, resulting in a hefty bill at car-return time.

It is also important to decide beforehand just who will be driving the car. Most companies now refuse to rent to drivers under 21 years old and add a surcharge of from $5 to $10 a day for drivers under 25. Also, if more than one person will be driving, there may be an extra charge. Some companies allow a spouse to drive at no additional cost; some have a one-time fee of $5 or $10; others add as much as $3 a day for each extra driver. These less-obvious expenses may offset what at first looks like a lower rental price. Think also about who will be riding in the car. Florida state law requires that children aged 3 or under must be secured in a separate, federally-approved child-restraint seat. All companies rent these for $2 or $3 a day. If you will need one, be sure to factor in that cost too and reserve the seat when you reserve the car.

Quoted rates do not include local taxes, Florida's road-use tax of $2.00 a day, or airport fees (usually a

one-time fee of about $3.00 if you rent at an airport).
Be sure to add these in when you are planning your
transportation budget.

Insurance coverage for damage to the car, sometimes called "loss/damage waiver" usually runs an
additional $9 to $13 a day and can substantially increase the cost. Although the coverage is optional,
rental companies make a lot of their money on it and
sometimes exert pressure on renters to take it. Find out
ahead of time whether your own car insurance (or
your credit card) covers rental cars. If either one does,
you may decide to decline the waiver. However anyone who is unsure about their coverage or does not
have auto collision insurance that covers rental cars in
the U.S. should take the collision/damage waiver. It is
expensive, but well worth the cost if anything hap-
pens.

You might want to consider picking your car up at
one city and returning it to another. Thus you might
fly into Miami, rent a car, travel through Florida, and
then fly out of Orlando or Panama City. That way you
can see far-flung parts of Florida with less driving.
Airlines sometimes permit arrival and departure from
different Florida cities for just a few dollars more, or
even the same price as a roundtrip ticket to one city.
And some car rental companies allow pick-up and
drop-off at any of their major airport offices in Florida
at no extra charge.

You can save money by calling to reserve a car well
in advance of your trip. Rates are often cheaper 30, 14,
or 7 days before the pick-up date. A few toll-free calls
will usually give you an idea of the going rate for the
dates and locations you want, and will often uncover
one or two companies with prices significantly lower
than the others. (Even if you rent at the last minute, it's
worth checking around; rates can vary substantially.)

Rental rates change from month to month and location to location so don't assume that the company that had the best deal on your last trip will necessarily yield the best bargain on this one.

Be forewarned that rental is difficult without a major credit card. At the time of rental, you will need to show at least one, as well as a valid driver's license for every driver. If you don't have a credit card, you may still be able to rent by filling out a cash qualification form ahead of time showing verified employment and then leaving a substantial cash deposit (often $300 or the rental cost plus 50%). Holders of a Sears charge card can use it to rent from Sears Rent A Car.

Once you have found a rate you can live with, reserve the car — rates can change faster than the time it takes to hang up the phone and place a second call. The agent will give you a confirmation number and when you arrive in Florida, a car of the size and cost you reserved should be waiting for you. At the time of rental, the agent may encourage you to "upgrade" but if you've made a considered judgement about what you want, stick to it. The company has to give you a free upgrade if it doesn't have the size you reserved.

Once you get your car — buckle up! Seat belt use is required in Florida. Two other rules to remember on the road — you can turn right on a red light, and you are required to turn on your headlights when it rains.

There are a few things to keep in mind as you plan your driving. Florida is *big*. It is 500 miles from the tip of the state to its northern border, and 400 miles from Jacksonville to Pensacola. Roads are good all over Florida, mostly flat and straight. However don't expect to sail along at high speeds. The maximum speed limit is 55 miles per hour, except on the interstates and the turnpike where it is 65 m.p.h. Traffic around major cities, especially in the south during the winter, can be

fierce. It is particularly bad near Disney World 8-9 a.m.
and 4-6 p.m. so if you are driving to the Orlando
airport around then, be sure to allow extra time. If you
spend much time off the major highways, remember
that, even without snow, it is possible to get stuck in
Florida. Sand can mire a car faster than you can shift
from forward to reverse and back again. In some
places, Florida seems like one big sand dune. Beware
of narrow back roads and beaches — even those that
allow cars. Parking can be hazardous too — keep two
wheels on the road if you pull off in a sandy area. Clay
roads have their own set of problems. They can be
slick as ice in wet weather.

Air

You can travel by air between most major Florida
cities. This is not the cheapest way to go, and certainly
doesn't give you a close-up view of the state, but it is
a quick way to get from one city to another. If you want
to get a birds-eye overview of the state, there are many
small charter companies that offer scenic flights. For
example, you can visit Fort Jefferson in the Dry Tortugas west of Key West by chartering a seaplane from
Key West Seaplane Service (5603 West Junior College
Rd., Key West: 305-294-6978, FAX 305-294-9521). Cost
is around $119 per person for a half day or $195 for a
full day. Flying time is approximately 40 minutes each
way. The flight to the island is at low altitude to allow
bird and fish spotting and the return trip is usually
higher to give a panoramic view of the area.

Train and Bus

You can travel by train with Amtrak to 22 cities in
the state. Foreign visitors can get a Florida Region Rail
Pass for $69 that provides unlimited travel with unlim-

ited stopovers within Florida. You will need to present a valid passport issued outside the U.S. or Canada. Call Amtrak 800-872-7245 for information.

Buses run with fair frequency between the larger cities and offer a reasonable and comparatively easy way to get around. Check with Greyhound/Trailways in Orlando (214-655-7000) or local bus stations. There are also bus tours to many of the state's main attractions. Information on these is available in hotel and motel lobbies or from local visitor centers.

Bicycle

Bicycles are becoming an increasingly popular way to explore Florida because of the excellent year around weather, flat terrain, and scenic vistas. In Florida the bicycle is legally defined as a vehicle with the same rights to the roadways and obligations to obey traffic laws as other vehicles. Especially pleasant cycling areas are found in the central and northern portions of the state, Captiva and Sanibel islands near Fort Myers, and in Shark Valley in Everglades National Park. If you plan to do much traveling by bicycle in Florida contact the State Bicycle Program (Florida Department of Transportation, 605 Suwanee St., M.S. 19, Tallahassee, FL 32301-8064; 904-488-4640). It has excellent information on trails and special conditions in all parts of Florida, local cycling clubs and events, and bicycle laws. Contact the Suwannee Bicycle Touring Company for information about bicycle route maps. Maps of several bicycle trails (e.g. Sugar Beaches, Canopy Roads, Crystal Springs, the Healing Waters Trail, Lakes-N-Hills, Withlacoochee Meander, and Land O-Lakes) are available for $1.00 each plus 6% tax from Florida Department of Transportation (Map & Publication Sales, Mail Station 12, 605 Suwannee St., Tallahassee, FL 32399-8064).

Boat

Water is everywhere in Florida and the Intracoastal Waterway runs all the way down the east coast. From this and other waterways, you can see a surprising amount of Florida. There are public marinas and boat ramps throughout the state and many motels provide overnight docking facilities for waterborne guests. Boating regulations and safety information may be obtained by contacting the Department of Natural Resources (Florida Marine Patrol, Boating Safety Program, 3900 Commonwealth Blvd., Tallahassee 32399; 904-487-3671). Regional chart packets for boaters may be obtained from the Florida Division of Tourism (126 West Van Buren St., Tallahassee 32301; 904-487-1462).

Every recreational vessel must carry, for each person on board, at least one United States Coast Guard-approved Personal Flotation Device (PFD). All vessels using Florida waters must be registered in Florida unless they are registered elsewhere and are only temporarily in Florida. Operating a vessel while under the influence of alcohol or drugs is a criminal offense in Florida with mandatory penalties. An "implied consent" law for boat operators gives law enforcement officials the right to chemically test breath, blood, or urine.

Some of the most beautiful places in Florida are accessible only by boat. However, don't despair if you can't bring your own. There are power and sail boat rental marinas throughout Florida and innumerable charter services as well. Check area visitor information centers, local marinas, or the telephone book yellow pages for details. Club Nautico, for example, rents boats all over Florida. Call 1-800-NAUTICO for information.

Canoe

Florida has hundreds of miles of scenic waterways suitable for canoeing. There are 36 state canoe trails, totaling over 950 miles, as well as trails in national parks, forests, and wildlife preserves. For copies of *Florida Recreational Trails System: Canoe Trails, Canoe Information Resources Guide,* and *Canoe Liveries and Outfitters Directory* write to the Florida Department of Natural Resources (Division of Recreation and Parks, Marjory Stoneman Douglas Building, 3900 Commonwealth Blvd., Tallahassee, FL 32399-3000; 904-487-4784). The Florida Association of Canoe Liveries and Outfitters (P.O. Box 1764, Arcadia, FL 33821) can also provide a list of private companies that organize canoe trips.

Other sources of information are: *Canoeing the National Forests in Florida* (USDA-Forest Service, National Forests in Florida, 227 North Bronough St., Suite 4061, Tallahassee, FL 32301; 904-681-7165), Everglades National Park (P.O. Box 279, Homestead, FL 33030: 305-247-6211), and Big Cypress National Preserve (Star Route, Box 110, Ochopee, FL 33943; 813-695-2000 or 813-262-1066).

Canoes offer an ideal way to traverse the national wildlife reserves. Contact Arthur R. Marshall Loxahatchee National Wildlife Refuge (Route 1, Box 278, Boynton Beach, FL 33437; 407-732-3684); J.N. "Ding" Darling National Wildlife Refuge (1 Wildlife Drive, Sanibel, FL 33957; 813-472-1100); and United States Fish and Wildlife Service (Region IV, Office of Public Use, Room 1240, 75 Spring St., Southwest, Atlanta, GA 30303; 404-331-0839).

There are numerous local canoe clubs in Florida as well as a state organization. Contact Florida Canoeing and Kayaking Association (Butch Horn, President, P.O. Box 837, Tallahassee, FL 32302; 904-422-1566). Two guidebooks on Florida's canoe trails are *Canoeing and Kayaking Guides to the Streams of Florida*. Vol I by Elizabeth F. Carter and John L. Pearce covers the north central peninsula and panhandle ($12.95) and Vol. II by Lou Glaros and Doug Sphar covers the central and south Peninsula ($10.95). Both describe each stream in detail and include maps, information on weather, water conditions, and local plants and animals. They are available from Menasha Ridge Press (P.O. Box 59257, Birmingham, AL 35259-9257; 1-800-247-9437; 205-991-0373; 919-732-9269).

Horseback

Horse trails have been developed in five of the state parks. These are: Jonathan Dickinson State Park (16450 S.E. Federal Highway, Hobe Sound, FL 33455; 305-546-2771); Myakka River State Park (13207 SR 72, Sarasota, FL 34241-9542; 813-924-1027); O'Leno State Park (Route 2, Box 307, High Springs, FL 32643; 904-454-1853); Paynes Prairie State Preserve (Route 2, Box 41, Micanopy, FL 32667; 904-466-3397); and Wekiwa Springs State Park (1800 Wekiwa Circle, Apopka, FL 32703; 305-889-3140). You can rent horses near Myakka from Myakka Valley Campground and Stables, Inc. (7220 Myakka Valley Trail; 813-924-8435). The campground also has tent sites and showers.

Withlacoochee State Forest has two horse trails — a one-day trail (14 miles), and a two-day trail (24 miles) with a primitive overnight camping area. The area includes a campground and a horse stable that will accommodate 20 horses. For information and reservations contact Withlacoochee Forestry Center (15019 Broad St., Brooksville, FL 33512; 904-796-5650). The Coldwater Recreation Area (Blackwater Forestry Center, Route 1, Box 77, Milton, FL 32570; 904-957-4201, 7 a.m. to 4 p.m. Central Time) located within the Blackwater River State Forest in the panhandle has 65 campsites and stables for 72 horses.

Near Kissimmee, Poinciana Horse World (3705 Poinciana Blvd., Kissimmee 407-847-4343) rents horses and arranges overnight trail ride campouts. If you like to ride on the beach, Sea Horse Stable (7500 1st Highway, Amelia Island, FL 32034; 904-261-4878) provides horses and guides. The cost is $25 for an hour and 15 minutes, by reservation only.

Foot

How would you like to explore the entire length of Florida by foot? When the Florida Trail is completed you will be able to walk from Big Cypress National Preserve in the south all the way to Blackwater State Forest in the north. Meanwhile you can traverse Florida on the completed sections that already total over 1,100 miles with enough continuous lengths of trail to provide either short walks or extended hiking trips with many overnight camping opportunities.

The Florida Trail is dirt-surfaced and is best hiked during the dry season (winter and spring). It passes through three major Floridian habitat regions, with mostly flat terrain and some rolling landscapes. Special permits or land owner permission is required for some sections. For more information write: The Florida Trail Association (P.O. Box 13708, Gainesville, FL 32604; 904-378-8823). The association publishes a regular newsletter, "Footprint," and has active chapters throughout the state which organize year-round programs of outdoor activities ranging from learning experiences and leisurely day outings to extended backpacking and canoeing trips.

There are many other opportunities for walking, as well. For additional routes look at *A Hiking Guide to the Trails of Florida* by Elizabeth F. Carter ($8.95; Menasha Ridge Press, P.O. Box 59257, Birmingham, AL 35259-9257; 1-800-247-9437; 205-991-0373; 919-732-9269). It is a highly readable sourcebook, complete with maps, data summaries, and photos. Most of the state and national parks and forests maintain walking and hiking trails that range from handicapped-accessible to strenuous, and from half mile round-trip nature trails to several-day excursions. Beaches also offer scenic opportunities for hiking, especially along the northeastern coast where there are miles of continuous, hard-packed sand. The finest hiking in the state is probably in central Florida with its generous sprinkling of lakes and springs and its large tracts of national forest.

If you prefer to take your walks in a more urban setting, there are innumerable walking tours in towns and cities throughout Florida. Check with the local Visitor Information Center to see if they have self-guided or docent-led walking tours of historic areas or special attractions.

CHAPTER 2

WHERE TO STAY —
WHAT TO DO

Home Base: Places to Stay

The Importance of Advance Reservations

Florida has been a tourist state for years and has a large number of accommodations. In fact, in some places it seems like there is nothing in sight but motels and condominiums. This doesn't mean, however, that one should expect to walk into a resort area during high season and find a place to stay. Every one of those hundreds of thousands of beds may be occupied. When you go to Florida in peak seasons (December to May in central and southern Florida and May to September in northern Florida) you want to have a bed with your name on it. Pumping quarters into a pay phone looking for a motel is no way to spend a vacation.

I speak about the value of advance reservations from the perspective of one who for many years refused to have my freedom of action limited by them. I've come around (at least partially) after spending frustrating hours of more than one vacation trudging from place to place looking for somewhere to stay — and finally ending up with the most ordinary (or dreary) of rooms at much more than I had budgeted. Not only do more people travel now than twenty years ago, they are more likely to make reservations ahead of time. In peak season in Florida the choice of last minute accommodations is slim. That's a fact of life.

Even during off-season, when advance reservations may not be as necessary, they can be a plus. Sometimes a little planning can guarantee you the best room in a beachfront motel for a very reasonable cost — a room that may not be available if you turn up on the door-step at three o'clock. And there is a certain warm home-coming feeling as you drive into a community knowing that a special room is waiting for you. Advance reservations are easy to make. Long distance phone calls are inexpensive, toll-free numbers are increasingly common, and more and more hotels are listing FAX numbers on their brochures.

Traveling Without Reservations: Minimizing the Down Side

I admit that I still travel without reservations part of the time, especially off season or during the week. It gives me the chance to try out a special-looking motel or inn that I happen to see. That's part of the fun of exploring Florida, at least for me, and I'm willing to take the occasional risk of a frustrating search and an unsatisfactory night's lodging. There are some ways to minimize that risk.

Always travel with a good accommodations guide or the 800-numbers of major motel chains, and a map. If you get stuck you can always find a phone booth and start making phone calls. Be prepared to give the motel you finally select a credit card number to guarantee the room if you will be arriving after 6:00 p.m. Otherwise get there fast. A good time to look for rooms in a crowded area, by the way, is between 4 and 6 p.m. That is when unclaimed reservations are canceled out.

Plan to arrive early at your destination so you can look around at what's available and make some preliminary inquiries. Early arrival also gives you the chance to stop in at the local visitor's center to pick up a listing of accommodations and perhaps some help in finding a place. If you see that there are plenty of rooms free, you can relax and look for something especially pleasant. On the other hand, if rooms are already scarce, you know to grab one when you find it, even if it isn't ideal, or to move on to a place that's less crowded while you still have time. Make inquiries about future openings in an area or place you really like. There may be space in the near future that you can reserve now and come back to.

You may want to reserve in advance just for the first night or two of your trip, especially if you plan to arrive in the evening. Then during the first day you can check out prices and availability of rooms. If things look really tight, you can move on or nail down any room you find. You may even be able to extend your stay in your initial hotel.

A Range of Choices

The most common accommodations in Florida are chain motels, small privately owned motels, and apartment hotels or condominiums. There are also a growing number of private houses for rent by the week or month, and some small or historic inns or bed and breakfast homes. House exchanges between individuals are also becoming an increasingly popular way of solving the accommodation problem. Some visitors settle down on the water in houseboats. And still others bring their accommodations with them and camp in tents, or recreational vehicles (RVs).

Florida puts out an annual guide to accommodations in the state. Write to the Florida Hotel & Motel Association (P.O. Box 1529, Tallahassee, FL 32302; 904-224-2888) or pick up a copy at any of the Florida welcome stations. Several popular guidebooks to Florida also have lists of accommodations. *Frommer's* has retained its reputation for unearthing interesting and reasonably priced places to stay for a generation. *Fodor's Florida* recommends inexpensive to expensive accommodations throughout the state. *Hidden Florida* (Ulysses Press, Sather Gate Station, Box 4000-H, Berkeley, CA 94704) includes accommodations in some of the smaller towns as well as in the larger cities. Some areas have a centralized reservation service through which tourists can book motels. For example, visitors can call for reservations in the popular Kissimmee-St. Cloud area in central Florida near Disney World (1-800-333-KISS).

The *AAA TourBook to Florida*, published by the American Automobile Association, is strictly mainstream, but it is a reliable source of clean, comfortable, reasonably priced places to stay. This annually updated guide is keyed to the AAA state map which prints in red the names of towns that have AAA-approved accommodations. Both are available in AAA offices; free to members, $8.95 to nonmembers. The guide lists approved accommodations by town with address, phone number, and prices for different seasons, and facilities. By leafing through you can get an idea about the general price ranges in different communities and the seasonal variation in rates.

Chain Hotels and Motels. The chains are everywhere in Florida. They all have toll-free numbers (listed below) and by calling you can quickly learn the availability and prices of rooms in any location in Florida. However, be careful! In areas like Orlando where a chain may have six or seven different motels in separate locations, it is important to specify which motel you want and to make sure you get the exact address and name of the one in which you have your reservation. Chain motels and hotels range in price and atmosphere from low budget to deluxe with everything in between. They may not be very interesting, but they generally ensure a fairly consistent level of good lodging.

Motel Chain Toll-Free Numbers
Best Western — 1-800-528-1234
Comfort Inn — 1-800-228-5150
Days Inn — 1-800-325-2525
Econo Lodge — 1-800-446-6900
Embassy Suites Hotels — 1-800-EMBASSY
Hilton Hotels — 1-800-HILTONS
Holiday Inns — 1-800-465-4329
Howard Johnson — 1-800-FLORIDA
Hyatt Hotels — 1-800-233-1234
La Quinta Inns — 1-800-531-5900
Marriott Hotels & Resorts — 1-800-228-9290
Quality/Rodeway Inns — 1-800-251-1962
Radisson Hotel — 1-800-333-3333
Ramada Hotel — 1-800-228-2828
Red Carpet Inns/Scottish Inns — 1-800-251-1962
Red Lion Hotels & Inns — 1-800-547-8010
Sheraton — 1-800-325-3535
Stouffer Hotels and Resorts — 1-800-HOTELS-1
TraveLodge — 1-800-255-3050
Westin Hotels — 1-800-228-3000
Wyndham Hotel — 1-800-822-4200

Location is all important in determining Florida hotel prices. The closer you are to the beach or to Disney World, the higher the price. If you are trying to keep costs low you may want to bed down a couple blocks in from the shoreline or a few miles from Mickey Mouse. Most resort areas in Florida have numerous public beach access points so you don't have to stay on the beach to spend the day there.

Privately Owned Small Hotels. Although chain motels may dominate the scene in major tourist areas and along the interstate highways, there are still many privately owned "Mom-and-Pop" motels in smaller communities and in older beach areas. These may be less glitzy than the big resorts; sometimes they look downright weather-worn. The "delightful small motel with flower-filled windows" described in a guidebook sometimes turns out to be a set of run-down cinderblock cabins with dead geraniums and cold water. But the discovery of special places that give one a sense of the history and mystery of Florida can yield great rewards, worth the occasional disappointment.

The best of the small motels are scrupulously clean and well maintained and often have some little touches that give them personality — colorful tiles in the bathroom, paintings by a local artist, carefully tended flowers, unusual landscaping around the pool. I remember one June morning in such a motel in the Florida Keys when I joined three or four other guests on the dock to feed the baby manatee who came each morning for her breakfast of lettuce. With its beat-up peddle boats, talking parrots in cages, and slow moving harmony with water and wildlife, the place gave me a better sense of what life had been like on the Florida Keys for the last 40 years than anything else on my trip.

Many of these small motels have a cadre of regular visitors who return periodically to stay for days or months and they usually get most of their guests by word-of-mouth. If you are planning to visit an area, it's worth asking friends with travel styles similar to yours if they have any special motels to recommend.

Apartments, Condominiums, and Houses. Imagine a beach house on stilts on one of the most beautiful stretches of shoreline in the world, or a luxury condo facing the ocean. It's possible and not financially prohibitive if you choose your place and time. Although business is brisk in season, a surprising number of rental apartments, condominiums, and houses sit empty many weeks during the year. They offer an ideal lodging solution for travelers who want space, cooking facilities, or rental by the week or month, and are willing to forego daily maid service. There is usually a minimum stay requirement of a week or more in season, but sometimes houses and condos can be rented for shorter periods off-season. Like the small motels, these can sometimes be hard to track down, but may be well worth the search.

Local chambers of commerce and visitor centers can usually send you lists of rental agents for such accommodations in their areas. Some are also included in hotel and accommodations guides. Many now have toll-free numbers. A good way to collect information about attractive apartments, condominiums, and houses is to look out for interesting places whenever you are visiting an area to which you expect to return. Stop in for price lists, information, and phone numbers to stow away for your next trip.

Small Inns and Bed and Breakfast Homes. Inns and B & Bs can offer distinctive accommodations. If you prefer staying in a place that has its own personality and expresses some part of Florida and its residents, you may want to seek them out.

"Bed-and-breakfast homes" and "bed-and-breakfast inns" are often confused. The "home" is a private home or apartment occupied by a family that occasionally rents out a spare room or two to overnight visitors. The "inn" is a small hotel, a business by which the proprietors earn their living. Inns can often be more expensive than a hotel, whereas a B & B home is supposed to charge 50% less than prevailing hotel rates in its area.

A good starting place for locating private inns is the *Guide to the Small and Historic Lodgings of Florida* by Herbert L. Hiller, published by Pineapple Press (P.O. Drawer 16008, Sarasota, FL 34239). This guide gives a page or two of description along with prices and phone numbers for over a hundred historic accommodations in the state. The Association of Smaller and Historic Lodging Properties of Florida (9601 East Bay Harbor Drive, Bay Harbor Island, Florida 33154; 305-868-4226) also distributes information on small inns in the state. Small lodgings often have a two or three night minimum, or add a surcharge for one night stays.

There are several bed-and-breakfast services in Florida through which you can get information about, and make reservations in B & B homes. Tallahassee Bed & Breakfast, Inc. (3023 Windy Hill Lane, Tallahassee, FL 32308; 904-385-3768) has accommodations around the capital. Bed & Breakfast of Volusia County (P.O. Box 573, De Leon Springs, FL 32130; 904-985-5068) has host homes in DeLand and surrounding areas. A & A Bed & Breakfast of Florida, Inc. (Brunhilde G. Fehner, General Manager, P.O. Box 1316, Winter Park, FL 32790; 407-628-3233, open 9 a.m. to 6 p.m.) has been providing accommodation services to visitors in the Orlando area since 1981. Double room prices range from budget to deluxe.

B & B Suncoast Accommodations of Florida (8690 Gulf Blvd., St. Petersburg Beach, FL 33706; 813-360-1753) specializes in beach towns along the west coast, but also lists a few homes in other parts of Florida. Palm Beach Reservation Service (Peggy Maxwell, Box 3025, Palm Beach, FL 33480; 407-842-5190) lists homes on the east coast as far north as Jupiter. Bed & Breakfast Co. Tropical Florida (P. O. Box 430262, Miami, Fl 33243-0262; 305-661-3270) lists accommodations all over Florida, some of them quite elegant. Bed & Breakfast of the Florida Keys, Inc. (P.O. Box 1373, Marathon, FL 33050; 305-743-4118) features a small number of homes throughout the keys, all air-conditioned and on the water.

One way to locate B & B reservation services, inns, or homes is to check the yellow pages of the phone book under "Bed and Breakfast Accommodations." Also, several national B & B directories include Florida inns and homes. Look at the *Official Bed and Breakfast Guide for the U.S. and Canada* by Phyllis Featheston and Barbara Ostler, available from the National Bed & Breakfast Association (148 E. Rocks Rd., P.O. Box 332, Norwalk, CT 06852). Others are *The Annual Directory of American Bed & Breakfasts* edited by Toni Sorter (Routledge Hill Press, Inc. 513 Third Ave S., Nashville, TN 37210); *Bed and Breakfast, USA* by Betty Rundback and Nancy Ackeman; *Bed and Breakfast, North America* by Norma Buzan; *Bed and Breakfast Directory* by Gail Parker; *The Complete Guide to Bed & Breakfasts, Inns, & Guesthouses in the U.S. and Canada* (Pamela Lanier, P.O. Box 20467 Oakland, CA 94620-0467); *Travel Discoveries* by Bob & Ellen Christopher; and *Hostlist* by the American B & B Association.

Home Exchange. Home exchange is one of the most exciting developments in the travel field. The logic is simple. People *here* would like to visit *there*. And people *there* would like to visit *here*. But often they can't do so because they can't afford lodging and because they don't know about each other. The object of the exchange listings is simply to provide a way for these people to get in touch with each other and discuss the possibility of swapping homes. The idea is catching on, expanding travel opportunities for people all over the world. It provides one of the nicest ways yet devised to visit places and meet people. All you need is a willingness to let someone else use your home and a listing with one of the several home exchange programs.

Two major exchange services have been in business for several years. Intervac US/International Home Exchange (Lori Horne & Paula Jaffe, P.O. Box 590504, San Francisco, CA 94119 415-435-3497; FAX 415-386-6853) has over 8000 listings around the world, of which the U.S. listings comprise less than 20%. Their fee for listing and three issues of their publication (February, April, and June) is $45.00 plus $12.00 for air postage from the printer in Europe. There is an extra charge to include a house photo. Deadlines are November 24, February 22, and April 17. Exchangers who do not want to list their home can join as an unlisted subscriber for $55 plus postage and receive the catalogues.

Vacation Exchange Club (Debby and Karl Costabel, P.O. Box 820, Haleiwa, HI 96712; 1-800-638-3841 (in Hawaii 638-8747) FAX 1-808-638-5184 or Compuserve 72520, 1414) has affiliates all over the world, mostly in Europe, and continues to expand its coverage yearly. It publishes two listings a year (February and April). Subscribers can list one home and receive both editions for $50.00. For an extra charge they can include a photo or list an additional home. Exchangers who do not wish to be listed can join and get both publications for $55.00. Application deadlines for listings are December 1st and February 5th.

Once the exchange books come out, listers are on their own to make arrangements directly with each

other. Families usually talk on the phone, send detailed information and pictures of their properties and
themselves, and discuss insurance or any special issues such as care of pets. They also swap information
about favorite restaurants, good fishing spots, and
special things to do and see. They often decide to swap
cars as well. An exchange can run from a weekend to
as long as a year.

Florida is one of the most popular states for exchange listings, in part because of its high number of
second-homes and its large population of retired people (many of whom are avid exchangers). Home exchange not only enables visitors to live like residents,
it also allows Floridians to explore different parts of
their own state. It is one of the best ways to get off the
beaten path.

Houseboat Rental. A unique way to tour parts of
Florida and solve your lodging problem at the same
time is to rent a houseboat. Houseboating is fun all
year round and boats are easy to operate and equipped
with all the comforts of an air conditioned home.

For information about cruising on St. John's River
contact Sanford Boat Rentals, (4370 Carraway Place,
Sanford, FL 32771; 407-321-5906 or toll-free 1-800-237-
5105); Three Buoys (2280 Hontoon Road, DeLand, FL
32720; 904-736-9422); or Hontoon Landing Marina
(2317 River Ridge Road, DeLand, FL 32720; 904-734-
2474). If you prefer to explore the Suwannee River, you
can get your home from Miller's Suwannee Houseboats (P.O. Box 280, Suwannee, FL 32692; 1-800-458-
BOAT or 904-542-73499). Houseboats give a unique
perspective on the Everglades and an especially pleasant way to see the Florida Keys. Contact Flamingo
Lodge (Flamingo, FL 33030; 305-253-2241) or Florida
Keys Sailing School (Mile Marker 85.9, P.O. Box 1202,
Islamorada 33036; 305-664-4009). The cost of house-

boat rental is lower during the week and off-season, ranging from around $1,100 to $1,700 per week.

Camping. Florida's good weather allows the option of camping year round. The state has over 50,000 camp sites in a wide variety of private campgrounds as well as in state and national parks and forests. Reservations are important for campsites, just as they are for other kinds of accommodations, especially during peak season. Camping fees in Florida vary greatly, depending upon the part of the state, the time of year, the number of people in a party, the length of stay, and the kind of services included.

Most state campgrounds accept reservations up to 60 days in advance. Sites may be reserved in person or by telephone, but not by mail. Call the parks between 8 a.m. and 5 p.m. in their local times. Only 50% of all campsites are reserved in each park, leaving the rest available year round on a first-come, first-served basis. The camping period in a state park may not exceed 14 days. Pets are not allowed. The basic camping fee covers four persons per campsite. There is a fee for each additional person, up to a maximum of eight. Daily fees range from a low of $9.00 off-season in less expensive campgrounds, to a high of over $20.00 for a waterfront location in one of the more popular parks. For general information about camping and fees contact the Florida Department of Natural Resources (Division of Recreation and Parks, Marjory Stoneman Douglas Building, 3900 Commonwealth Blvd., Room 613, Tallahassee, FL 32399; 904-488-7326). If you plan to do much camping in Florida's parks, you will want to get *Florida Parks: A Guide to Camping in Nature* by Gerald Grow (Longleaf Publications, P.O. Box 4282, Tallahassee, FL 32315).

An annually up-dated list of private campgrounds in the state is available from the Florida Campground

Association (1638 N. Plaza Drive, Tallahassee, FL
32308-5323; 904-656-8878). For reservations and information call toll-free in Florida, 1-800-FLA-CAMP.
Most private campgrounds allow pets on a leash, although some have restrictions on the size or type of
pet and set aside certain sections of the park for them.

What to Do

Florida's easy pace usually mellows out even the
die-hards who work at vacation. If it doesn't, there is
still more than enough to do to keep the vacationing
workaholic busy. Travelers who succumb to Florida's
spell may decide they don't have to do *everything*.
Their problem is deciding which activities they do
want to do. There is a lot of choice.

Florida's Parks

Some of the finest recreational activities in the state
are found within Florida's outstanding network of local, state and national parks and forests. Two national
seashores (Canaveral and Gulf Islands) and two national parks (Everglades and Biscayne) lie in the state.
Thousands of acres of land in the state are designated
National Forests, including Apalachicola, Osceola,
and Ocala.

The system of over 125 state parks is especially note-
worthy. The objective of the Florida Park Service is to
manage its parks, preserves, recreation areas, and botanical and geological sites as natural systems and as
examples of the plant communities prevailing in 1513,
when the first Spaniards arrived. Through the ongoing
land acquisition program of the state parks and a special Environmentally Endangered Lands Program, the
state has acquired a representative sample of every

major plant community in Florida. Park lands are restored to their earlier condition through the re-establishment of natural ecological processes and native vegetation. Thus they serve as natural museums in which we can catch glimpses and scents of the Florida which the early explorers experienced.

State park fees for Florida residents are $1.00 for vehicle and driver, and 50 cents for each vehicle passenger, walk-in, and cyclist. For nonresidents they are $2.00 for vehicle and driver, and $1.00 for each vehicle passenger, walk-in, and cyclist. Annual passes are available for $50.00 per Florida resident family; $80 per non-resident family; $25 per resident individual; and $40 per nonresident individual.

Florida's parks offer something for everyone. Most have picnic areas, playgrounds, swimming pools, and open areas for families seeking activities for children and space for family gatherings. They offer fishing sites, boat slips, canoe runs, and hiking and nature trails. The parks differ from one another in what they offer and how they are designed, but all share high standards of cleanliness, good maintenance, and knowledgeable and service-oriented staffs. Most have good access to restrooms and other facilities for the physically challenged. Individual parks with historic sites are described in Part II of this book; wilderness areas and beaches are detailed in Parts III and IV. For a brochure describing all the state parks write to the Department of Natural Resources (Division of Recreation and Parks, 3900 Commonwealth Blvd., Tallahassee, FL 32399-3000) or ask at any park entrance gate.

Good Eating

One way to explore a region is to try its native foods and local specialties. Florida is especially rich in fish, seafood, and fresh fruits and vegetables. If you like seafood or fish you will be in heaven here. It is everywhere — fresh, delicious, and especially fine if you pull it in yourself, or eat it in an outdoor waterfront cafe or along a fishing pier. Florida's southern heritage comes through strongly in its cooking — deep fry is still the preference in most Florida restaurants. But the options are growing and you can now get your fish broiled in most places. Apalachicola oysters from the panhandle are famous the world over and available throughout Florida most of the year, on the half-shell or however you want them.

Annual Seafood Festivals give you a good chance to try different specialties and enjoy entertainment and a variety of other activities as well. A particularly pleasant one, in the very heart of oyster country, is the November Florida Seafood Festival at Apalachicola (P.O. Box 460, 128 Market St., Apalachicola, FL 32320; 904-653-8051). You couldn't find a better setting for seafood consumption than this charming riverfront town where you can watch the fishing boats unload their catch. Oyster shucking and eating contests are two of the more popular highlights.

Fish isn't all they serve in Florida. Gator tail is a tender, tasty meat that is worth a try. Once you have, you may well add it to your list of "must-haves" for whenever you are in Florida. Steak is good too — after all, Florida is one of the major cattle producing states in the country. In addition to "southern cooking" and its close relative, "cracker cooking," both of which are much more varied than you might expect, the state is home to several ethnic cooking traditions. Cuban and Latin American restaurants serving picadillo, black beans, chicken and yellow rice, and fried plantains are common throughout southern Florida. Greek cooking dominates the Tarpon Springs area above Tampa, and crops up throughout the state. The influence of the Caribbean Islands is strong here as well. Conch chowder is ever different, but always wonderful all through the Keys. The Miccosukee Indians along the Tamiami Trail serve pumpkin and fry breads and special Indian burgers. If you prefer your food gourmet-style, you can find that too, in topflight restaurants throughout the state.

For dessert there is always key lime pie, which should be yellow if it is the real thing, or that rich southern standby, pecan pie. And of course, those famous Florida oranges! They are plentiful and cheap everywhere from October through May. You can buy them by the box, bag, or bushel. You can squeeze them, peel them, or slice them. Almost as popular as the oranges are the grapefruit. A whole range of other exotic tropical fruits are available as well. Finally, if none of these appeal to you and you really prefer to have your food dished up by fast-food chains, you will still be in heaven. Every chain has a host of outlets in Florida.

One of the newest gastronomical activities in Florida is winery tours. There are several wineries in the state. **Lafayette Vineyards and Winery** (6505 Mahan Dr., Tallahassee, FL 32308; 904-878-9041, hours vary by season) covers 38 of the original 23,040-acre grant awarded by the U.S. Congress to the French Marquis de Lafayette for his service in the Revolutionary War. The modern winery began producing in 1983.

Lakeridge Winery & Vineyards on U.S. 27 west of Orlando (19239 U.S. 27 N, Clermont, FL 34711-9025; 1-800-476-8463 or 904-394-8627) offers complimentary tours and wine tasting Mon.-Sat. 10 a.m.-6 p.m. and Sun. noon-6 p.m. **Chautauqua Vineyards** north of Panama City on I-10 at U.S. 331 (P.O. Box 1308, 1330 Freeport Road, DeFuniak Springs, FL 32433; 904-892-

5887) is open for tours and tasting — Mon.-Sat. 10
a.m.-6 p.m. and Sunday 1-6 p.m. **Eden Vineyards Winery and Park** ten miles east of I-75 on SR 80 near Alva
(813-728-9463) is open daily 11 a.m.-5 p.m. and offers
in addition to tours and tasting a deli and picnic area,
tram ride, and nature walk.

If you plan to do most of your own meal preparation
or want to stock up on picnic fare, you will enjoy the
wide selection of foods in the several large supermarket chains in Florida. Most have bakeries that turn out
fresh breads and pastries daily, good meat and frozen
food sections, and delis and seafood/fish counters
with a wide selection of prepared or quick-preparation
foods. Fruits and vegetables are inexpensive and
good. You can also find a wide selection of wines and
beers. Every town has a major supermarket somewhere around it, often in a shopping mall on the outskirts.

If you can't find a supermarket, you can surely locate a small convenience store, complete with gasoline
pumps and often open 24 hours a day. There are several chains of these and they are scattered along roads
all over Florida. Their stock is not inspiring and could
send the health-food advocate into a sugar/fat coma,
but you can always get hot coffee, a pre-packaged
sandwich, bread, a few canned goods, juice, milk, cold
drinks, packaged nuts, and other basics.

If you particularly enjoy food, one of the ways to
explore an area is to browse through local cookbooks
and even try cooking a few specialties on your own.
*Tropic Cooking: The New Cuisine from Florida and the
Islands of the Caribbean* by Joyce LaFray Young is a
delightful introduction to tropical flavors and ingredients. It is available from local bookstores, or The Ten
Speed Press (900 Modoc, Berkeley, CA 94707). The
Great Outdoors Publishing Company (4747 28th St.

North, St. Petersburg, FL 33714) includes three inexpensive cookbooks: *How to Cook your Catch* by Rube Allyn, *Catch and Cook Shellfish* by Dorothy Raymond, and *Famous Florida Recipes* by Lowis Carlton. Look also for *Country Cookin', Cracker Cookin', Famous Florida Restaurants and Recipes, Underwater Gourmet, Cuban Home Cooking,* and *Florida's Best Recipes (Less Than 5 Ingredients)*.

Annual Events

You can find special events going on in Florida any weekend of the year. Some are unique to a particular town, expressive of the community's own place in the culture or history of the state. Others, like the annual seafood festivals, are celebrated in many communities across the state. If you like special events and want to time your visit around one, write the local chambers of commerce and ask for a list. Keep in mind, however, that lots of other folks will be going too. Advance reservations for lodgings may be essential.

Gone Fishing

What more appropriately symbolizes Florida than a fish flopping up from sparkling water on a taut fishing line! Anglers line the bridges and piers, sit solitary beside a pole stuck in the sand, wade along the tidelands, and fight with the big ones on deep sea charter boats. For many visitors and residents, Florida is synonymous with fishing. And well it should be. The fishing — any kind of fishing — is good!

For information about fresh water fishing contact Florida Game and Fresh Water Fish Commission (Division of Fisheries, 620 South Meridian St., Farris Bryant Building, Tallahassee, FL 32399-1600; 904-488-1960) or regional offices (Northwest 904-265-

3676; Northeast 904-752-0353; Central 904-732-1225; South 813-644-9269; and Everglades 407-683-0748). The Game and Fresh Water Fish Commission puts out a handbook for each region that includes descriptions of the kinds of fish commonly caught and popular fishing areas, a list of fishing camps, fishing and tackle tips, and the best months to catch different varieties.

Fresh water anglers are required to carry valid fishing licenses (resident $8.50 a year; nonresident $26.50 a year or $11.50 for 10 days). Residents 65 years of age or over can obtain a free license. Children under 16 do not need a license.

Saltwater anglers can get information from the Department of Natural Resources (3900 Commonwealth Blvd., Tallahassee, FL 32399-1600; 904-488-7326). Licenses for saltwater fishing became necessary beginning January 1, 1990. The fees collected from licenses have been designated by the Florida legislature for improving and restoring fish habitats, building artificial reefs, researching marine life and its habitats, and educating the public about fishery resources. Annual license fees for residents are $14.00. Nonresidents can buy a one-year license for $32.00, or a 7-day one for $17.00. An additional license stamp of $2.00 is necessary for either snook or crawfish. Children under 16 and Florida residents over 65 do not need licenses.

Many communities have fishing clubs and contests. Guides for all types of fishing abound in Florida. Inquire at any chamber of commerce or at local bait and tackle shops and marinas. Another good source of information is the Florida Chapter of the American Fisheries Society (P.O. Box 1903, Eustis, FL 32727-1903), which has a large booklist of fisheries books, available through mail order. From them you can get *Florida Aquatic Habitat and Fishery Resources* edited by William Seaman, Jr. ($15) and *Fisherman's Guide: Fishes of the*

Southeastern United States by C. S. Manooch, III. ($24.95).

Swimming

Do we even need to talk about swimming? Florida's beaches and its year-round climate are famous the world over. If you are really serious about swimming, as opposed to playing in the surf, you may prefer the gulf side of Florida where beaches are gently sloping and the water is often calm. There you can stroke up and down the shore for as long as you want. The Atlantic Ocean usually provides bigger waves, but both coasts have times and places of calm and surf.

There is also a lot of opportunity for swimming in Florida's interior, especially in the north central part which is sprinkled with lakes, springs, and rivers. Since Florida's soil is sandy, there are sandy beaches everywhere — not only along the Gulf and ocean, but also beside delightful small lakes and slow-moving rivers. Swimming pools are plentiful as well and in some luxury resorts they can be spectacular. Many pools, especially in the south, are open and warm year around. Most beachfront resorts give water-loving guests the best of all possible worlds — pools right beside the beach. Part IV of this book, "Search for the Perfect Beach," is dedicated to beachcombers.

Scuba Diving and Snorkeling

Divers and snorkelers flock to Florida for its clear Gulf waters, deep springs, and coral reefs along the keys. These reefs with their tropical fish populations, are among the finest in the world. For information on diving in Florida contact the Department of Commerce, Division of Tourism, Office of Sports Promotion (Collins Building, Suite 510 E, Tallahassee, FL 32399-2000; 904-488-8347).

Two Florida parks are devoted to diving and snorkeling. **The John Pennekamp Coral Reef State Park** at MM 102.5 (P.O. Box 487, Key Largo, FL 33037; 305-451-1202) features an unusual visitor center with touch tanks, and a giant reconstruction of a living patch reef in a circular aquarium. It offers scuba and snorkeling tours daily (305-451-1621). **Biscayne National Park** and **Biscayne Aqua Center** (Biscayne National Park Headquarters, end of 328th St., east of Florida City; P.O. Box 1369, Homestead, FL 33090-1369; 305-247-2400) give access by boat to 181,500 acres of islands and underwater reefs. Closeby is the Key Largo Coral Reef National Marine Sanctuary, encompassing about 178 nautical square miles, most of which lies out in the Atlantic Ocean north and east of Key Largo. Both experienced and novice divers can find innumerable dive shops in the area offering charter boats and instruction.

Looe Key National Marine Sanctuary (Rt. 1, Box 782, Big Pine Key, FL 33043; 305-872-4039) is one of several sites established by the National Oceanic and Atmospheric Administration to protect and manage special marine areas throughout the coastal waters of the United States. It consists of a submerged section of the Florida reef tract located 6.7 nautical miles southwest of Big Pine Key in the lower Florida Keys. The wide range in depths makes the reefs accessible to both the beginning snorkeler and the experienced diver. The sanctuary area includes several shipwrecks including the remains of the H.M.S. *Looe*, a British frigate that sank in 1744.

Florida also has an active program of artificial reef building along several portions of the coast. Fort Lauderdale started building artificial reefs several years

ago when it established Lowrance Artificial Reef.
Since then, more than two dozen derelict freighters
and other vessels have been sunk off the coast of
Broward County, primarily around Fort Lauderdale
and Pompano Beach. Baby fish find shelter in them,
and soft and hard corals adhere readily to the steel and
grow rapidly. The reefs have gained great popularity
with scuba divers and one in particular, the Mercedes
I, is now a major diving center.

Divers may want to look at two diving and snorkeling guides: *Florida's East Coast*, and *The Florida Keys*
($11.95 each). They detail each dive, giving depth, con-
dition, difficulty, and photo tips. The books are available in bookstores or by mail from The Book Passage
(1-800-321-9785). If you are curious to learn more
about what you see down under you can order *Diver-
Snorkelers Guide to Fishes/Sea Life* by F. J. Stokes (12.95)
from American Fisheries Society (5410 Grosvenor
Lane, Suite 110, Bethesda, MD 20814-2199).

Water Activities

Have you ever floated down a scenic wild river in
an inner-tube? Now is the time. North central Florida
is the place. Head for the tubing rivers to drift for
miles between vine-draped banks. Those who prefer
stand-up sports can find plenty of places to water ski
and rent a boat and equipment. To see how the pros do
it, visit Cypress Gardens with its world-famous water-
ski revue which performs several times daily on Lake
Eloise. Surfers and those who like to watch the sport
may want to check out the Central Florida District
Surfing Contest held in October sponsored by the Eastern Surfing Association. The premiere surfing locale in
Florida is Sebastian Inlet State Park, midway down the

east coast. There is also good surfing below Fort Pierce on Hutchinson Island.

Boardsailing enthusiasts will find kindred spirits around Melbourne, on the east coast. The U.S. Boardsailing Team has trained in South Brevard County since 1984 and the area hosts some of the country's most prestigious boardsailing championships each year. Each spring the team offers a series of intermediate-to-advanced instructional clinics. Beginners can find instruction at either of two boardsailing shops in the area: Longitude 80 Windsurfing in Indian Harbour Beach (407-773-1720) and Calema Boardsailing in Merritt Island (407-453-3223). For details on the U.S. Boardsailing Team's training, regatta, and/or clinic schedule, write USBT (P.O. Box 360804, Melbourne, FL 32936; 407-242-2424).

Other Sports

You don't have to like water to enjoy Florida. You can keep very busy without ever going near it. Baseball spring training camps every March attract over a million fans. Some of our most famous tennis champions, for example Chris Evert, learned to play in Florida and have clubs here. For information about clubs, tournaments, and courts, contact the Florida Tennis Association (801 N.E. 167 St. Suite 301, North Miami Beach, FL 33162; 305-652-2866). Golf thrives in Florida as well. There are over 1,000 golf courses in the state and the number continues to grow. For a directory of courses by county and a schedule of tournaments, send a check or money order for $3.95 to the Florida State Golf Association, (P.O. Box 21177, Sarasota, FL 34238; 813-921-5695).

If you are interested in riding or horseracing, you can visit some of the most famous horse breeding and training centers in the world near Ocala. There are over 600 farms in the state, and each day of the week at least one is open to visitors. For a list of farms and their hours, contact the Florida Thoroughbred Breeders Association (4727 N.W. 80th Ave., Ocala, FL 32675; 904-629-2160 or FAX 904-629-3603). If you do plan to visit one of the farms, be sure to call before you go.

Birdwatching

Whether you are a serious birdwatcher or a more casual observer of the feathered scene, there is a lot to see in Florida. It has more water birds and rare species than any other state. Human "snowbirds" aren't the only ones to fly south in the winter. Many northern bird species migrate to the Florida peninsula and fill the lagoons and glades of the bird sanctuaries and wildlife refuges. There are several birdbooks to help you figure out which you are seeing. *Florida's Fabulous Waterbirds* and *Florida's Fabulous Land Birds* are two. Also helpful are Golden's Field Guide *Birds of America* and two of the Great Outdoors Series *Birds of Florida*, a reprint of an older book by Francis Wyly Hall, and *Seashore and Wading Birds* (Great Outdoors Publishing Co, 4767 28th Street North, St. Petersburg, FL 33714).

The Florida Audubon Society (1101 Audubon Way, Maitland, FL 32751; 305-647-2615) has special events and chapters all over Florida. Membership in the state association includes local chapter membership and a subscription to *The Florida Naturalist*. The society's **Madalyn Baldwin Center for Birds of Prey** (1101 Audubon Way, Maitland, FL 32751; 305-647-2615, open 10 a.m.-4 p.m. Tues.-Sat. with daily tours at 11 a.m., free) is dedicated to rehabilitating injured birds of prey (eagles, hawks, owls, falcons, vultures, and ospreys). Its specially constructed aviary for birds with permanent injuries provides a unique educational experience for visitors.

The **Suncoast Seabird Sanctuary**, on the Gulf Coast below St. Petersburg (18328 Gulf Blvd., Indian Shores, FL 33535; 813-391-6211, open 9 a.m. to dark) cares for almost 5,000 injured birds a year. **Corkscrew Swamp Sanctuary** (on the west coast near Bonita Springs on SR 849 off Rt 41;813-992-2591) is one of Florida's finest wilderness refuges. Some years it shelters nesting wood storks, and it always has a wide variety of birds. There are other refuges scattered throughout Florida, most open to the public.

Looking For Wildflowers

Florida has over 3500 species of wildflowers, scattered over the state in a great diversity of habitats. Many showy species bloom along the roadsides, and state parks have nature trails and boardwalks where you can view wildflowers in natural settings. If you watch for wildflowers wherever you go, you will soon be discovering them in the most unexpected places — parks and rest areas, near bridges, and overpasses, even growing on trees. Many of the flowers can only be found in Florida — and many with endangered or threatened status are protected by law. To help in identification, look for a brochure put out by the Florida Department of Agriculture and Consumer Services or locate one of several books such as *Florida Flowers* from Great Outdoors.

Art, Theater, and Music

So much emphasis is put on Florida's outdoor activities that the state's art, theater and music resources are often overlooked. They are extensive and continually expanding, especially in the larger cities. For information contact local chambers of commerce and visitor's centers.

Shopping

Bathing suits and sportswear dominate the shopping scene. You may want to travel light and buy your casual clothes here. They are colorful, interesting, and reasonably priced. If you prefer high fashion, you can find that too. **Worth Avenue** in Palm Beach is one of the best known shopping streets in Florida, lined with chic boutiques selling everything from locally-made specialties to internationally famous labels. On the west coast, **St. Armand's Circle**, in Sarasota, decorated with statues from Ringling's art collection, has a different atmosphere but is equally well known to discriminating shoppers. Interesting boutiques and giftshops abound in all resort areas with prices ranging from reasonable to out-of-sight.

Flea markets are springing up everywhere and are great fun as well as a good way to experience the diversity and entrepreneurial ingenuity of modern Floridians. Several of these markets are huge, with hundreds of booths in both roofed and open areas. Many operate only on weekends, but a few do business every day. They sell souvenirs, crafts, antiques, plants and flowers, fresh produce, clothes and most everything else you can imagine. Local tourist brochures advertize area markets. **Flea World**, between Orlando and Sanford (take exit 50 off I-40, turn right on Hwy. 17-92, and travel one mile), advertises itself as "America's largest flea market." It is open Friday, Saturday, and Sunday, 8 a.m.-5 p.m. and has 1500 dealer booths, 15 food concessions, 2 petting zoos, entertainment, and parking for 4,000 cars over 104 acres.

Precautions

Florida beat back many of the early explorers because they were unprepared for the rigors of its climate and environment. Today we travel in relative comfort, even luxury. But we move still in a natural world that can be harsh and fickle. We walk under the same tropical sun that downed Spanish noblemen, provide flesh for the descendants of the insects that crazed the French Huguenots, and stand as vulnerable before the high waters and thrashing winds of a hurricane as any human has ever stood.

Sunblock is a must — preferably one with a high number. Any visitor to Florida who has ever had a sunburn will tell you just how omnipresent the sun in the sunshine state is — and what it feels like on sunburned skin, even through long sleeves. Sunburn is probably the number one killer of vacation fun in Florida. It's better to take it slow the first few days than to have the first day be the last day of outdoor fun.

Insects, especially mosquitoes, are an inescapable part of Florida in some places and at some times of year. If you plan outdoor excursions in wet season, take insect repellent and clothes to cover arms and legs. Even if you expect to be near stores, don't count on buying your insect repellent. If you need it, everyone else will too. Like Mother Hubbard, you may find the shelf bare.

Florida's wildlife is one of its most interesting attractions. However many species have become rare as their natural habitats have been invaded by human development and activities. We can help them survive by leaving them alone, especially when they are nesting, by disposing of trash properly, by driving power boats slowly in manatee areas, and by not feeding them.

Alligators, endangered for several years and protected by law, are now becoming more common. You can often see them along streams and lakes. Generally they are afraid of humans and will stay away from you unless you attempt to feed or otherwise bother them. Although snakes are common in Florida, most are harmless. If you prefer not to see any, stay on trails and avoid wading through swamps and palmettos.

Water safety is important everywhere in Florida. Watch children carefully, never swim alone, swim in guarded areas only, and don't rely on flotation devices as life preservers. Many beaches have a flag warning system — red means danger; yellow means caution; and green means water conditions appear safe. However even in waters rated as safe, swimmers should exercise caution. Water conditions can change rapidly.

Allow for the Unexpected

Advance planning is good to help you narrow down where you want to go and what you want to do. It enables you to get reservations ahead of time that will help insure a pleasant, minimally hassled trip. But it's important also to remain open to the unexpected. Florida really does have a magic and the best trip is one that allows some room for the unplanned, the unexpected chance to try something new. Or the freedom to stay put in a beautiful spot, even though your itinerary says it is time to move on.

PART II

FLORIDA'S FRONTIERS:

FROM PREHISTORIC TIMES TO THE SPACE AGE

Any exploration of Florida must be a journey through time as well as space. In some ways, in some places, the land is much the same as it was before the Europeans arrived. Hurricanes still thrash across the peninsula. The sun still sets magnificently over the Gulf. Direct descendants of prehistoric palmetto bugs still walk with the arrogant majesty of a long-surviving species across the floors of wealthy and poor alike. The tropics are hard to tame in the short-run or the long-run.

Florida spans American history in a way no other state does. It was the site of the first European settlements and is today the place from which we launch our most far-flung exploration of the universe. The peninsula has drawn pioneers, entrepreneurs, dreamers, and scoundrels from every walk of life and nationality. In some respects it typifies America. Yet it is singularly its own place. The influences of Spain, the Indians, the American South, the newcomers who have flowed across its borders, and the tropics themselves have blended to produce Florida's own unique atmosphere. In order to appreciate what is special about Florida we need a sense of its history.

CHAPTER 3

IN THE FOOTSTEPS OF INDIANS AND CONQUISTADORS

The earliest settlers in Florida were prehistoric Indians who lived about 12,000 to 8,000 B.C. As far as we know, the peninsula has been continuously inhabited since that time. The more recent Indians, who lived in the area from around 200 B.C. on, have left evidence of their lives throughout Florida in high mounds built of shell and earth. When the Europeans arrived in the sixteenth century, they found five main tribes of Indians: the Timucuan in central and northeast Florida; the Apalachee in northwest Florida, the Tocobaga around the Tampa Bay area at Crystal River and Cedar Key; the Calusa in the southwest; and the Tequesta who lived east of the Calusa and south of Cape Canaveral.

The Indians were agile, strong, and deadly accurate with bows and arrows. They decorated themselves brilliantly with elaborate tattoos, strings of beads and rattles, and bright feathered mantles. The men wore their long hair piled high in a knot and put inflated fish bladders, dyed red, in their ears. The women left their hair unbound and wore skirts off flowing moss.

The arrival of the Spanish in 1513 brought the ultimate decline and extinction of the original Florida

Indians, who numbered over 100,000 at their peak. The period of co-existence between the two cultures was difficult for both Indians and Europeans.

There are many sites in Florida that preserve the remains of both prehistoric and European culture. Visits to several of them will give you a good sense of Florida's early history. Another way to walk in the shoes of the early residents and explorers is to visit the state parks which have been preserved as they were when the Europeans first saw them. Here you can stand and imagine the lives of the Indians who called this place home for thousands of years, and also feel the awe and fear of those first explorers who tried to tame a land so different from the one they had known in Europe.

The Prehistoric Indians in Florida

Imagine what Florida must have looked like 12,000 years ago, at the end of the great Ice Age, when human beings first discovered it. The seas were lower and Florida probably was twice as wide as it is now. The climate was drier and cooler and big game animals roamed savannahs and grasslands. The earliest inhabitants were the nomadic hunters and gatherers we call Paleo-Indians. Their weapons and the bones of the large animals they hunted are found along the Silver-Springs run and at shallow fords on rivers in north-central Florida.

Over time, at a pace that seems incredibly slow by modern standards, the Indians changed their lifestyle. They became more settled and discovered they could eat shellfish and a wider variety of plants and animals. Eventually they discovered how to make pottery and began to farm and live in settled communities.

Those who lived along Florida's western coast after

about 200 B.C. have come to be called Pre-Columbian Mound Builders. By 700 A.D. they had a centralized political system and could build elaborate linear embankments and mounds of shell and earth which they used for ritual purposes, fields, and houses. These Indians were all sun worshipers, resorting to human sacrifices in hard times. Lines of descent were traced through the mother and there were some instances in which women ruled the tribes.

Much of what we know about Florida's prehistoric Indians comes from the reports of early Europeans who described what they saw when they first arrived. We know most about the Timucuan Indians because of the drawings of the French artist LeMoyne, who came to Florida in 1564 with the French Huguenots. The Timucuan language was understood in all parts of the peninsula, and the Spanish missionaries used it for catechisms and texts. The Apalachee Indians in northwest Florida were especially powerful because the chiefs were united in a strong league. Their area was reported to be the richest in Florida and their warring abilities were well known among the other tribes, who urged the Spanish north into their territory.

We can see evidences throughout Florida of the thousands of years of habitation of these prehistoric Indians. They represent the longest period in Florida's history and a life lived in harmony with the land. Travelers who let their imaginations free when they visit the sites of these ancient villages and ceremonial mounds may feel the flow of these years and perhaps even envision a tall, agile Indian gliding through the lagoon in a dugout canoe.

Prehistoric Indian Sites

Although many Indian mounds have been destroyed, others remain at least partially intact, especially along the Gulf coast and in the Everglades. Some
of the most accessible archaeological sites and museums with Indian artifacts are listed here by region,
from north to south. Some have interpretative displays
or opportunities to watch archaeologists at work. Although there may not be a lot to see at Indian mounds,
they represent thousands of years of human habitation
and are the best source we have for clues about how
the earliest Floridians lived.

Northwest Region

The **Indian Temple Mound** (139 Miracle Strip Parkway, Fort Walton; 904-243-6521, open 11 a.m.-4 p.m.
Tues.-Thur.) served as a sort of county seat for the
many villages in this area. There were wooden structures with thatched roofs and totems with carved bird
heads on the mounds. The people gathered here on
feast days and for consultation with the chief or head
medicine man, and for trade. When a leader died, the
temple was destroyed and another temple was built.
The small museum beside the mound shows Indian
artifacts illustrating over 100,000 years of life in the
Choctawhatchee Bay area.

The **Lake Jackson Indian Mounds** (1313 Crowder
Road, north of SR 10 near Tallahassee; 904-562-0042,
open daily 8 a.m.-sunset, free) were probably in the
main town of Apalachee visited by De Soto in 1539.
From 1200 to 1500 A.D. it was a large ceremonial center. Small villages and single-family farm plots were
located nearby.

Today the Lake Jackson mounds look like ordinary, low hills in a picnic area. Two of the unprotected mounds were indeed treated like ordinary hills; they were torn down for fill dirt. As one was being bulldozed, archaeologists were allowed to dig it, and found some of the most important artifacts yet discovered in Florida. Today 41 acres of the complex are protected within the state site and archaeologists have been examining it periodically since 1940.

San Luis Archaeological and Historic Site (2020 Mission Rd., Tallahassee, FL 32304-0250; 904-487-3711, open daily) is located high on a hilltop west of downtown Tallahassee. It was the site of an important Apalachee Indian village and is also believed to have been the site of one of the Spanish missions. It contained a large Indian council house, a Christian church, a Spanish fort, and many homes and outbuildings. It was burned by its inhabitants as they sought to escape British invaders in 1704. Visitors can take free guided tours and from February to May may be able to watch archaeologists at work. Exhibits along the trails tell the story of the early inhabitants, as well as today's search for the past.

Northeast Region

Paynes Prairie State Preserve (off U.S. 441 just outside Gainesville; 904-466-3397) has Indian artifacts that date back to 10,000 B.C. in the visitor's center.

The **Florida Museum of Natural History** (Museum Road, University of Florida, Gainesville, FL 32611; 904-392-1721, open Mon.-Sat. 9 a.m.-5 p.m., Sun. 1-5 p.m., free) is the largest natural history museum in the South. The collections of the Department of Anthropology provide a systematic record of human life in

**PREHISTORIC INDIANS AND EUROPEAN EXPLORERS
MAP OF SITES**

PREHISTORIC INDIANS AND EUROPEAN EXPLORERS

SITES TO VISIT

1. AMELIA ISLAND MUSEUM OF HISTORY, 233 South 3rd St., Fernandina Beach, FL 32034; 904-261-7378.

2. CRYSTAL RIVER STATE ARCHAEOLOGICAL SITE, 3400 N. Museum Pt., Crystal River, FL 32629; 904-795-3817, open daily 9 a.m.-5 p.m.

3. DAYTONA MUSEUM OF ARTS & SCIENCES, 1040 Museum Blvd. Daytona Beach; 904-225-0285, open Tues.-Fri. 9 a.m.-4 p.m., Sat. noon -5 p.m.

4. DE SOTO NATIONAL MEMORIAL, 75th St. N.W., Bradenton, FL 34209-9656; 813-792-0458, open daily 8 a.m.-5 p.m., free.

5. FLORIDA MUSEUM OF NATURAL HISTORY, Museum Road, University of Florida, Gainesville, FL 32611; 904-392-1721, open Mon.-Sat. 9 a.m.-5 p.m., Sun. 1-5 p.m., free.

6. FORT CAROLINE NATIONAL MEMORIAL, 12713 Fort Caroline Road, Jacksonville, FL 32225; 904-641-7155.

7. FORT MATANZAS NATIONAL MONUMENT, on SR A1A, 14 miles south of St. Augustine, open daily 8:30 a.m.-5:30 p.m., free.

8. FORT MYERS HISTORICAL MUSEUM, 2300 Peck St., Fort Myers, FL 33901; 813-332-5955. open Mon.-Fri. 9 a.m.-4:30 p.m. Sun. 1-5 p.m.

9. FORT SAN MARCOS DE APALACHEE, P.O. Box 27, St. Marks FL 32355; 904-925-6216, open Thur.-Mon. 9 a.m.-5 p.m.

10. GUANA RIVER STATE PARK, 2690 S. Ponte Vedra Blvd., Ponte Vedra Beach, FL 32082; 904-825-507.

11. HISTORIC KEY WEST SHIPWRECK MUSEUM, 510 Greene St., Key West, FL 33040; 305-292-9740, open daily 10 a.m.-6 p.m.

12. HONTOON ISLAND STATE PARK, 2100 W. French Ave., Orange City, FL 32762; 904-734-7158.

13. INDIAN KEY STATE HISTORICAL SITE, accessible by State Park ferry, Mile Marker 78, Indian Key Fill; 305-664-4815, open 8 a.m.-sunset.

14. INDIAN TEMPLE MOUND, 139 Miracle Strip Parkway, Fort Walton; 904-243-6521, open Tues.-Thur. 11 a.m.-4 p.m.

15. LAKE JACKSON INDIAN MOUNDS, 1313 Crowder Road, Tallahassee; 904-562-0042, open daily 8 a.m.-sunset, free.

16. MADIRA BICKEL MOUND, U.S. 19, north of Sarasota, c/o Gamble Plantation, 3708 Patten Ave., Ellenton, FL 34222; 813-722-1017, open 8 a.m.-sunset.

17. MCLARTY STATE MUSEUM, Sebastian Inlet State Recreation Area, A1A, Melbourne Beach, FL 32951; 407-984-4852.

18. MEL FISHER'S MARITIME HERITAGE SOCIETY MUSEUM, 200 Greene St., Key West; 305-296-9936, open daily 10 a.m.-6 p.m.

19. MUSEUM OF ARCHAEOLOGY, 203 Southwest 1st Ave., Fort Lauderdale, FL 33301; 305-525-8778, open Tues.-Sat. 10 a.m.-4 p.m., Sun. 1-4 p.m.

20. PAYNES PRAIRIE STATE PRESERVE, U.S. 441, Gainesville; 904-466-3397.

21. PENSACOLA, Visitors Information Center, 1401 East Gregory St., Pensacola, FL 32501; 904-434-1234; 800-874-1234.

22. SAN LUIS ARCHAEOLOGICAL AND HISTORIC SITE, west of Tallahassee, c/o Museum of Florida History, Tallahassee, FL 32399-0250; 904-488-1673, open daily.

23. SOUTH FLORIDA MUSEUM, 201 10th St. West, Bradenton FL 34205; 813-746-4132, open Tues.-Fri. 10 a.m.-5 p.m., Sun. 1-5 p.m., guided tours available.

24. ST. AUGUSTINE, Visitor Information Center, 10 Castillo Dr., St. Augustine; 904-824-3334 or Chamber of Commerce, P.O. Drawer O, St. Augustine, FL 32085; 904-829-4581.

25. ST. LUCIE COUNTY HISTORICAL MUSEUM, 414 Seaway Drive, Fort Pierce; 407-468-1795, open Wed.-Sat. 10 a.m.-4 p.m.

26. TOMOKA STATE PARK, 2099 North Beach St., Ormond Beach, FL 32174; 904-677-3931.

27. TURTLE MOUND, Appolo Beach, Canaveral National Seashore; 904-428-3384, open daily during daylight hours.

Florida, including a reconstruction of a Timucuan Indian site.

Central West Region

The **Crystal River State Archaeological Site** (3400 N. Museum Pt., Crystal River, FL 32629; 904-795-3817, open daily 9 a.m.-5 p.m.) is one of the major pre-Columbian sites in the state. It was an important ceremonial and cultural center, continuously occupied for at least 1,600 years, from 200 B.C. to 1400 A.D. Crystal River includes temple mounds, burial grounds, and middens (refuse mounds). It probably had a permanent population of about 30, and as many as 7,500 annual visitors.

A unique feature of Crystal River is a stone calendar with ceremonial stones (stelae) which enabled the Indians to determine the approximate date of the winter and summer solstices. They are the only stelae in North America north of Mexico, and they suggest that there was contact between the Florida Indians and those in the Yucatan. Excavators have found over 450 graves. One has been cut away to show an open crypt which contains remains treated with a preservative and encased in glass for observation. The complex has a small museum from which trails lead to points of interest.

The **South Florida Museum** (201 10th St. W. Bradenton, FL 34205; 813-746-4132, open Tues.-Fri., 10 a.m.-5 p.m., Sun. 1-5 p.m., guided tours available) houses a large and varied Indian collection with life-size dioramas portraying Indian life in early Florida.

The **Madira Bickel Mound** (off U.S. 19 just north of Sarasota on Terra Ceia Island; c/o Gamble Plantation; 813-722-1017, open 8 a.m.-sunset) may be part of the village of Ucita, described by the De Soto expedition-ers. It was begun about 1,200 years ago and shows at least three periods of Indian culture, spanning 700 years. There are no picnic tables or facilities here.

Central East Region

The ferry ride to **Hontoon Island State Park** (contact: Blue Spring State Park, 2100 W. French Ave., Orange City, FL 32762; 904-734-7158) is very short, but it transports passengers from the busy world of the 1990s to a place full of nature and history and free of cars. A replica of a Timucuan Indian totem of an owl that was found here alerts the visitor that this place belonged to others long ago. The walking path to the Indian Mounds in the southwest corner of the island starts out wide and worn but narrows, as travelers turn back, until it is just a thin line.

There are two mounds here, built from discarded shells of snails, the Indians' staple food, gathered from the shallows of the St. Johns River. From the far corner of one mound, a giant live oak, with a trunk six feet across, winds around, then leans far out and up over the swamp, just as it must have done when the Indians threw their shells here.

The ferry slip for Hontoon Island State Park is a little hard to find. It is on a vacant lot in the midst of a residential area. The park is off SR 44, south of Deland. Go south on Old New York Road, then south on Hontoon Road, and follow the sign onto River Ranch Road.

In **Tomoka State Park** (three miles north of Ormond Beach off N. Beach Street; 904-677-3931) an historical plaque in a pleasant picnic area marks the site of the Timucuan Indian village of Nocoroco, near the junction of the Tomoka and Halifax rivers. Alvaro Mexia discovered the village in 1605 when he was traveling northward on an expedition to explore the east coast south of St. Augustine. The spot is typical of the sites chosen by the Indians for their villages, surrounded by a fish-filled lagoon and protected from hurricanes by the barrier island to the east. Near the village site is a large art deco sculpture of Indian figures by Fred Dana Marsh. The Indian braves wear their hair in topknots customary to the Timucuan Indians. This juxtaposition of ancient Indian site and 1930's art gives a uniquely Floridian quality to the quiet picnic area.

The **Daytona Museum of Arts & Sciences** in Daytona Beach (1040 Museum Blvd. off Nova Rd, .5 mile south of U.S. 92; 904-225-0285, open Tues.-Fri. 9 a.m.-4 p.m., Sat. noon-5 p.m.)has a wing with displays on the pre-history of Florida.

Turtle Mound in Canaveral National Seashore (Appolo Ranger Station; 904-428-3384, open daily during daylight hours) is located within sight and sound of our explorations into outer space. Together the Indian mound and the space center represent the extremes of human habitation and exploration — as far back as we have been able to go in prehistory and as far ahead as we can dream. The 35 foot high mounds of seashells discarded by the Surreque Indians over six centuries ago are visible 15 miles out to sea, an important landmark. Turtle Mound is in the northern half of Cape Canaveral National Seashore, reachable from New Smyrna Beach but not from the southern portion of the seashore.

Southwest Region

Fort Myers Historical Museum (2300 Peck St., Fort Myers, FL 33901; 813-332-5955, open Mon.-Fri. 9 a.m.-4:30 p.m., Sun. 1-5 p.m.) displays materials from when the site was a Calusa Indian settlement. Ceremonial, burial, and refuse shell mounds are found throughout the area including Mound Key, Pine Island, Cabbage Key, and Useppa Island.

Southeast Region

The **Museum of Archaeology** (203 Southwest First Ave., Fort Lauderdale, FL 33301; 305-525-8778, open Tues.-Sat. 10 a.m.-4 p.m., Sun. 1 p.m.-4 p.m.) includes in its collection the 2000 year old skeleton of a Tequesta Indian girl. It also has shell picks, bone points, weapons, tools, pottery, ornaments, and other artifacts from the Ice Age forward.

Indian Key State Historical Site (reachable by state park ferry, launch dock at Mile Marker 78 on Indian Key Fill; 305-664-4815, open 8 a.m.-sunset) has a long history of Indian occupation. Early expeditions described a "town of seven or eight houses, built of timber and covered with palm leaves." Because of the dearth of excavations we know relatively little about everyday village life among these Indians. It is certain that after glacial times the rise of the water level in the Gulf has drowned earlier sites, which now lie off shore.

The boat ride to Indian Key and the tour take about three hours. If you plan to use the park ferry, call ahead for reservations because schedules depend upon the season and trips require a minimum number of passengers.

The End of Prehistoric Indians in Florida

The Spanish wanted to bring Christianity to the Indians and by the mid-1600s an estimated 30,000 Indians lived around the missions. But the Spanish also brought diseases to which the Indians had no immu-

nity. Small pox and measles spread like wildfire. By
the early 1700s, less than two hundred years after the
Spanish first arrived, these peoples who had walked
the beaches and fished the waters of Florida for over
12,000 years were all gone, victims of disease, raids by
slavers from the English colony in South Carolina, and
wars to protect their homelands from the new explorers. As their populations dwindled, inland parts of
Florida were infiltrated by Creek Indians from central
and western Georgia, who in time became known as
Seminoles.

The European Explorers

The Europeans did not settle easily on the land. The
fate of Florida over its early years was dominated by
three main forces: European history, Florida's climate,
and the original Indians. Of the three, perhaps climate
was the most telling. The dreams of several of its
would-be conquerors were laid waste by hurricane
gales, swarms of insects, tropical foliage that withstood even the sharpest machete, and insufferable heat
and humidity.

Although the Spanish dominated the early exploration and settlement of Florida, they vied constantly
with France and England for the area. Four nations
attempted to conquer Florida, but ultimately only one,
America, claimed it. In contrast to the Indians, the
Europeans did not know how to live in harmony with
the land.

The earliest explorers faced unfriendly Indians at
every turn. Some historians argue that the Indians'
hostility to the Spanish explorations grew out of prior
unpleasant — though unrecorded — encounters. Evidence certainly exists for early unofficial sightings of
Florida either by the Spanish or the English. A Spanish

map of 1502 depicts a peninsula like Florida and a report from 1511 describes a land near the Bahamas with water of eternal youth.

In 1513 Juan Ponce de León arrived near present-day St. Augustine and claimed the land for Spain. The shore in **Guana River State Park** below Jacksonville (2690 South Ponte Vedra Blvd., Ponte Vedra Beach, FL 32082; 904-825-5071) is believed to be close to his first landing place in the New World. Ponce de León returned in 1521 to set up a colony on the southwestern coast, but quickly gave up because of hostile Indians. A few years later, in 1528, another Spaniard, Panfilo de Narváez, tried again, without success, near Pensacola with 5 vessels and 240 people.

In 1539 Hernando De Soto came to Florida to mount a major expedition north from present day Tampa Bay. De Soto was 39 years old — a dashing, handsome man, wealthy and famous from his conquests in Peru. He planned carefully and brought with him an army of 622 soldiers, numerous servants and slaves, a dozen priests to Christianize the natives, artisans to build boats and bridges, as well as 223 horses, mules, 300 domestic pigs, greyhounds, and bloodhounds.

De Soto's precise landing remains in historical doubt. Some historians believe it was in Tampa Bay. Others believe he landed further south, perhaps near Charlotte Harbor. It was the beginning of a four-year journey that covered eleven of the present United States, and left De Soto and more than 300 of the original group dead.

The **De Soto National Memorial** south of Tampa (75th Street N.W., Bradenton, FL 34209-9656; 813-792-0458, open daily 8 a.m.-5:30 p.m., free) commemorates De Soto's landing and expedition. At the visitor center a film dramatizing the journey is shown hourly, and there are displays about the conquistadors. From early

December to mid-April, staff members wear De Soto-era costumes and give demonstrations of how the Spanish explorers lived in America.

The De Soto Trail has been marked at five mile intervals from Inverness on the West coast above Tampa, to the state line, above Tallahassee, so that the expedition may be followed through Florida. The Spaniards wintered the first year on the shores of Lake Ayavalla (now Lake Jackson) near Tallahassee and the first Christmas mass in the present U.S. was celebrated there, probably near the Lake Jackson Indian Mounds mentioned earlier.

European attempts at settlement continued despite setbacks. A hurricane greeted Tristán de Luna's settlers at Pensacola Bay in August 1559. They left after only two years. The French, not to be outdone by the Spanish, attempted settlement in 1562 and again, more successfully in 1564, when they established Fort Caroline, near St. Johns River.

Fort Caroline National Memorial, (12713 Fort Caroline Road, near Monument Road, Jacksonville, FL 32225; 904-641-7155) includes a reconstructed version of this fort.

The Spanish wasted little time in responding to this challenge to their possession. Pedro Menéndez de Avilés was sent in 1565 to dispose of the French settlers, who were disliked not only because they were interlopers on Spanish land but also because they were Protestant Huguenots. And dispose of them he did — with the help of a major hurricane that scattered and wrecked a fleet of French ships bringing reinforcements. **Fort Matanzas National Monument** (14 miles south of St. Augustine, on SR A1A; open daily 8:30 a.m.-5:30 p.m., free) marks the spot where Menéndez captured and killed the French.

While Menéndez was preparing to meet the French

troops, he established the first permanent settlement in the United States — St. Augustine. From there the Spanish fanned out across northern Florida, building a chain of forts and missions. Their main fort was **Fort San Marcos de Apalache** on the Gulf coast, south of Tallahassee (State Historic Site, P.O. Box 27, St. Marks, FL 32355; 904-925-6216, open Thur.-Mon. 9 a.m.-5 p.m.). The site had been used by the Spanish on their earliest expeditions, even before the establishment of St. Augustine. Narvaez had stopped in 1528 with 300 men and built the first ships made by white men in the New World. De Soto spent time there, as well, on his expedition in 1539. By 1679 a wooden fort was in place and by the 1680s there was a settlement of some consequence. The Spanish erected a large stone fort in 1739 and San Marcos de Apalache continued to play a role in the area's history as a mission, a trading center, a port, and a fort throughout the period of European settlement.

After the earlier disastrous attempts to settle along Pensacola Bay, the Spanish concentrated on the east coast and their line of missions from St. Augustine to San Marcos de Apalache. In 1686, however, Florida's gulf coast again captured Europe's attention and nations raced for its possession. The Spanish got there first and established Pensacola in 1693. The French arrived in 1698 and moved on to sites now known as Biloxi, Mobile, and New Orleans. Except during 1719-1723 when France and Spain were at war and Pensacola alternated between French and Spanish control, the two colonies coexisted peaceably. Pensacola, on the verge of a great wilderness area and isolated from the other Spanish colonies, remained relatively undeveloped through the Spanish period.

Until the mid-1600s, the English stayed well to the north, leaving Florida to the Spanish, except for a raid on St. Augustine by Sir Francis Drake in 1586. However as the American colonies thrived in the 1700s, England eyed Spanish Florida with growing interest and began to step up its pressure on Spanish towns and missions. James Oglethorpe invaded Florida from Georgia in 1740, besieging St. Augustine for 27 days. Although he finally withdrew, beaten by Spanish tenacity and Florida's summer climate, the attack weakened Spain's hold on the territory. England put additional pressure on Spain by capturing Havana during the Seven Years' War. At the war's end, England was able to trade it to Spain for Florida. In 1763, after generations of Spanish rule, Florida became British. Spanish residents from the 900 houses in the well-established Spanish community of St. Augustine and the frontier town of Pensacola took up their belongings and sailed to Cuba and Mexico.

The British had great plans for Florida. They divided it into two provinces, East Florida with St. Augustine as capital and West Florida with Pensacola as capital. In Pensacola the British engineer, Elias Durnform, created a city plan that can still be seen today around the Seville Square historic district.

The English established a plantation economy much like that in their colonies to the north and promised settlers land grants and other benefits. They made tentative peace with the local Indians, a dissident branch of the Creeks who had moved in from Georgia to take up residence in the villages deserted by the original Florida Indians.

Although St. Augustine and Pensacola thrived under British rule as wealthy loyalist refugees flooded into Florida from the north, Britain was too distracted with the American Revolutionary War to ever really develop Florida. Spain, eager to get Florida back, took advantage of her distraction and in 1781 recaptured

Pensacola. By 1783 it regained all of Florida and began to colonize in earnest, offering generous land grants to both Spanish people and the new Americans. But the European presence in North America was shrinking and Spain found it increasingly difficult to maintain control of the territory. When the United States bought 828,000 miles of French-owned land through the 1804 Louisiana Purchase, Spanish Florida was surrounded by the U.S.

Spain's policy of giving protection to runaway slaves was a constant source of conflict with Americans just across the border. The Blacks got on well with Florida's Indians and often lived in the same or nearby villages. The term Seminole meaning "run-away," had come into use during the British era and began to be applied to both groups. American raiding parties frequently crossed the border to search for slaves in Indian villages.

The small border town of **Fernandina Beach** on Amelia Island, just northeast of Jacksonville, was a particular target for border skirmishes. Reclaimed by Spain with the rest of Florida in 1783, it went through a rapid sucession of owners. The U.S. government conducted its first "covert" actions against the town in the early 1800s to try to stop a brisk slave trade, pirating, and possible British takeover. In 1812, 200 Americans from Georgia captured it and declared it the "Republic of Florida." Violent opposition from both Spain and England led to an American withdrawal, but in 1817 Sir Gregor MacGregor, a Scottish champion of South American independence, conquered it again and raised the Green Cross of Florida over the city.

The Spanish ousted him too, but a few months later another American (a former member of Congress from Pennsylvania) gathered together a band of privateers and raised his own personal flag over Fernandina.

This flag was quickly replaced by the flag of Mexico, put up by a French pirate named Luis Aury. United States citizens moved in next in a covert action to claim the area for their country. Though none of these assertions of dominance were significant in their own right, they showed Spain's inability to protect its northern borders.

The **Amelia Island Museum of History** (233 South 3rd St., Fernandina Beach, FL 32034; 904-261-7378) includes maps, charts, pictures and memorabilia of the area. There are occasional guided tours of the museum and the historic district.

Florida's European Capitals — St. Augustine and Pensacola

The number one place to learn about European exploration of Florida is, of course, St. Augustine. However Pensacola, though less well known, is rapidly gaining its own fame.

St. Augustine

There is so much to see and do in St. Augustine that a good first stop should be the **Visitor Information Center**, (10 Castillo Dr.; 904-824-3334, open 8 a.m.-5:30 p.m. daily). At the center you can see two orientation movies "Dream of an Empire" and "Struggle to Survive," each shown once an hour from 9:30 a.m. to 5:30 p.m. daily (admission $2 for one movie; $3 for both; children under 15 $1 for each). Get tickets in advance to be sure of seating. For more information contact Museum-Theater, (5 Cordova St., St. Augustine, FL 32084; 904-824-0339). The information center also has guided tour information and St. Augustine Historical Society walking tour brochures which have pictures and brief descriptions of points of special interest. There are two tours — one starting at the oldest house and one starting from the main plaza.

Autos are not the recommended mode of transportation in St. Augustine. Find a good parking space early in your visit and get rid of your car! The narrow winding streets, dead ends, one way streets, and swarms of people damp a driver's enjoyment quickly. St. Augustine is a good walking city, but also has alternatives for those who want something a little easier on the feet. **Sightseeing trains** (170 San Marco Ave., St. Augustine, FL 32084; 904-829-6545) give a good overall orientation, and allow riders to get off and on at major attractions. Tickets are good for the length of visit. Another alternative is a carriage ride in one of **Colee's Sightseeing Carriage Tours** operated by St. Augustine Transfer Co., established in 1880. Carriages are located on the bayfront near the entrance to the Fort (P.O. Box 604, St. Augustine, FL 32085; 904-829-2818, 8:30 a.m.-6 p.m. daily). Visitors in June can enjoy the **Spanish Night Watch Ceremony** on the third Saturday of the month. Local historians recreate life as it was when the settlement was ruled by Spain. There is a parade and candlelight procession with soldiers in full-dress as the town is officially locked for the night with a traditional ceremony.

Summer visitors can attend the *"Cross and the Sword,"* the state's official play about St. Augustine's founding and early days, performed by a cast of singers, dancers, and actors in the outdoor amphitheater in Anastasia State Park, south of the city off SR A1A. The production is produced in partnership with the Florida School of the Arts, a state-supported professional arts school for high school and college students seeking careers in art, dance, music, and theater. (Performances are at 8 p.m. daily except Sunday, admission is

$8 for adults, $4.00 for children 6-12. For reservations call 904-471-1965).

The **Castillo de San Marco** (open daily 9 a.m.-5:45 p.m.) is located at Castillo Drive between Avenida Menendez and the river, right across from the visitors center, an easy landmark close to the town's Spanish era attractions. There is an admission fee for the inside of the fort, but you can walk around the grounds without charge. The earliest forts on this site were wooden and quickly fell victim to fire, humidity, and shoddy construction. Feeble though they were, they provided the Spanish settlement's main protection from 1565 to 1675. In 1672, ground was broken for Castillo de San Marcos and by 1695 the basic fortress was completed, built of coquina, a soft yellow stone formed from solidified masses of sand and shells. The stone was quarried on Anastasia Island, hauled by oxcart, and floated on barges across the river. Earthworks were added in the early 1700s, but it was not until 1756 that the royal coat of arms was placed over the gate to signify completion. The British added a second floor to the fort during their occupation and the Americans renamed it Fort Marion when they took over in 1825. It remained active until 1900 and in 1924 it was declared a National Monument.

St.Augustine's **Restored Spanish Quarter** is a preservation area across the street from the castillo, open daily from 9 a.m.-5 p.m. In this 18th-century Spanish colonial village guides and craftsmen dressed in period clothing recreate the daily lifestyles of the time. Enter the Spanish Quarter on historic St. George Street, south of the Old City Gate. The area includes the Oldest Schoolhouse. Nearby is the **Sanchez House**, perfectly restored with a fountain in the courtyard and antique furniture inside. It is open from 9:30 a.m.-5 p.m. daily, free. The **Oldest House** (14 St. Francis

Street, open daily 9 a.m.-5 p.m.) stands in a quiet residential neighborhood south of the plaza and the Bridge of Lions among many of St. Augustine's surviving Spanish colonial houses. The house and its furnishings reflect the different cultures of its owners down the centuries. Admission includes two adjoining museums with archaeological and historical exhibits and free parking. A National Historic Landmark, it is owned by the St. Augustine Historical Society.

In the **Government House Lobby** (48 King St., open Mon.-Fri. 8 a.m.-5 p.m., free) the Preservation Board displays a large collection of Hispanic artifacts unearthed in continuing excavations in the region. Exhibits change monthly.

The **Mission of Nombre de Dios** (27 Ocean Ave.; 904-829-5696) is easy to spot. A great cross soars 208 feet above the easternmost point of the mission, believed to be the site of the first Roman Catholic mass ever celebrated in the U.S. Connected to it is the Shrine of Our Lady of Le Leche. The **Old Spanish Treasury**, built by the king of Spain between 1690 and 1695, is a fascinating place with a strong room, treasury chests, rare furniture and paintings, pieces of eight, and many other authentic relics. The **Tovar House** (22 St. Francis Street), was marked on the Puente map of 1764. Originally a one-story coquina dwelling, a second story was added during the British era (1763-1783). It is known as the House of the Cannonball because a large cannonball is said to have lodged in the east wall during the bombardment of St. Augustine by the English under General Oglethorpe in 1740.

When the British moved into St. Augustine in 1763 they took over existing Spanish buildings in a well-established city. Although the city retained its Spanish flavor then as it does today, several sites from the British era are still visible. Both the Government

House (48 King Street) on the plaza, where the British governor lived, and Peck House, a neighboring town house where the Lieutenant Governor lived, were modified to English tastes. The modern Episcopal church on the plaza occupies the site of the Spanish bishop's house which was first transformed by the British into an Anglican church and later into a statehouse. St. George Street in the Historic District includes reconstructed wooden shops and houses erected by the British immigrants. The Saint Francis Barracks stand on the site of a Spanish monastery which the British transformed into a barracks.

Pensacola

Pensacola's atmosphere is different from that of St. Augustine's. The town was isolated from other settlements for many years, perched on the southern edge of an extensive North American interior wilderness. The first permanent settlement on the city's present site was made in 1752 after a hurricane destroyed an earlier community on Santa Rosa Island. Because of its location, it was a major Indian trading center. The settlers who built homes along the bayfront and Seville Square were of mixed Scottish, French, Spanish, and British heritage, and many free Blacks also lived in the area.

The city's historic areas are charming and renovation, restoration, and archaeological exploration are actively underway. Stop at the **Visitor's Information Center** (1401 E. Gregory St., Pensacola, FL 32501; 904-434-1234; 800-874-1234) for information about the historic areas. The **Seville Historic District**, listed in the National Register of Historic Places, runs along Pensacola Bay near I-10 and SR 98. There you will find restored houses, shops, and restaurants clustered around the old square. Within the area is **Historic Pensacola Village** (904-444-8905, open 10 a.m.-4:30 p.m. Mon.-Sat.). Tickets allow entry to all village sites — Museum of Industry, Museum of Commerce, several historic houses, and the Colonial Archaeological Trail.

In the complex you can tour the French colonial Lavalle House, a survivor of the second Spanish period (1763-1821), and the Julee Cottage Museum of Black History housed in one of Pensacola's oldest houses, the home of a "free woman of color." The Quina House, a Spanish-French Creole cottage built about 1821, and the Dorr House, a Greek revival house built in 1879, are also in the village. The Colonial Archaeological Trail has exhibits explaining the British fort site and its relationship to different eras of Pensacola's history.

In **Seville Square** look for **Old Christ Church** (Zaragoza and Adams Streets) built in 1832, one of the oldest churches in Florida and now the home of the Pensacola Historical Museum. **The Barkley House** (410 South Florida Blanca St.) is one of the oldest masonry residences in Florida. Barkley, a prosperous merchant of British background, built the house for his wife who grew up in New Orleans. The style is often called a "high house" because of its elevated first floor. The construction resembles that of the early masonry homes of New Orleans and Louisiana. The cannons in Plaza Ferdinand were left by the English and the Spanish. Pensacola has many houses and buildings from the late 1800s and early 1900s as well, not only in the Seville District, but also in nearby **Palafox Historic District** and the **North Hill Preservation District**.

Pensacola also has some interesting fortifications dating from early times. Although there are no remains of the earliest Spanish forts, a small portion of one of the British forts, Fort George (1779-1781) has been excavated and restored as **Fort George Park** (Palafox and La Rua Streets). Parts of one Spanish fort from the later period also remain. The **Battery San Antonio** (Water Battery, 1797-1821), sometimes called "**Fort San Carlos**" is in the general area of the earlier **Fort San Carlos de Barrancas**. Visitors can see rooms or bombproofs in the rear wall made of earth, brick, and stucco. Restored by the National Park Service and administered by the Gulf Islands National Seashore; it is open to the public and guided tours are available.

Spanish Treasure

The Spanish early discovered the swift Gulf Stream that ran along Florida's coasts. For many years it was the route by which they took the great treasures of meso-America back to Spain. The ships were prey to pirates of many nationalities, and the Windward Squadron, a fleet of armed Spanish naval vessels, patrolled the Gulf of Mexico. But the squadron could not protect the treasure ships from the natural environment.

Many were shipwrecked in storms and hurricanes, and stories of riches buried under land and sea have tantalized generations of tourists and treasureseekers alike. There are several museums along the central east coast of Florida that display the riches retrieved from the wrecks of these hapless ships. In fact the central and southeastern coasts of Florida are known as the Treasure Coast and the Gold Coast for the riches that either washed up along the shore or were hoped-for by local residents.

The **McLarty State Museum** (Sebastian Inlet State Recreation Area, 9700 South A1A, Melbourne Beach,

FL 32951; 407-984-4852) is located on the site of an old
Spanish salvage camp. It displays relics from 18th-cen-
tury ships wrecked off the nearby coast. Archaeologists believe an Indian mound near the inlet may
contain the skeletal remains of some of the first European settlers in Florida. They suspect that shipwreck
survivors may have been captured by the Ais tribe and
lived near here with them at least three years before
the founding of St. Augustine. A large cross of shells
over the grave of a chief shows that someone had
introduced him to Christianity.

Another treasure museum, **St. Lucie County Historical Museum** (414 Seaway Drive, Fort Pierce; 407-
468-1795, open Wed.-Sat. 10 a.m.-4 p.m.) specializes in
artifacts from the 1715 wreck of a Spanish treasure
fleet bound from Havana. Exhibits show how divers
locate the many wreck sites off this stretch of coast.

The treasure display which most catches our imagination because of its recent origin is **Mel Fisher Maritime Heritage Society Museum** (200 Greene St., Key
West, FL 33040; 305-296-9936, open daily 10 a.m.-6
p.m.). Fisher is a modern treasure salvor whose most
spectacular discoveries were made in 1985 when he
found the much sought-after treasure ships which
sank in a hurricane in 1622, the *Nuestra de Atocha* and
the *Santa Margarita*. The cache of gold, silver, and em-
eralds is enormous, estimated to be around four bil-
lion dollars, but visitors don't see much of the find.
Although the building is large, only one small room is
devoted to treasure. There is also a National Geographic film concerning the treasure salvors which
plays all day. The **Historic Key West Shipwreck Museum** (510 Greene St., Key West, FL 33040; 305-292-
9740, open daily 10 a.m.-6 p.m.) displays Spanish
treasure in the city's old city hall, recently restored by
the Historic Key West Preservation Board.

Much of the treasure reportedly lost or buried off the Florida coast remains undiscovered. Although serious salvors spend thousands of dollars on equipment, trained divers, and detailed charting of the ocean's bottom, and even then rarely succeed, amateurs can at least hope for some glimpse of a gold coin as they scratch the sand for shells.

New Footsteps on the Land

In 1819 Spain, realizing it could no longer control its Florida territory in the face of shrinking European holdings in North America and increasing American pressure on its borders, sold Florida to the U. S. for five million dollars and United States' agreement to surrender its claim to Texas. The loss of Florida was a hard blow for Spain, but the territory had never met its expectations. The gold the explorers had hoped to find never materialized and though springs flowed freely, none was magical enough to keep soldiers and settlers alive in the face of assaults from nature, hostile Indians, and other contenders for the territory. The last of Florida's prehistoric Indians passed from the land in the early 1700s. By the early 1800s, the Europeans had left as well.

The Americans took over eagerly. As explorers, however, they were no more respectful of the Indians than the Europeans had been. Whereas the Spanish sought gold and souls from the Indians, the Americans wanted land and security for the settlers. The Spanish had attempted to bring Florida's Indians into a Christian heaven. The United States wanted to push them out — away from the lands which Americans wanted to homestead. At first they pushed them into Florida's inhospitable interior; then they tried to remove them altogether, to barren lands in the Oklahoma territory. The story of the Seminole Indian Wars in Chapter 4 chronicles the final conflict between explorers and Indians.

CHAPTER 4

FIGHT FOR A
HOMELAND

AMERICANS AND THE
SEMINOLE INDIANS (1817-1859)

By the time the United States acquired Florida in 1821, many Americans had already settled there and the American army had been operating inside its borders against the Seminole Indians for several years. Jackson's raids against the Seminoles in the First Seminole War set the scene for much of the territory's history over the next 40 years. Only in the extreme isolation of Key West did settlement proceed untroubled by these tensions.

The Seminoles were Creek Indians who had separated from their main tribe and moved into Florida from Georgia to occupy the villages left empty by the original Florida Indians. Their number also included many runaway black slaves, who settled in their towns or established villages of their own nearby. The Seminoles had gotten along well with the British and continued to live in relative freedom under the Spanish. Spanish Florida, in fact, became a haven for both runaway Blacks and Indian refugees of many tribes who poured in from Alabama and Georgia after the Creek War of 1813-1814, tripling the Indian population in a few years.

There were three Seminole wars. The first, from 1817-1818, was fought in northern Florida when the area still technically belonged to Spain. The second, 1835-1842, erupted when the Americans attempted to remove all Indians from Florida by 1836. This was an especially bitter and costly war for both sides in which the Indians destroyed a large number of plantations and homesteads scattered through northeast Florida. Settlement of Florida came to a virtual standstill during this period as the American army attempted to push the Indians down into the less-populated Everglades region. Although the war was officially over in 1842, some Seminoles stayed in Florida and tension remained high. Conflict broke out again in 1849 and the army began to build a chain of forts to keep the Indians in the south. From 1855-1859, in the Third Seminole War, the army pursued the Indians into the Everglades. At the end of this war, almost all Indians were forcibly removed from Florida.

There are many sites throughout Florida associated with the Seminole wars, which can tell us a lot about both the Indians and the settlers from this period.

First Seminole War (1817-1818)

Americans were not tolerant of the Seminoles, even when Florida was still Spanish. They accused them of harboring runaway slaves and stealing livestock. Plantation owners in the southern states sent bands of slave catchers into Florida to raid villages, and the American army, under command of General Andrew Jackson, made numerous forays across the border. Two sites from the First Seminole War can be visited today in the Florida Panhandle. **Fort Gadsden State Historic Site** in the interior along the Apalachicola River (6 miles SW of Sumatra, off SR 65; 904-670-8988, open

daily 8 a.m.-sunset, free) has an open-sided interpretative center with a miniature replica of the fort and
remnants of earth fortifications from this period. **San
Marcos de Apalache,** below Tallahassee (at the southern end of SR 363; 904-925-6219, open Thur.-Mon. 9
a.m.-5 p.m.) features a visitor center with historical
exhibits about General Jackson's visit as well as about
the earlier Spanish era. Both played an important role
in starting the war.

Fort Gadsden had been built by the British as a base
against the U.S. during the War of 1812. After the war,
the English left the fort to a group of free Blacks,
escaped slaves, and Indians. It quickly became known
as the Negro Fort and drew many settlers who farmed
nearby and traded along the river. General Jackson
viewed the fort with growing alarm and accused its
occupants of making raids over the border into Georgia. Tension between Jackson's army and the fort in-
tensified and in 1816, after four Americans were killed
by Indians, U.S. forces surrounded it.

Fighting broke out when the commander refused to
surrender, and a red hot cannon ball from an American
gunboat landed in the fort's powder magazine, blowing up the buildings. Only thirty of the three hundred
occupants survived. Two years later, during the course
of the First Seminole War, the Americans rebuilt Fort
Gadsden as a supply base.

But it took another incident to officially start the
war. In 1817, when Jackson and his troops were again
operating in Spanish territory, he attempted to arrest
Neamathla, a Seminole chief. He then moved southeast and seized San Marcos de Apalache, a Spanish fort
and settlement on the Gulf coast. There he executed
two captured British citizens whom he suspected of
inciting Indian raids, creating a diplomatic crisis between the U.S., Great Britain, and Spain. Jackson with-

AMERICANS AND THE SEMINOLE INDIANS
MAP OF SITES

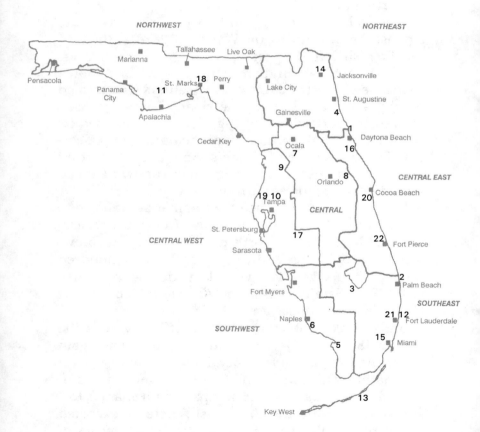

AMERICANS AND THE SEMINOLE INDIANS

SITES TO VISIT

1. ADDISON BLOCKHOUSE STATE HISTORIC SITE, Tomoka State Park, 2099 North Beach St., Ormond Beach, FL 32174; 904-677-3931, accessible by boat.

2. BATTLE OF THE LOXAHATCHEE RIVER, Jonathan Dickinson State Park, 16450 S.E. Federal Highway, Hobe Sound, FL 33455; 407-546-2771, guided tours.

3. BRIGHTON SEMINOLE INDIAN RESERVATION, northwest of Lake Okeechobee SR 78.

4. BULOW PLANTATION RUINS STATE HISTORIC SITE, 3 miles west of Flagler Beach on SR 100, then south on CR 2001; P.O. Box 655, Bunnell, FL 32010; 904-439-2219.

5. CHOKOLOOKEE ISLAND, Everglades; see commemoration on grounds of Florida Capital in Tallahassee.

6. COLLIER-SEMINOLE STATE PARK, south of Naples on U.S.1; Rt. 4 Box 848, Naples, FL 33961; 813-394-3397.

7. DADE BATTLEFIELD STATE HISTORIC SITE, off SR 476, west of U.S. 301, P.O. Box 938, Bushnell, FL 33513; 904-793-4781, open Thur.-Mon. 9 a.m.-5 p.m.

8. FORT CHRISTMAS MUSEUM, County Road 420, 1300 Fort Christmas Rd., Christmas; 305-568-4149, open Tues.-Sat. 10 a.m.-5 p.m., Sun. 1-5 p.m.

9. FORT COOPER STATE PARK, 3100 S. Old Floral City Rd., Inverness, FL 32650; 904-726-0315.

10. FORT FOSTER, Hillsborough River State Park, 15402 U.S. 301 North, Thonotosassa, FL 33592; 813-986-1020, open weekends and holidays with tours on the hour, transportation by van from the park entrance.

11. FORT GADSDEN STATE HISTORIC SITE, 6 miles SW of Sumatra, off SR 65; 904-670-8988, open daily 9 a.m.-sunset, free.

12. FORT LAUDERDALE HISTORICAL SOCIETY, 219 Southwest 2nd Ave., Fort Lauderdale, FL 33301; 305-463-4431.

13. INDIAN KEY, reached by boat from state park ferry, Indian Key Fill at Mile Marker 78; c/o Lignamvitae Key State Botanical Site, P.O. Box 1052, Islamorada, FL 33036; 305-664-4815.

14. KINGSLEY PLANTATION STATE HISTORIC SITE, 11676

Palmetto Ave., Jacksonville, FL 32226 ; 904-251-3122, open 8
a.m.-5 p.m., guided tours daily.

15. MICCOSUKEE INDIAN VILLAGE and FLORIDA ANNUAL
INDIAN ARTS FESTIVAL (Dec. 26 to Jan. 1) U.S. 41; P.O. Box
44021, Miami, FL 33144; 305-223-8388 (weekends) or
305-223-8380 (weekdays).

16. NEW SMYRNA SUGAR MILL STATE HISTORIC SITE, west
of SR 44, south on Mission Drive; P.O. Box 861, New Smyrna,
FL 32170; 904-428-2126, open daily except Mon., free.

17. PAYNES CREEK STATE HISTORICAL SITE, just off U.S. 17,
SR 664-A; P.O. Box 547, Bowling Green, FL 33834;
813-375-4717.

18. SAN MARCOS DE APALACHE, end of SR 363 in St. Marks;
904-925-6219, open Thur.-Mon. 9 a.m.-5 p.m.

19. SEMINOLE CULTURAL CENTER, 5221 N. Orient Rd.,
Tampa; 813-623-3549.

20. SEMINOLE INDIAN AND PIONEER FESTIVAL, Brevard
Community College, Cocoa Campus, 1519 Clearlake Rd.,
Cocoa, FL 407-632-1111, free.

21. SEMINOLE NATIVE VILLAGE and TRIBAL FAIR AND
RODEO (mid-February), 3551 N. State Rd. 7, Hollywood, FL.;
305-961-4519, open Mon.-Sat. 10 a.m.-5 p.m., Sun. 9 a.m.-2
p.m.

22. ST. LUCIE COUNTY HISTORICAL MUSEUM, 414 Seaway
Dr., Fort Pierce, FL 34949; 464-6635, open Wed.-Sat. 10 a.m.-4
p.m., free.

drew from the area, presumably to go back across the border to the United States, but the war was underway. Jackson's dislike of Indians was well-known to Indians and Anglos alike and his attacks on the Seminoles during the First Seminole War were infamous. His troops burned towns, seized corn and livestock, and killed and captured the people.

The Indian Removal Plan

In 1821, the United States finalized its purchase of Florida. American control brought a level of settlement that the peninsula had not experienced since the days of the prehistoric Indians. It also set the scene for a fierce battle between the Indians and the settlers. American settlers, assuming the legality of their European and American land grants, flooded into the territory taking over lands which the Indians believed were rightfully theirs. Hostility grew, fueled by the strong anti-Indian policy of Andrew Jackson who became the territory's first governor.

Governor Jackson launched an all-out attack on the Seminoles and herded them into a small reservation in the interior of the peninsula. But the settlers were pouring into these areas too. The Florida Legislative Council declared in 1829 that the Seminole reservation was in the "pathway of our settlers and has seriously impeded the settlement of the fairest part of Florida."

So new plans were made, spearheaded by Jackson, to move the Seminoles out of Florida altogether. At an 1832 meeting at Paynes' Landing near Silver Springs, the Seminole leaders were urged by white officials to move to the Arkansas Territory (now Oklahoma) and in 1833 they made an inspection trip to the new lands. While there, they were persuaded to sign a document promising removal of all Seminoles from Florida by

1836. Some Seminoles, including a young warrior called Osceola, rebelled against the plan and began to organize resistance. As the time for "Removal" drew near, hostilities between Indians and settlers mounted. By late 1835, a growing number of incidents were setting nerves on edge throughout the territory. Osceola was thrown into prison for six days at Fort King (Ocala) when he spoke out against the whites.

Second Seminole War (1835-1842)

The Dade Massacre
There is no sign today of a long column of American soldiers winding slowly on the Old Fort King Military Road with their six pound cannon. No sign either of canny Seminole Indians lying in wait in the palmettos. But the wary visitor to **Dade Battlefield State Historic Site** in Bushnell, midway between Tampa and Ocala in central Florida (off SR 476, west of U.S. 301; P.O. Box 938, Bushnell, FL 33513; 904-793-4781, open Thur.-Mon. 9 a.m.-5 p.m.) checks the palmettos a second time, just to be sure, remembering that Major Francis Langhorne Dade and his 105 men had seen no Indians either, moments before they were ambushed here on a rainy December morning in 1835.

It's hard to imagine violence here. Today the State Historical Site, also a National Monument, lies serenely in the Florida sunshine. The soldier statue who guards the modern visitor's center stands relaxed, unstartled. A path winds through ancient oaks tracing the army's route, the drama long ago weathered off the round, white columns that mark the spots where Major Dade and his officers fell. The low structure of evenly hewn logs that identifies where survivors of the first round of attack threw up their makeshift breastwork gives no hint of the desperation with which the soldiers rolled their cannon into position to aim at an enemy they could not see.

Major Dade and his men had started out from Fort Brooke (Tampa) in late December 1835 to tramp the 100 miles through Florida's interior to Fort King (Ocala). They knew their mission was dangerous. They did not realize, however, that the Indians were in control of the interior and had vowed to prevent any reinforcements from reaching Fort King. The first five days of Dade's trek wound through swamp land more familiar to Indians than white men. The Indians moved in front of them, burning bridges so the army had to ford rivers and float their cannon on a raft. However, as the army moved onto a broad open tract that signaled the beginning of the high country, their spirits began to rise. They were almost two-thirds of the way along, with the most dangerous terrain behind them.

Suddenly the trees and clumps of palmetto came alive with shots as Chief Alligator, Chief Jumper, and 180 Seminoles opened fire. After the first onslaught, the remaining troops hastily threw up a log breastwork for protection, but there was little they could do and their six-pound cannon was soon silenced. Two soldiers, mistaken for dead, survived the attack and managed to crawl back to Fort Brooke to report the battle. The Seminoles were jubilant. Their own losses were light — three dead and five injured. And the warrior Osceola, on that same day, had murdered the Indian agent at Fort King who had earlier ordered his imprisonment. The massacre, which is reenacted each year on the Saturday nearest to December 28, was the first of a series of raids by the Indians that culminated in the Second Seminole War.

Florida's Early Plantation Era Comes to an End

The December 1835 Indian raids and subsequent hostilities terminated a fascinating but brief chapter of Florida history as plantations all along the east coast were ransacked and burned. Ruins of several of these plantations can still be seen along the northeast and central east coast, especially around Ormond Beach and New Smyrna.

Addison Blockhouse State Historic Site (in Tomoka State Park, 2099 North Beach St., Ormond Beach, FL 32174; 904-677-3931, accessible by boat) has earthworks and the ruins of the plantation kitchen which served as a blockhouse during the war, a large fireplace, and a corner tower. There is a visitor's center and guided tours.

The large chimneys at the **Bulow Plantation Ruins State Historic Site** (3 miles west of Flagler Beach on SR 100, south on CR 2001; P. O. Box 655, Bunnell, FL 32010; 904-439-2219) show the scale of the plantation's sugar operation before the mill was burned down in January 1836. In its time it was one of the most glamorous and wealthy of all Florida's plantations. Major Bulow of Charleston, Georgia, a descendent of an aristocratic German family, acquired 4,675 acres of wilderness in 1821. When he died a few years later he left everything to his young son, John, who managed the estate and lived like a prince. John James Audubon visited the plantation while on a collecting and painting trip in 1831 and spoke of his "most hospitable treatment." Young Bulow's plantation life came to a sudden end in late December 1835, when the Seminoles rampaged through the countryside. A hastily constructed fort was thrown up near the house and for a few weeks it served as a shelter for other local families whose homes were burned. Then it served briefly as a military center and hospital until it was abandoned on January 23, 1836 because of the great number of Indians in the area. John Bulow left the plantation forever that night and died a few months later at the age of 27.

All that is left today of this once thriving plantation are several wells, a spring house, the crumbling foundations of the mansion, and coquina ruins of the sugar mill, ghostly reminders of the fiery end of a long-gone period of Florida's history. There is a brooding quality about the place. You can walk between the sugar mill's walls or simply sit and contemplate the juxtaposition of grandeur and wilderness that this plantation and others like it must have represented. The site has an interpretative center, guided tours, and a nature trail.

New Smyrna Sugar Mill State Historic Site (west of SR 44, south on Mission Drive; P.O. Box 861, New Smyrna, FL 32170; 904-428-2126, open daily except Mon., free) contains the ruins of the Gruger and Depysler Sugar Mill, also destroyed in the same series of raids. Most of the coquina walls and their magnificent arches have survived, along with some machinery and restored kettles. Several other sugar mills from this era have been reclaimed by Florida's vegetation, and lie in ruins in isolated areas.

If you want to see an intact plantation house from this period, head to Fort George Island near Jacksonville to visit **Kingsley Plantation State Historic Site** (11676 Palmetto Ave., Jacksonville, FL 32226; 904-251-3122, open 8 a.m.-5 p.m., guided tours daily). Kingsley is believed to be the oldest plantation house in Florida and has been restored and furnished in its original style.

Battles in a Long War

The Dade massacre, the murder of the Fort King Indian agent by Osceola, and the rampages against plantations, stirred the ire of American military leaders and politicians and signaled the beginning of the Second Seminole War, the longest and most expensive Indian war in American history. The action ranged widely over Florida from the heavily populated northern sections to the wilderness of the Everglades. Everywhere settlers were killed and farms and plantations were destroyed. One of the early battles took place in April 1836 southwest of Ocala near Inverness at **Fort Cooper State Park** (on SR 39, two miles southeast of Inverness; 3100 South Old Floral City Rd., Inverness, FL 32650; 904-726-0315). The fort was hastily constructed to protect sick and wounded soldiers against a two-week siege by a large Seminole force during a U.S. campaign to surround these Indians in the swamps and hammocks of an area known as the Cove of the Withlacoochee. The campaign, although elaborate, proved fruitless. A marker notes where the fort formerly stood and guided tours are available upon request. Each year, on a weekend in early April, a Fort Cooper Commemorative Day is held, at which park staff and volunteers in period clothing recreate the event.

Shortly after the Dade Massacre, the military began to construct a series of log forts, one day's march apart, in an attempt to secure the wilderness territory and provide supply depots for soldiers in the field. Visitors today can see the remnants of these forts at several historic sites.

The history of **Fort Foster**, is representative of many of them. It has been restored with an interpretative center and stands in Hillsborough River State Park northeast of Tampa (15402 U.S. 301 North, Thonotosassa, FL 33592; 813-986-1020, open weekends and holidays with tours every hour, transportation by van from the Park entrance). Park rangers dressed as soldiers carry replicas of weapons and other equipment of the period.

The fort lies in the flood plain near a crossing of the Hillsborough River on the Fort King Military Road. This was the ford that Major Dade and his men took on their ill-fated march from Fort Brook (Tampa) to Fort King (Ocala), just three days before their massacre. After the massacre and the start of the Second Seminole War, military strategists decided to construct a fort and a bridge to protect the crossing and supply army units in the field.

Over the next sixteen months the fort went through periods of construction and abandonment before it was permanently vacated in June 1837. The first fort, thrown up in March 1836, was called Fort Alabama, in honor of the Alabama volunteers who built and manned it. After two months it was abandoned and actually blown up. Then in December it was re-established, named this time for Lt. Col. William Foster who was in charge of rebuilding it.

When this second fort was completed in January 1837, it was turned over to 50 sailors who faced continuous harassment from the Seminoles until mid-March when the Indians agreed to move south of Hillsborough in preparation for emigration to the west. Gradually the sailors were replaced by men from the 2nd Artillery and as the fighting moved south, the fort was no longer involved in ongoing battles with the Seminoles. Boredom and ill health were the greatest problems of the men in this and other forts. The Americans were finding out what the Spanish, British, and French had learned only too well — the primary enemies in Florida were climate, insects, and disease.

At one time there were 350 men assigned to the post, but fortunately there were rarely that many present. Because there was so little room inside the fort, most of the soldiers slept in tents. The cramped quarters, dampness, and insects led to increasing ill-health and in April 1837 the post physician recommended withdrawal. The fort once again served as a supply depot during the following winter but then was abandoned permanently as the Indians were pushed further south toward the Everglades.

On a quiet day it is possible to imagine the sound of soldiers' axes cutting logs for the fort, the curses of sailors who longed for the sea, and the almost imperceptible rustle of proud Indian warriors in the underbrush as they plotted against the intruders who were trying to take away their homelands. The trails along the river and around the fort help us understand the natural environment in which Indians and Europeans settled and fought. The fort itself gives us a sense of both the human drama and the daily boredom of the struggle.

Collier-Seminole State Park on the edge of the Everglades (17 miles south of Naples on U.S. 1; Rt 4 Box 848, Naples, FL 33961; 813-394-3397) has a replica of one of the blockhouses from this period with a small museum inside.

The Fort Christmas Museum, in an Orange County park east of Orlando, also has a replica of a fort from the Second Seminole War (County Road 420, 1300 Fort Christmas Rd., Christmas, FL; 305-568-4149, open Tues.-Sat. 10 a.m.-5 p.m., Sun. 1-5 p.m.). An audio-visual in the storehouse gives the history of the Seminole Wars.

There was brief hope that the war might come to a

quick end in 1836 when the head chief of the Seminoles, Micanopy, sent word that he was ready to negotiate. He sent Osceola and two other Indians to meet with U.S. officials, but while the group was negotiating a cease fire, a body of U.S. troops approached and opened fire on the Indians. Osceola and his two companions escaped but the incident escalated hostilities for another year. Peace seemed close again in the middle of 1837 when many Indians, tired of fighting, agreed to emigrate. Others refused, however, and vowed to fight on, angered by rumors that they would be settled among their arch enemies, the Creeks, and that their black allies would be returned to slavery. Osceola, who had lead the fight for the Indians' homeland from the beginning, carried on the battle until late 1837 when he was captured, through treachery, while under a flag of truce. He died a few months later in a dungeon in Fort Moultrie, South Carolina. But even the loss of Osceola's leadership did not end the war.

The **Battle of the Loxahatchee River** was fought in January 1838 on the southeastern coast of Florida just above West Palm Beach within the present day Jonathan Dickinson State Park (16450 S.E. Federal Highway, Hobe Sound, FL 33455; 407-546-2771). A sign in the park explains the battle. There are guided tours, and an interpretative demonstration by a park ranger dressed as a mounted horse soldier brings the historic event to life.

In December 1838, in a new attempt to terminate the war, Cherokee Indian chiefs were brought to Florida to persuade the Seminoles to move west of the Mississippi River. The initial meeting occurred at a place now known as Tosohatchee State Reserve east of Orlando (3365 Taylor Creek Rd., Christmas, FL 32709; 407-568-5893). This effort proved no more successful than the others.

As the war moved south, even residents of the Florida Keys felt the Indians' rage. **Indian Key** (c/o Lignumvitae Key State Botanical Site, P.O. Box 1052, Islamorada, FL 33036; 305-664-4815, reached by boat from Indian Key Fill on U.S. 1) was a small thriving community of 35 inhabitants, including the well-known physician-botanist, Dr. Henry Perrine, who introduced more than 200 plants to tropical Florida. The dominant force of the community was Jacob Housman, a wealthy salvager, who in 1840 was trying to negotiate a contract with the government to hunt and kill Indians at $200 a head. But the Indians beat him at his own game. They attacked Indian Key on August 7, 1840, destroying the community and killing 16 people, including Dr. Perrine. Indian Key has trails and markers that explain its history.

By the time Florida became a state in 1845, the majority of the Seminoles had been killed or removed from the peninsula. A few, however, retreated into the swampy reaches of the Everglades. The Second Seminole War had cost the United States a great deal — more than 1,500 men, an unknown number of civilian settlers, and twenty million dollars. Yet it had not won peace.

Settlement in Florida came to a halt at the height of the war and for a period afterwards the area experienced economic depression. Fields abandoned during the conflict remained half-cleared and overgrown. With the admission of Florida as a state in 1845, however, settlement not only picked up, it took off. White settlers continued to demand total removal of the Indians.

Third Seminole War (1855-1859)

Billy Bowlegs, Chief of the Seminoles, tried to avoid trouble but slavers continued to capture Blacks and some Indians, even in the Everglades. In 1849, three Seminoles attacked and killed two clerks at a trading post along Paynes Creek, near present-day Wauchula in central Florida, an incident which helped precipitate the Third Seminole War.

In **Paynes Creek State Historical Site** on SR 664-A just off U.S. 17 in central west Florida (P.O. Box 547, Bowling Green, FL 33834; 813-375-4717) a square white monument marks the graves of the two men from the Kennedy-Darling trading post. The Seminole leaders, hoping to avoid conflict, declared the killers renegades, pursued them, and turned them over to U. S. authorities. But American anti-Indian sentiment still ran high.

The brooding silence of Paynes Creek collapses time. You can visualize perhaps, as you stand in that small clearing, the five Indians creeping from the palmettos on a steaming July day in 1849 to open fire on the new trading center, built to keep them in Florida's interior, away from their established trading posts and American settlers on the Gulf Coast. You may feel a flash of the anger and frustration that both settlers and Indians must have felt as they fought for lands they believed were rightfully theirs.

Displays in the visitor's center illustrate the park's history as well as a fascinating comparison of the dress of the Seminole Indians and Scottish Highlanders who had migrated to the frontier earlier. The Scots and Indians were similar in their hardiness, fierce fighting ability, and independence, and apparently got on well together. Over the years the clothing of the Indians came to resemble that of the Highlanders with a bright-colored knee-length skirt, broad shoulder straps, pouches decorated with tassels, and diamond patterned garters over leggings. On Indian heads, Highland bonnets turned into wrapped turbans, complete with ostrich plumes.

Near the Paynes Creek visitor's center is the site of Chokonikla, one of a chain of forts built by the army after the trading post incident. These forts, designed to keep the Indians in the south, were put up every ten miles in a line from the Manatee River on the Gulf coast below Tampa Bay to the Indian River on the east coast. Chokonikla, like many of the other forts, was abandoned within a year as the Third Seminole War moved south.

While it was in service, however, it housed 223 men, including a regimental band. No battles were fought there, but a number of men died, victims of malaria and fever. On one occasion, 153 of the 166 troops of the fort were either sick, on detached duty, or under arrest. Archeological excavation was conducted in 1982 and the fort's main outlines are marked on the ground.

From 1856-1858 the army pursued the Indians into the Everglades, penetrating further than white men had ever been before. As they went, they mapped and explored the area for the first time.

In the final stages of the Third Seminole War, a major army expedition was based on **Chokolookee Island**. The plan was to converge from all sides on the hiding places of the Seminoles in the Everglades and Big Cypress Country, rounding them up for transportation to the west. In November 1857 a group of mounted volunteers from Fort Myers led by Captain John Parkhill traveled up the Turner River and discovered and destroyed a recently deserted Indian settlement and two large Indian fields. The next day the

Indians ambushed them, killing Captain Parkhill and five others. A statue on the grounds of the Florida Capital in Tallahassee commemorates this event. Little by little, through other such skirmishes, almost all of the remaining Indians were forcibly removed from Florida and the Seminole Wars came to an end.

Seminole Indians Today

A small number of Seminole Indians, an estimated 200-300, withstood all relocation efforts and formed the nucleus of Florida's present Seminole Indian population. There are two language groups, the Musk-ogee-speaking Cow Creek Seminoles and the more numerous Miccosukee. Their numbers have been increasing steadily since the early 1900s. They rarely intermarry and most remain full-blooded Indians.

Today visitors can learn about the Seminole Indians at the **Miccosukee Indian Village** (on U.S. 41 25 miles west of Miami, P.O. Box 440021, Miami, FL 33144; 305-223-8388 weekends or 305-223-8380 weekdays). The village is owned and operated by the Miccosukee Tribe of Indians and includes a museum, demonstrations and sales of arts and crafts, an airboat tour of a typical hammock village where a Miccosukee family still lives, and a restaurant that features a variety of Indian dishes. If you want to compare what you see in the village with the original communities, visit the **Seminole Cultural Center** in Tampa (5221 N. Orient Rd; 813-623-3549), or **The Fort Lauderdale Historical Society** (219 southwest 2nd Ave., Fort Lauderdale, FL 33301; 305-463-4431) which has a scale model of a Seminole Indian village, complete with arts and crafts.

You can also see Indian artifacts at the **St. Lucie County Historical Museum** (414 Seaway Dr. in Fort

Pierce FL 34949; 464-6635, open Wed.-Sat. 10 a.m.-4 p.m., free).

In Hollywood, Florida the local Seminole tribe operates a **Seminole Native Village** (3551 N. State Rd. 7; 305-961-4519, open Mon.-Sat. 10 a.m.-5 p.m., Sun. 9 a.m.-2 p.m.) which, in addition to the usual wildlife displays and alligator wrestling, features paintings of Seminole life and legends by Guy La Bree, widely known as the "Barefoot Artist." La Bree, a white man with an extensive knowledge of Seminole traditions, was asked by tribal leaders to paint Seminole subjects. Today Chief James Billie holds the world's largest collection of La Bree's works, which can be purchased only from the artist's home in Arcadia, Florida.

There are several Seminole Indian festivals in the state. At the Florida Annual Indian Arts Festival held at the Miccosukee Village from December 26th to January 1, over forty tribes gather to dance, sing, exhibit, and perform. In Hollywood, Florida the Indians hold a Tribal Fair and Rodeo in mid-February. Brevard Community College holds a Seminole Indian and Florida Pioneer Festival each October on its Cocoa campus (1519 Clearlake Rd., Cocoa, FL; 407-632-1111, free).

Many of the state's Seminole Indians live on the Brighton Seminole Indian Reservation northwest of Lake Okeechobee (off SR 78) in much the same way as they have for centuries. Here is uncommercial Indian life. The Indians inhabit houses, like other Floridians, but their lifestyles remain close to the earth and their tribal rituals.

CHAPTER 5

UNDER THE
CONFEDERATE FLAG

Floridians had little time to adjust to peace at the end of the last Seminole war. Even before it was over, economic, ideological, and social undercurrents were pulling Florida, along with the rest of the nation, toward civil war. After becoming a part of the United States, Florida had become increasingly Southern in its orientation, even though its long Spanish history distinguished it in some important ways. Its extreme climate and infertile land did not yield crops easily and agriculture here was highly labor intensive. Although Spanish Florida had provided a haven for escaped slaves, American Florida, with its plantation economy, had been built on slave labor and remained heavily dependent on it. Immigrants from other southern states, who poured across its northern borders as the Seminole Indian wars moved down toward the Everglades, reinforced the southern perspective.

When Florida became a state in 1845, the population, mostly concentrated in the northwest along the Georgia border, numbered 66,500, about half of whom were slaves. Through the 1840s and 1850s, Florida remained highly dependent on imports for survival. It produced cotton, turpentine, lumber, vegetables, cornmeal, and pasture grasses. Everything else came from outside. Although railroads were beginning to be developed and there was a line between Jacksonville on the east coast and Cedar Key on the Gulf coast, there were no railroads connecting Florida with the rest of the country. Supplies arrived primarily by water through the three main Gulf ports: Pensacola, St. Marks, and Apalachicola.

Floridians, along with other Southerners, had come to regard themselves as culturally different from people outside the region. There were sharp economic differences between the industrial North and the agricultural South, as well as disagreement about the acceptability of slavery. For years the country had attempted to maintain a delicate balance of interests between the North and the South. In 1860, after the November election of Abraham Lincoln as President, that balance was lost and the nation toppled into Civil War.

In December 1860, South Carolina, always a firm supporter of states' rights, became the first state to secede from the Union, followed shortly after by Mississippi. Florida was the third state to withdraw, on January 10, 1861. By the time of Lincoln's inauguration in March 1861, seven states had seceded and established the Confederate States of America, with Jefferson Davis as President.

Although a sizable percentage of Floridians opposed secession, once the decision was made they committed themselves to the war. With only about 140,000 people, half of whom were still slaves, the state had few soldiers to defend either the state or the Confederacy. Forts and arsenals, relatively unused in recent years, suddenly became important again. Even before Florida's secession, both state and federal officials had begun to jockey for control of the state's strategic posts. Several forts were at stake: the three forts at Pensacola (Barrancas, McRee, and Pickens);

Fort Clinch at Amelia Island; Fort Marion (the Castillo de San Marcos) at Saint Augustine, and Forts Taylor and Jefferson at Key West. Over the course of the war, some forts changed hands several times. Today you can trace the story of Florida's involvement in the War Between the States through displays in these forts and at the major battle sites.

Florida Forts

Pensacola

Federal officers at Pensacola decided quickly that they could hold only one of the area's three forts. They evacuated Fort Barrancas and Fort McRee, and on January 10, the day Florida's secession was ratified, took control of then unoccupied **Fort Pickens**, which they saw as the most strategically important. It was a massive fortification on Santa Rosa Island with a five-sided plan and five bastions which incorporated over 20 million bricks. In 1829 when building was started, the fort was much closer to the water. Over the intervening years wind and waves have expanded the island almost three-quarters of a mile to the west. Fort Pickens is now in **Gulf Island National Seashore** (Fort Pickens Road; 904-932-5302, museum open daily 9 a.m.-5 p.m. with guided tours and summer activities).

At the same time federal forces took control of Fort Pickens, federal reinforcements for the fort set sail from Boston. The Union forces sent to repair the fort found that their main problem was to reverse its defenses. Although it had been designed to protect against attack from the sea, in this war the fort needed protection from the mainland.

The Confederates issued three demands for the surrender of Fort Pickens. Each was refused. Ironically,

UNDER THE CONFEDERATE FLAG
MAP OF SITES

NORTHWEST

NORTHEAST

1
Marianna
Tallahassee   Live Oak
11
2
6
5
Pensacola
St. Marks   Perry
3
Jacksonville
Panama
City
Lake City
8
St. Augustine
Apalachia
Gainesville
Cedar Key
Ocala
Daytona Beach

CENTRAL EAST

Orlando
Cocoa Beach
Tampa
CENTRAL
St. Petersburg
CENTRAL WEST
10
Fort Pierce
Sarasota
Palm Beach
Fort Myers
SOUTHEAST
Naples
Fort Lauderdale
SOUTHWEST
Miami
7 4
Key West 9

UNDER THE CONFEDERATE FLAG

SITES TO VISIT

1. BATTLE OF MARIANNA, Marianna, FL (near Florida Caverns).

2. BATTLE OF NATURAL BRIDGE, six miles east of Woodville, off SR 363; Natural Bridge State Historic Site, c/o San Marcos de Apalache State Historic Site, P.O. Box 27, St. Marks, FL 32355; 904-929-6216, open 8 a.m.-sunset, free.

3. BATTLE OF OLUSTEE, between Jacksonville and Lake City; State Historic Site, P.O. Box 40, Olustee, FL 32072; 904-752-3866, museum open Thur.-Mon.

4. EAST MARTELLO MUSEUM, 3501 S. Roosevelt Blvd., Key West; 305-296-3913.

5. FORT BARRANCAS, FORT MC REE, and FORT PICKENS, (BATTLE OF SANTA ROSA ISLAND) Fort Pickens Road; Gulf Islands National Seashore, P.O. Box 100, Gulf Breeze, FL 32561; 904-932-5302, museum open daily 9 a.m.-5 p.m.

6. FORT CLINCH STATE PARK, 2601 Atlantic Ave., Fernandina Beach, FL 32034; 904-261-4212.

7. FORT JEFFERSON NATIONAL MONUMENT, Dry Tortugas, accessible by boat or plane from Key West.

8. FORT MARION (Castillo de San Marco), 1 Castillo Drive East, St. Augustine, FL 32084, open daily 9 a.m.-5:45 p.m.

9. FORT ZACHARY TAYLOR STATE HISTORIC SITE; P.O. Box 289, Key West, FL 33041; 305-292-6713, open Wed.-Sun., 8 a.m.-5 p.m.

10. GAMBLE PLANTATION STATE HISTORIC SITE, 3708 Patten Ave. (U.S. 301), Ellenton, FL 34222; 813-722-1017, open Thur.-Mon., 9 a.m.-4 p.m., entrance by tour only, on the hour.

11. OLD FORT PARK, Tallahassee.

Colonel William H. Chase, the Florida officer called upon to lead the attack against Fort Pickens, had supervised its construction several years earlier, before he had retired from the U.S. Corps of Army Engineers. He knew its strengths only too well. Assault would be costly, and success unlikely. Furthermore, Florida Senators still in Washington advised Florida's Governor Perry to avoid bloodshed. U.S. President Buchanan, hoping to avoid war, at least until Lincoln was inaugurated in March, arranged with Florida Senator Mallory the "Pickens Truce," in which it was agreed that the Union would not reinforce the fort, and the Confederate States would not attack it.

Fort Pickens, along with federally controlled Fort Sumter in South Carolina, raised the ire of Confederates. Both commanded Confederate harbors, with the United States flag flying high. Yet even after Lincoln's inauguration, both sides held back for a time, reluctant to precipitate war. Although the *USS Brooklyn* arrived off Pensacola with troops aboard, they did not land. On March 29, 1861 Lincoln's cabinet voted to reinforce Fort Pickens, but due to a series of miscommunications the federal troops were not sent ashore.

Finally on April 12, 1861 the Confederates began firing on Fort Sumter and forced the surrender of federal troops. On April 15, Lincoln called for federal troops to enforce the nation's laws. Five more states promptly joined the Confederacy. The Civil War had begun. Immediately afterwards, federal troops were landed at Fort Pickens, and Lincoln declared a naval blockade of the Southern states.

The Confederates stepped up their strengthening of **Fort Barrancus,** on a bluff overlooking the bay, by adding auxiliary batteries along the coast. As Confederate troops arrived, they settled into temporary camps north of the fort. Their spirits were kept high in the first months of the war by reports of early successes by the Southern armies.

By Fall, the Union troops under Colonel Harvey Brown numbered 2,000 and Confederate troops on shore, commanded by General Braxton Bragg, numbered 7,000. On October 9, in the first major engagement in Florida, known as the Battle of Santa Rosa Island, a Confederate attack on Fort Pickens was thwarted. On November 22, 1861 the Union forces returned the challenge. The guns of the fort and of the battleships *Niagara* and *Richmond* opened fire, concentrating their bombardment on **Fort McRee**, a brick masonry fort across the channel from Fort Pickens on a narrow neck of land then called Fosters Bank and today known as Perdido Key. The location necessitated a unique design, resembling a broad stubby airplane wing with rounded ends. Plans for the 1840 fort, believed to be the only one of its kind in the United States, are on file at the **Pensacola Historical Museum** (located in Old Christ Church, 405 South Adams St.; 904-433-1559).

The Confederates held Fort McRee, but it was badly damaged and the Federal offensive continued. On February 27, 1862 Pensacola was ordered abandoned by the Confederates. The troops and materials were needed in other parts of the South. By May 9, 1862 the evacuation was complete. Pensacola remained in Union hands for the rest of the war.

Fort McRee was so badly damaged in the Civil War that it was not repaired. Its crumbling walls were washed away in the hurricane of 1906 and today the site itself is under water, a result of heavy erosion of land on that side of the channel.

Fort Barrancas and the Advanced Redoubt to the north are now part of **Gulf Islands National Seashore**.

They have been recently restored by the National Park Service and are open to the public with guided tours.

Fernandina Beach

Fort Clinch, on the north end of Amelia Island in Fernandina, was taken quietly by the Confederates just before Florida's secession. It had been started in 1842 and only partially completed by 1861. The Confederates established batteries in the fort, around the town, and in other strategic locations on Amelia Island to protect against attack by sea. In early 1862, however, the federal army captured several South Carolina and Georgia coastal islands, effectively isolating Fernandina. Confederate General Robert E. Lee authorized his forces to withdraw from the area and by March 3 the northern army controlled it. The Federal troops immediately began to complete the fort, but it never played a major role in the war nor engaged its guns in battle, even though it was of strategic importance.

Today in **Fort Clinch State Park** (2601 Atlantic Ave., Fernandina Beach, FL 32034; 904-261-4212) rangers dressed in Union uniforms carry out the daily chores of a garrison soldier in 1864. This well-preserved fort, on the shore of Cumberland Sound, provides an opportunity to walk through vaulted brick passageways and along bastions and get a real feel for the life of a working fort. Exhibits on its history are displayed in the Interpretive Center. Campfire programs and guided walks are provided seasonally.

Jacksonville

Although no forts remain in Jacksonville for modern visitors to see, the city was of interest to both the Union and the Confederacy. It changed hands four times and suffered from friend and foe alike. When the Confederates left before the first invasion by Federal troops in March 1862, they burned eight sawmills and over four million board feet of lumber as well as iron works and a boat under construction.

St. Augustine

Fort Marion, (Castillo de San Marco) in St. Augustine was quickly occupied by the Confederates at the time of Florida's secession. One of the first actions of the fort's new commander, Captain George Couper Gibbs, was to order that all the east coast lighthouses be extinguished to make navigation more difficult for the Union blockaders. A group of Confederates moved down the coast, dismantling the lights as they traveled. St. Augustine had little strategic importance in the national conflict. By early 1862 it was evacuated by the Confederates, along with other towns on the coast, and fell under Union control. In early March, the day before the U.S. Navy anchored in the mouth of the harbor, Confederate soldiers, accompanied by many of the town's civilians, departed for the interior. Although the change of authority was outwardly peaceful, there was hostility. Several women of the town, strong supporters of the Confederacy, cut down the town's flagpole to keep the Union flag from flying over St. Augustine.

There are few distinctively Civil War-period sites in St. Augustine. **Castillo de San Marco** (1 Castillo Drive), the city's main landmark, has some exhibits from the days when it housed both Confederate and Union troops. The U.S. Army barracks in St. Augustine during the Civil War, restored to its former design in 1922, is now the state headquarters for the Florida National Guard. **The Gun Shop and Museum of**

Weapons (81C Kings St.; 904-3829-3727, open 10 a.m.-6 p.m in winter and 10 a.m.-8 p.m. in summer) includes some Civil War guns within its collection.

Key West

In Key West, Captain James M. Brannan, commander of U.S. forces there at the time of secession, vowed he would not surrender control of the island's defenses even though he had only 44 men and no authority to act. In the hope of gaining a more secure position, he moved his men secretly, at night, across the island from their barracks to **Fort Taylor**, then still incomplete. Once there, he worked quickly to repair the barracks and mount defenses. Although Confederate supporters made one attempt to take the fort, the Union position was never seriously challenged. Key West was an important outpost for the Union because numerous blockade-running ships were detained in its harbor, guarded by Fort Taylor's cannons, a severe loss to the South. Fort Taylor's 10-inch-Rodman and Columbiad cannons had a range of three miles, an impressive deterrent against Confederate takeover attempts.

Federal troops also occupied **Fort Jefferson** in the Dry Tortugas. Like Forts Pickens and Taylor, Fort Jefferson had become obsolete before it was completed and had never been garrisoned. It was never the scene of any military or naval action but served a dramatic role as a military prison during and after the war. Its most notable inmates were the "Lincoln Conspirators," four men convicted of complicity in the assassination of President Abraham Lincoln. One of these, Dr. Samuel Mudd, was involved only because he innocently set the broken arm of John Wilkes Booth after he had assassinated Lincoln. Mudd spent two years here before he was pardoned on account of his help during the 1867 yellow fever epidemic at the fort.

Both forts can be visited today. **Fort Zachary Taylor State Historic Site** (P.O. Box 289, Key West, FL 33041; 305-292-6713, open Wed.-Sun. 8 a.m.-5 p.m.) has been recently excavated and is open to the public. The fort was started in 1845 as part of a plan for a number of forts along the Florida coastline. It is constructed in the shape of a trapezoid on a shoal off the southwestern shore of the city, with three sides facing seaward and the long side with the main entrance facing land.

The fort is remarkable in many respects. The outstanding brickwork was laid by German and Irish expert craftsmen using bricks from Pensacola and Virginia. The building has sanitary facilities flushed by the tide and a desalination plant which produced drinking water from the sea as early as 1861. Today it houses one of the finest collections of Civil War armaments in existence.

Fort Jefferson National Monument, (c/o U.S. Coast Guard Base, Key West, FL 33040; 305-247-6211) is accessible only by boat or plane. Sometimes dubbed the Gibraltar of the Gulf, the fort has walls 50 feet high and 8 feet thick and covers most of the 16 acre Garden Key, 68 miles from Key West.

At the fort there is an excellent self-guiding tour, introduced by an explanatory slide show. Visitors can roam freely over the key which has a small beach, snorkeling, and interesting wildlife. Facilities are few (no housing, no water, no supplies) so bring everything you think you might need. Key West Seaplane (Murray's Marina, 5603 Junior College Road, on Stock Island; 305-294-6978) flies twice a day for half-or full-day trips.

The **East Martello Museum** (3501 S. Roosevelt Blvd., Key West; 305-296-3913), housed in an 1862

Civil War brick fortress, displays Key West memorabilia. The fort's tower, with vaulted ceilings, has a good view of the surrounding area.

The Federal Blockade — A Waiting Game

The federal blockade, instituted as soon as the Civil War started, posed grave problems to a state so dependent on shipping for survival. Early in the war, as a result of the Union control of Pensacola, St. Augustine, and Key West, Florida found itself surrounded by federal forces on all sides except the north. Blockade ships sat off the coast and moved in and out, almost at will. **Cedar Key**, for example, along the big bend on the Gulf coast, was raided by federal ships early in 1862. Sailors and marines from the *USS Hatteras*, out of Key West, landed and destroyed the railroad wharf and depot, several boxcars of military supplies, the telegraph office, and a turpentine storehouse. They captured four schooners, three sloops, one ferryboat, a sailboat, and a launch. Only a lieutenant and 22 men were present to protect the railway terminus.

Apalachicola, another of Florida's key ports, fared little better. At the start of the war a command was assigned to protect it, but numbers dwindled and the defense force was finally disbanded. Most of the town's population fled 90 miles upriver to Ricco's Bluff. The Confederate military strategy for Florida was to concentrate strength in the interior of the state, ready to move to any area that was menaced by federal forces. Floridians had worried from the beginning of the war that the Confederacy would give low priority to the protection of Florida. These fears quickly proved to be well founded. The main contingents of

Florida troops were moved to other parts of the south and fought in every major battle in the Civil War. Few were left at home to protect their own state.

Civil War Battles in Florida

Florida saw little action within its own borders until early 1864. The largest battle in the state, the **Battle of Olustee** (Olustee Battle State Historic Site, P.O. Box 40, Olustee FL; 904-752-3866, museum open Thur.-Mon.) was fought about halfway between Jacksonville and present day Lake City. On February 7, 1864 Union transports had brought troops to Jacksonville for the fourth time. The soldiers moved on westward, marching inland for several days in the first major threat to Florida's interior. The Confederate General Finegan withdrew in front of the Union forces until he reached Olustee, 13 miles from Lake City, where he felt he had the greatest natural advantage. His troops took up positions on a line about a mile-and-a-half long running between Ocean Pond on the north and a large cypress swamp on the south. The two armies were about evenly matched, each with about 5,000 men.

Fighting raged for several hours until finally the Federal army began to retreat. The Confederates had secured the interior of Florida and their supply lines, and had captured some much-needed equipment.

If you visit the Olustee Battlefield in late February, you can see the battle re-enacted by volunteers dressed in Union and Confederate uniforms. The battlefield is accessible by a trail and the battle lines are well marked by signs. A small museum introduces and interprets the battle and the larger context in which it occurred. Olustee battlefield is a good place to learn about the Civil War.

The next major engagement in Florida, the **Battle of**

Marianna, occurred a few months later in September, 1864. On September 18, Federal General Alexander Asboth moved out from Fort Barrancas in Pensacola with 700 mounted men to capture scattered rebel forces in Washington and Jefferson counties, liberate any Federal prisoners held there, find recruits for the Union forces, and locate horses and mules. After four days, the Federal army reached present-day De Funiak Springs; the next day they surprised the village of Eucheeana; and the day after that they reached Marianna, a trading center for Jackson County with 500 inhabitants.

The townspeople had been warned and put together what defense they could — about 150 youths and old men in a home guard group dubbed the "Cradle and Grave Company" and a handful of Confederate regulars home on sick leave. They constructed a barricade of logs and old wagons, but could not protect their flanks. When they were fired upon from the rear, they had no choice but to surrender. The women and children of the community sheltered from the battle in nearby Florida Caverns (3 miles north on SR 167; 2701 Caverns Road, Marianna, FL 32446; 904-482-9598) a fascinating cluster of underground caves. Reenactment of the battle occurs here every October.

The last major engagement in Florida, the **Battle of Natural Bridge,** (Natural Bridge State Historic Site, six miles east of Woodville off U.S. 363 on Natural Bridge Road (SR 354); c/o San Marcos de Apalache, P.O. Box 27, St. Marks, FL 32355; 904-925-6216, open 8 a.m.-sunset, free) took place early in 1865, close to the end of the war. As a result of a Confederate victory, Tallahassee was the only Confederate state capital east of the Mississippi River never to fall into Union hands. Military strategists had feared an attack on St. Marks and Tallahassee for a long time. It finally came in March

1865. The federal forces were eager to neutralize the port at St. Marks so that it would not become a center for blockade-running activity by the Confederates. They also wanted to capture the state capital and destroy the railroad and Confederate supplies. On the morning of March 4, fourteen Union vessels landed about a thousand troops under the command of General John Newton, who started marching inland toward the capital. At the same time, U.S. naval commander William Gibson attempted to steam up the St. Marks River to take Fort Ward and Port Leon, but his ships ran aground in the shallow waterway.

Confederate riders raced to the capital to warn the residents, who immediately began to construct Fort Houston on the outskirts of the city. These breastworks are still in place in Old Fort Park. Everyone organized in defense. Old men from Quincy formed a company, the Gadsden Greys, in which no member was younger than 50. Wounded men came out from their sickrooms. Cadets from the West Florida Seminary came too, some as young as twelve, in a company nicknamed the "Baby Corps."

These volunteers, along with the Florida reserves, took the offensive. They got to the railroad bridge at Newport and burned it before the Union troops arrived, forcing them to move up toward Natural Bridge where the St. Marks River goes underground and they could cross on land. By the time they arrived at Natural Bridge, the Confederates, under the command of Brigadier General William Miller, were entrenched in a huge crescent which was waiting to converge out of the forest on the Federal troops. The Confederates repulsed two assaults before the Union troops finally retreated to their ships. The Confederates pursued them for twelve miles, then waited at the bridge for three days to be sure they would not return. Then they marched back in triumph to Tallahassee.

The city was jubilant. Tallahassee was safe and Confederate losses were less than the Union's. And the Baby Corps had come back intact. The capital began to plan a celebration concert for all its defenders.

But elsewhere the Confederate cause was going badly, and on April 1, just a few days after Tallahassee had been saved, John Milton, governor of Florida, committed suicide. He realized what the capital's residents were not yet willing to admit. The Confederacy's fall was very near. A week later General Lee surrendered the Confederate forces to General Grant. The news of the end of the war arrived in Tallahassee at the height of the festivities celebrating the victory of Natural Bridge.

Once a year the conflict is re-enacted, but the rest of the time the Natural Bridge battlesite is a quiet place that speaks for itself. The long arc of breastworks and indentations that mark the graves of those who died are still visible. A monument commemorates all those who served. A sand road leads from the battleground into the woods, the road down which the Union troops retreated to their ships. Here one can get a feeling for the tragedy that was the Civil War — a war whose wounds still have not fully healed.

After the War...

Federal troops took over Florida on May 20, 1865. But the state still had one page to add to the history of the Civil War. In late May 1865 the Confederate secretary of state, Judah P. Benjamin, took refuge in the Gamble Mansion near Ellenton, inland from the Gulf coast near present-day Bradenton, while Union troops searched for him and other cabinet members. After the fall of the Confederacy, Benjamin had made his way south, crossing the Suwannee River on May 15 disguised as a Mr. Howard. He arrived at Gamble Mansion on May 20 and hid there while friends found a boat. On May 23 he sailed from Sarasota Bay, escaping by a hazardous and circuitous route to England, where he became a leading member of the English Bar. **Gamble Mansion** is now a State Historic Site (3708 Patten Ave (U.S. 301), Ellenton, FL 34222; 813-722-1017, open Thur.-Mon. by tour only, on the hour 9:00 a.m.-4:00 p.m.). It was built in the 1840s by Major Robert Gamble, of a primitive form of concrete "tabby" composed of water, oyster shells, and sand. Once the headquarters of an extensive sugar plantation along the Manatee River, it is the only antebellum plantation house surviving in south Florida.

The end of the Civil War threw Florida, along with other Confederate states, into social, economic, and political chaos. The end of the war signaled the end of an era. The labor intensive, limited crop economy collapsed. Black workers were no longer tied to the plantations and the white male population was badly depleted — one in eight had perished in the war. Money was in short supply as well. Wealthy plantation families had put everything into Confederate bonds. For many, defeat brought severe poverty. Large land holdings were broken up and sold for taxes. Houses were abandoned and many slid, like the Indian villages and Spanish missions before them, under the verdant Florida vegetation.

Florida fared better than other southern states in many ways. Sherman did not march there and the transfer of control in Tallahassee was accomplished without widespread destruction. However, reconstruction in Florida, as elsewhere in the South, brought first confusion and absence of authority, then eventually federal occupation and control. Corruption, violence, and resistance were rampant. The state was under military government from 1865 until it was readmitted to the Union on June 25, 1868 and economic instability continued unabated.

After the Civil War, an assortment of refugees converged on Florida, attracted by the same features that had enticed so many earlier explorers and adventurers. Deserters and veterans from both sides found their way to Florida to log, farm, and pillage. John Muir, traveling to Cedar Key during the height of Reconstruction, noted that the transients he encountered in Florida were the roughest he had seen anywhere. But along with the carpetbaggers and drifters came new settlers who looked beyond the political turmoil and economic uncertainty to a new life. Florida itself began to move in new directions, tentatively at first, and then with the roar of the railroad builder's wheels of iron.

CHAPTER 6

THE MANY FACES OF FLORIDA

(1870-1930)

As the nation recovered from the War Between the States, settlers and tourists flowed into Florida in an ever-widening stream. They came from many places, for many reasons. Some — including impoverished small farmers from Georgia, Alabama, and the Carolinas — hoped simply to make a living for their families. Tourists from the North, "Snowbirds," came seeking health and comfort in the mild winters. Capitalists with money to invest came to gain power and riches. Poor but optimistic entrepreneurs came in search of quick wealth. Many of the African-Americans who had helped to build Florida as slaves stayed and continued the process as free men and women. They were joined by other African-Americans who flocked to Florida for the same reasons everyone else did — the warm pleasant winters and a chance to make a living. Cubans came to work in the cigar factories and to escape violence and political repression; Greeks came in pursuit of sponge beds. All these individuals, with their varied economic enterprises and cultural traditions, created many different Florida lifestyles and experiences. The gap in life style between the Black turpentiner and the railroad magnate was about as far, on any dimension, as one could imagine, while the Cubans' Latin zest for dance and music stood in sharp contrast to the stoic endurance of the Southern Cracker. And some Yankee entrepreneurs brought a slippery knack for making a buck that was foreign to many old-time Florida settlers.

Life on America's last eastern frontier ranged from hard and primitive to glamorous and opulent. Individuals each in their own way plunged into Florida's wilderness, leaving their tracks and their handiwork everywhere. The people who flowed into the state created not one Florida, but many Floridas. They all shared its resources and the vicissitudes of its weather, but how those factors shaped their lives and enabled them to shape the land varied greatly. Modern explorers who try to understand Florida in this period will find very different scenes, depending on whose footsteps they follow. And out of those many Floridas comes the Florida we experience today.

The Pioneers

For the earlier pioneers and homesteaders Florida was a land of opportunity for people who wanted a new start or simply the prospect of better circumstances. Life in most parts of the state remained hard. Homes and settlements were isolated, and travel was difficult. Florida Crackers, as the small farmers were called, were courageous, tough, and self reliant. They needed all three attributes in an environment that remained as hostile to them as it had been to the state's first explorers. Like them, they were the victims of malaria-carrying mosquitos, dysentery, typhoid fever, yellow fever, hookworm, and insects. Florida soil did not prove to be as fertile as they had hoped, markets were far distant, and roads were barely passable.

These pioneers left a legacy of homes and small farms from which the state's communities and cities grew. It is these pioneers that Marjorie Kinnan Rawlings described in her Pulitzer prize-winning book *The Yearling*, as well as in *Cross Creek* and *The Big Scrub*. In 1928 Rawlings moved to northeast Florida where she managed a citrus grove and wrote. She was stirred by this place and felt that a country with such wilderness and silence as Florida's *big scrub* must have some pronounced effect upon the character of the people who lived there. Her biographer, Gordon Bigelow, notes that her mature life and literary career "can be understood only in terms of her discovery of Florida in 1928, and this was for her as much as for Ponce de Leon four centuries earlier, a true discovery." Rawlings' house is now a State Historic Site, preserved just as she left it.

There are historic sites from the pioneer era throughout Florida.

Northwest Region

Pensacola's **Museums of Industry and Commerce** (205 East Zaragoza St., Pensacola, FL 32501; 904-444-8905, open Mon.-Sat. 10 a.m.-4:30 p.m.) depict the history of the every day life of West Florida. East of Pensacola, in an area that did not get conveniences like electricity, telephones, and paved roads until the 1940s, the **Valparaiso Historical Museum** (115 Westview Ave., Valparaiso, FL 32580; 904-678-2615, open Tues.-Sat., 11 a.m.-4 p.m., free) displays pioneer household utensils, farm tools, an old cotton gin, old maps, and photographs.

DeFuniak Springs became the winter home of the New York Chautauqua in 1885 and was an early center for cultural, educational, and religious activities. For a self-guiding walking tour of the historic homes sur-

THE MANY FACES OF FLORIDA - A
THE PIONEERS
Map of Sites

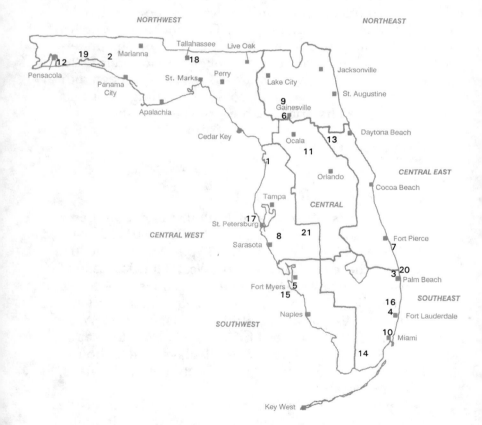

THE MANY FACES OF — FLORIDA

SITES TO VISIT—THE PIONEERS

1. CRYSTAL RIVER, Citrus County Historical Society, 1 Courthouse Square, Invernesss, FL 32650.

2. DEFUNIAK SPRINGS, Chamber of Commerce, P.O. Box 29, DeFuniak Springs, FL 32423; 904-892-3191.

3. DUBOIS HOUSE, P.O. Box 1506, Jupiter, FL 33486; 305-747-6639, open Sun. 1-3:30 p.m. or by appointment.

4. FORT LAUDERDALE

—HIMMARSHEE VILLAGE, historic preservation area along the New River. See especially King Cromartie House, 229 S.W. Second Ave., open weekends during the winter.

—STRANAHAN HOUSE, 333 S. Federal Highway; 305-524-4736, open Wed., Fri., Sat. 10 a.m.-4 p.m.

5. FORT MYERS HISTORICAL MUSEUM, 2300 Peck St. (½ mile east of U.S. 41 at Jackson St. & Peck St.); 813-332-5955, open Mon.-Fri. 9:30 a.m.-4:30 p.m., Sun. 1-5 p.m.

6. GAINESVILLE NORTHEAST HISTORIC DISTRICT, 306 N.E. 6th Ave. Gainesville, FL; 904-374-2197, open Mon.-Fri. 9 a.m.-5 p.m., Sun. 1-4 p.m., free.

7. GILBERT'S BAR HOUSE OF REFUGE, Hutchinson Island, 301 Southeast MacArthur Blvd., Stuart; 407-225-1875, open Tues.-Sun. 1-4:15 p.m.

8. MANATEE VILLAGE HISTORICAL PARK, 6th Ave. & 15th St. East, Bradenton, Manatee County Historical Commission, 604 15th St., E., Bradenton FL 34208; 813-749-1800, ext. 4075, open weekdays 9 a.m.-5 p.m., Sun. 2-5 p.m. Also in Bradenton, Old Main Street historic district.

9. MARJORIE KINNAN RAWLINGS STATE HISTORIC SITE, CR 325; Rt. 3 Box 92, Hawthorne, FL 32640; 904-466-3672, open daily 9 a.m. to 5 p.m., tours every half-hour.

10. MIAMI

—BARNACLE STATE HISTORIC SITE, 3485 Main Highway (Coconut Grove); 305-448-9445, open Thur.-Mon. 9 a.m. -5 p.m., tours at 10:30, 1:00, and 2:30.

—CAULEY SQUARE AREA, 22400 Old Dixie Hwy., Goulds; 305-258-3543.

—COCONUT GROVE historic area.

140 EXPLORINGEXPLORING FLORIDA

11. MOUNT DORA, off U.S. 41, 25 miles NW of Orlando;
Chamber of Commerce, P. O. Box 196, Mount Dora, FL 32757;
904-383-2165.

12. PENSACOLA MUSEUMS OF INDUSTRY and COMMERCE,
Historic Pensacola Village, 205 East Zaragoza St., Pensacola,
FL 32501; 904-444-8905, open Mon.-Sat. 10 a.m.-4:30 p.m.

13. PIONEER SETTLEMENT FOR THE CREATIVE ARTS, SR 40
& 17, near Barberville, West Volusia Tourist Center, 336 N.
Woodland Blvd., Deland, FL 32720; 904-749-2959, open
Mon.-Fri. 9 a.m.-3 p.m.

14. REDLAND HISTORIC DISTRICT, near Homestead, with
Fruit and Spice Park, 24801 S.W. 187 Ave.; 305-247-5727, open
daily 10 a.m.-5 p.m., tours Sat. and Sun. 1 and 3 p.m.

15. SANIBEL ISLAND HISTORICAL MUSEUM, Dunlop Road;
813-472-4648, open 10 a.m.-4 p.m., free.

16. SINGING PINES CHILDREN'S MUSEUM, 498 Crawford
Blvd. Boca Raton, FL; 407-768-6875.

17. ST. PETERSBURG

—HAAS MUSEUM VILLAGE COMPLEX, 3511 Second Ave.
South, St. Petersburg, FL; 813-327-1437, open Thur.-Sun. 1-5
p.m. (closed September).

—HERITAGE PARK, 11909 125th St. N., Largo; 813-462-3474,
open Tues.-Sat. 10 a.m.-4 p.m., Sun. 1-4 p.m., tours every
half-hour.

—PINELLAS COUNTY HERITAGE PARK, 407 S. Garden Ave.,
Clearwater, FL; 813-866-2662.

18. TALLAHASSEE, Chamber of Commerce, 100 N. Duval St.;
904-224-8116, open Mon.-Fri. 8:30-5:30 p.m.

—GOVERNOR'S MANSION, 700 North Adams St.; 904-488-4661
open September-May, Mon., Wed., Fri. 10 a.m.-noon, free.

—JUNIOR MUSEUM, 3945 Museum Drive, Tallahassee, FL
32304; 904-575-1636, open Tues.-Sat. 9 a.m.-5 p.m., Sun. 12:30
to 5:00.

—MUSEUM OF FLORIDA HISTORY, R. A. Gray Building, 500 S.
Bronough St., Tallahassee, FL 32399-0250; 904-488-1484, open
Mon.-Fri. 8 a.m.-4:30 p.m., Sat. 10 a.m.-4:30 p.m., Sun.
noon-4:30 p.m., free.

—OLD CAPITAL, Monroe St. & Apalachee Parkway;
904-487-1902, open Mon.-Fri. 9 a.m.-4:30 p.m., Sat. 10
a.m.-4:30, Sun. noon-4:30 p.m.

—UNION BANK, 295 Apalachee Parkway; 904-488-1484, open
Tues.-Fri. 10 a.m.-4:30 p.m., Sat.-Sun. 1-4:30 p.m.
19. VALPARAISO HISTORICAL MUSEUM, 115 Westview Ave.,
Valparaiso, FL; 904-678-2615, open Tues.-Sat. 11 a.m. to 4 p.m.,
Sun. 2:30-4:30 p.m., free.
20. WEST PALM BEACH POST OFFICE, murals by Steven
Dohanos depicting barefoot mailmen.
21. ZOLFO SPRINGS PIONEER PARK, SR 64 & 17; 813-735-0330.

rounding the town's almost perfectly round springfed
lake contact the Chamber of Commerce (P.O. Box 29,
DeFuniak Springs, FL 32423; 904-892-3191).

In **Tallahassee** (Chamber of Commerce, 100 N. Duval St., Tallahassee, FL 32302; 904-224-8116) you can
hop on a replica turn-of-the-century streetcar to tour
the historic Adams Street Commons and the rest of the
downtown area. This part of Tallahassee retains the
flavor of a Southern town square with restored buildings including the Governor's Club, a 1900's Masonic
lodge, Gallie's Hall built in 1874, and the 150 year-old
Union Bank (295 Apalachee Parkway; 904-488-1488;
open Tues.-Fri. 10 a.m.-1 p.m., Sat. and Sun. 1-4:30
p.m.). If you want to get some idea about the role
banks played in the development of early Florida, you
may want to tour the bank. You can also tour the
Governor's Mansion (700 North Adams St.; 904-488-
4661, Sept.-May, Mon., Wed., Fri. 10 a.m.-noon, free)
and the restored 1902 **Old Capitol** (Monroe St. and
Apalachee Parkway; 904-487-1902, open Mon.-Fri. 9
a.m.-4:30 p.m., Sat. 10 a.m.-4:30 p.m., Sun. noon-4:30
p.m.). You can get a good view of both local and state
history at the **Museum of Florida History** (R.A. Gray
Building, 500 S. Bronough St., Tallahassee, FL 32399-
0250; 904-488-1484, open Mon.-Fri. 8 a.m.-4:30 p.m.,
Sat. 10 a.m.-4:30 p.m., Sun. noon-4:30 p.m., free). The

**THE MANY FACES OF FLORIDA-B
MAP OF SITES**

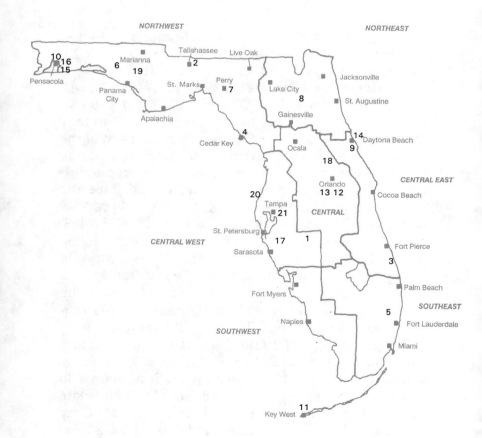

NORTHWEST

NORTHEAST

10
16
15

Marianna

6   19

Tallahassee   Live Oak

2

Pensacola

Panama
City

St. Marks

Perry

7

Lake City

8

Jacksonville

St. Augustine

Apalachia

Gainesville

Cedar Key

4

Ocala

14
Daytona Beach

18

9

CENTRAL EAST

Orlando
13 12

Cocoa Beach

20

Tampa

21

CENTRAL

St. Petersburg

17   1

Sarasota

Fort Pierce

3

Fort Myers

Palm Beach

SOUTHEAST

Naples

5

Fort Lauderdale

SOUTHWEST

Miami

11
Key West

CENTRAL WEST

THE MANY FACES OF FLORIDA—B

SITES TO VISIT

1. ARCADIA ALL-FLORIDA CHAMPIONSHIP RODEO, P.O.
   Box 1266, Arcadia, FL 33821; 813-494-2014 in July and March.

2. BLACK ARCHIVES RESEARCH CENTER AND MUSEUM,
   Carnegie Library, Florida Agricultural and Mechanical
   University, Tallahassee, FL; 904-599-3414.

3. BLACK HERITAGE FESTIVAL, Martin County Black Heritage
   Association, P.O. Box 2279, Stuart, FL 34995.

4. CEDAR KEY STATE MUSEUM, P.O. Box 538, Cedar Key, FL
   32625; 904-543-5350.

5. DAVIE RODEO ARENA, Griffin and Davie Rds, Davie FL
   33314; 305-434-7062.

6. EDEN STATE GARDENS, off SR 24; P.O. Box 26, Point
   Washington, FL 32454; 904-231-4214, open daily 8
   a.m.-sundown, tours on the hour.

7. FOREST CAPITAL STATE MUSEUM, 204 Forest Park Drive,
   Perry, FL 32347; 904-584-3227, Florida Forest Festival in
   October.

8. GOLD HEAD BRANCH STATE PARK, 6239 SSR 21, Keystone
   Heights, FL 32656; 904-473-4701.

9. HOWARD THURMAN HOME, 641 Whitehall St., Daytona
   Beach; 904-258-7514.

10. JULLEE COTTAGE, Historic Pensacola Village, 210 E.
    Zaragoza St., Pensacola, FL 32501; 904-444-8905, Museum of
    Black History.

11. KEY WEST CONCH HOUSES, Old Town, between Caroline
    & Angela Sts. and Duval & Francis Sts.; Key West Welcome
    Center, 3840 N. Roosevelt Blvd., Key West, 33040, FL;
    305-296-4444.

12. KISSIMMEE COW CAMP, Lake Kissimmee State Park, 14248
    Camp Mack Rd, Lake Wales, FL 33853; 813-696-1112, tours
    Sat., Sun. and holidays 9:30 a.m.-4:30 p.m.

13. KISSIMMEE TOWN, Chamber of Commerce, 320 Monument
    Ave., Kissimmee, FL 32741; 407-847-3174; Silver Spurs Arena,
    407-847-5118.

14. MARY MCLEOD BETHUNE FOUNDATION, 640 Second
    Ave., Daytona Beach, FL 32115, contact 904-255-1401, open
    Mon.-Fri. 9 a.m.-4 p.m..

15. NAVAL LIVE OAKS AREA, U.S. 98, Gulf Islands National Seashore, P.O. Box 100, Gulf Breeze, FL 32561; 904-932-5302.

16. PENSACOLA NORTH HILL PRESERVATION DISTRICT, Palafox at Belmont St.; Chamber of Commerce, P.O. Box 550, Pensacola, FL 32593; 904-438-4081.

17. PIONEER PARK MUSEUM, BONE MIZELL MONUMENT, SR 64 & 17, Zolfo Springs; 813-735-0330.

18. THE SENATOR, Seminole County Park, General Hutchinson Parkway, Longwood.

19. ST. ANDREWS STATE RECREATION AREA, 4415 Thomas Drive, Panama City, FL 32408; 904-234-2522.

20. TARPON SPRINGS
—SPONGERAMA, 510 Dodecanese Blvd., Tarpon Springs, FL 34689; 813-942-3771.
—ST. NICOLAS GREEK ORTHODOX CATHEDRAL, 30 N. Pinellas Ave., Tarpon Springs 34689; 813-937-3540.

21. YBOR CITY, Chamber of Commerce, 1800 E. 9th Ave., Tampa, FL 33605; 813-248-3712.
—YBOR CITY STATE MUSEUM, 1818 9th Ave., Tampa, FL 33605; 813-247-6323, open Tues.-Sat. 9 a.m.-5 p.m. except noon to 1 p.m.
—YBOR SQUARE, 1901 N. 13th St., P.O. Box 384, Tampa, FL 33601; 813-247-4497.

Tallahassee Junior Museum 3945 Museum Drive, Tallahassee, FL 32304; 904-576-1636, open Tues.-Sat. 9 a.m.-5 p.m., Sun. 12:30-5:00 p.m.) is a 55-acre farm-zoo-park-plantation about 6.5 miles southwest of the city on Lake Bradford. It ensures fun and education for all ages, not just children. Look particularly for the 1880s farm, complete with farm animals and demonstrations, and the one-room schoolhouse.

Northeast Region

Gainesville's Northeast Historic District is a 63-

block area of 290 historic buildings listed on the National Register of Historic Places, which reflects architectural styles prevalent in Florida from 1880 through the 1920s. You can start a self-guided tour of the area at the Thomas Center (306 N.E. 6th Ave., Gainesville; 904-374-2197, or call 904-373-2787 for a 24-hour activities hotline, open Mon.-Fri. 9 a.m.-5 p.m., Sun. 1-4 p.m., free).

Marjorie Kinnan Rawlings' house (CR 325; Rt. 3 Box 92, Hawthorne, FL 32640; 904-466-3672, open daily 9 a.m.-5 p.m. with tours every half hour) is typical of Cracker houses of the era, with open porches and numerous windows to allow cross ventilation. The kitchen is set off by a breezeway to keep its heat from warming up the other rooms. In nearby Hawthorne, the Yearling Cross Creek Restaurant (Blue Gill Drive and CR 325) serves meals made with recipes suggested by Rawlings in her *Cross Creek Cookbook*.

Central West Region

Crystal River north of Tampa, once a bustling fish and mill town, is being restored to its 19th century look with ornate street lights, verandas, and covered walkways. You can explore the area with an historic walking tour map from the Citrus County Historical Society (1 Courthouse Square, Inverness, FL., 32650). In Clearwater, **Pinellas County Heritage Park** (407 S. Garden Ave.; 813-866-2662), has 10 acres of historical buildings, including a log cabin, a cane mill, an old barn, and a turn-of-the-century house with original furnishings.

The **Tampa/St. Petersburg** area has three pioneer museums. At **Heritage Park** in Largo (11909 125th St. North; 813-462-3474, open Tues.-Sat. 10 a.m.-4 p.m., Sun. 1-4 p.m., tours every half hour) you can visit a

13-room mansion from the early 1900s and a log house that is one of the oldest buildings in the county. The **Haas Museum Village Complex** in St. Petersburg (3511 Second Ave. South; 813-327-1437, open Thur.-Sun. 1- 5 p.m. except in Sept.) preserves a number of the city's old homes dating back to 1850.

The **Manatee Village Historical Park** in Bradenton (The Manatee County Historical Society, 604 15th St. E., Bradenton, FL 34208; 813-749-1800, Ext. 4075, open weekdays 9 a.m.-5 p.m., Sun. 2-5 p.m.) includes a historic courthouse, church, and a "cracker gothic" house built in 1912. The city also has an historic Main Street, lined with buildings from the early 20th century, for which a self-guiding tour map is available.

Zolfo Springs **Pioneer Park** (SR 64 & 17; 813-735-0330) located on the Peace River is a preservation-receational area that has board-and-batten structures from the area's frontier days.

Central Region

Mount Dora (off U.S. 41, 25 miles NW of Orlando; Chamber of Commerce, P.O. Box 196, Mount Dora, FL 32757; 904-383-2165), today a quaint New England-style town famous for antiques, was first homesteaded in 1873. Its oldest building, **Lakeside Inn** (100 S. Alexander St.; 800-556-5016), a spacious yellow, white-trimmed Tudor-style resort, is full of gables, bays and windows, covered walkways, and touches of old Florida. **The Donnelly House**, (Donnelly St. between 5th and 6th Avenues), built in 1893 by the town's first mayor, J.P. Donnelly, is ornate and castle-like with stained glass and carved trim. Another landmark, the old ice house, is now the Ice House Theater, home of a community theater group which mounts productions year-round. The local museum (off Baker St. between

4th and 5th Avenues; 904-383-3642) called the **Royel-
lou Museum**, in commemoration of the town's name
before 1883, occupies the former city jail and houses
memorabilia of the community's earlier days.

Central East

The Pioneer Settlement for the Creative Arts (on SR
40 & 17 near Barberville; West Volusia Tourist Center,
336 N. Woodland Blvd., Deland, FL 32720; 904-749-
2959, open Mon.-Fri. 9 a.m.-3 p.m.) gives demonstrations of the lifestyles of early settlers. It includes a
bridgehouse, moved from the St. Johns River at Astor,
commissary store from a turpentine establishment,
and a post-and-beam barn. Displays in the museum
are constantly rotated. The settlement holds a "Country Jamboree" on the first weekend of November with
entertainment, arts and crafts displays, and home
cooked country food.

The lower half of Florida's coast was so isolated in
the 1870s that the government built six houses of refuge as havens for shipwrecked sailors. Today only one
is left, **Gilbert's Bar House of Refuge** on Hutchinson
Island (301 Southeast MacArthur Blvd., Stuart; 407-
225-1875, open Tues.-Sun. 1-4:15 p.m.). This clapboard
house, with the surf pounding at its doorstep, is the
oldest structure in the area. The refuge has several
rooms furnished much as they were when stranded
sailors stayed there.

Southwest Region

The **Fort Myers Historical Museum** (2300 Peck St.,
Fort Myers, FL 33901; 813-332-5955, open Mon.-Fri. 9
a.m.-4:30 p.m., Sun. 1-5 p.m.) has scale models of First
Street in Fort Myers and local buildings.

The **Sanibel Island Historical Museum** (Dunlop

Road; 813-472-4648, open 10 a.m.-4 p.m., free) is a
typical old Florida pine house that was moved to
Sanibel in 1982.

Southeast Region

The **Dubois House** near Jupiter (P.O. Box 1506, Jupiter, FL 33486; 407-747-6639, open Sun. 1-3:30 p.m. or by
appointment) was built in the late 1890s on top of a
20-foot-high Indian shell mound. The house and its
furnishing have been preserved by the Loxahatchee
Historical Society much as they were in the early part
of the 20th century. The Boca Raton **Singing Pines
Children's Museum** (498 Crawford Blvd., Boca Raton;
407-768-6875) is housed in what is said to be the oldest
unaltered woodframe building in the city and includes
a Florida cracker cottage constructed of Dade County
pine and timber found on the beach. The museum
focuses on pioneer Florida memorabilia.

Until the railroad came in the 1890s, mail was deliv-
ered along the southeastern coast of Florida by barefoot mailmen who walked the hundred mile stretch of
beach from Palm Beach to Miami, taking three days
each way. You can see murals by Steven Dohanos depicting these mailmen at the **West Palm Beach Post
Office**. There is a memorial plaque at Hillsborough
Inlet, near Pompano, to James E. Hamilton, one of
these mailmen who lost his life in the line of duty in
October 1887. The novel, *The Barefoot Mailman* by
Theodore Pratt (Mockingbird Press) portrays the pioneer Florida of this area.

Fort Lauderdale has many historic buildings. The
oldest is **Stranahan House** (333 S. Federal Highway at
Las Olas Blvd.; 305-524-4736, open Wed., Fri., Sat. 10
a.m.-4 p.m., admission includes tour). It is a two-story
frame building put up in 1901 by one of the city's first

citizens, Frank Stranahan. When Stranahan arrived in 1893 he found only a few white settlers clustered in a little camp along the banks of the New River. His house served Seminole Indians and local pioneers as Fort Lauderdale's trading post in the early 1900s, and later as a public hall and family home. Stranahan committed suicide when he lost everything in the Great Crash of 1929, but his wife continued to live in an attic room of the house until she died in 1971. The house was a restaurant for a time in the 1970s before the Fort Lauderdale Historical Society acquired and restored it. On Friday nights the Historical Society sponsors a social, much like those the Stranahans hosted in the early days of the Fort Lauderdale settlement. They are from 6-8:30 p.m. and admission includes the tour, wine and hors d'oeuvres.

Himmarshee Village, along the New River in Fort Lauderdale, is an historic preservation area. A self-guided tour booklet of this historic New River area, *Cruising Down the River* by Pamela Euston, is full of photographs and descriptions of the early houses. It is available from Broward County Cultural Affairs Council (Main Library Building, 100 S. Andrews Ave., Fort Lauderdale, FL 33301) or the visitors bureau. Look especially for the **King Cromartie House** (229 S.W. Second Ave., Fort Lauderdale, FL 33315; 305-764-1665, open weekends during the winter). It goes back to 1907 and is laden with antiques which show how creative the pioneers had to be to survive.

One of **Miami's** best known historic areas is **Coconut Grove**, now a lively artists' colony. There are more 19th-century buildings here than in any other area of Southern Florida. The town was the product of the friendship that developed between Charles and Isabella Peacock and Commodore Ralph Munroe, an innovative and environmentally conscious boat designer from Staten Island, New York. In 1882 Munroe encouraged the Peacocks to build a hotel, the first on the south Florida mainland. Soon a spirited, industrious, and diversified community grew up around it, a mixture of Bahamians, Key West Conchs, New England intellectuals, and hopeful settlers. Commodore Munroe's home is now the **Barnacle State Historic Site** (3485 Main Highway; 305-448-9445, open Thur.-Mon. 9 a.m.-5 p.m., with tours at 10:30, 1:00, and 2:30). The Barnacle gives the modern explorer a chance to re-enter the past and see and feel what Coconut Grove and the Miami area were like during homesteading days. Also near Miami is the **Cauley Square Area** (22400 Old Dixie Hwy., Goulds; 305-258-3543), where houses built by Dade County pioneers have been restored into antique shops and boutiques.

The **Redland Historic District**, north of Homestead, includes several homes, a church, and the **Fruit and Spice Park** (24801 SW 187th Ave.; 305-247-5727, open daily 10 a.m.-5 p.m.). In the park, part of the Metropolitan Dade County Park and Recreation Department, you can see an old schoolhouse (1906), a coral rock building (1912), and the Bauer-Mitchell House (1902), the oldest known house in the area. The latter is a fine example of pine pioneer construction, with crude beams, tongue-and-groove ceiling and a big porch. The Park itself is a 20 acre grove planted with over 500 varieties of fruit, spices and herbs, the only garden of its kind in the United States. There are tours on Sat. and Sun. at 1 and 3 p.m. for a small fee.

Lumber Barons and Turpentiners

Early Florida was rich in lumber (especially live oak, pine, and cedar) and in naval stores (rosin, tar, pitch, and turpentine). These were exploited first by the British and then by the Americans, and provided a livelihood for many early Floridians and an economic base for many towns.

Live oaks were particularly valued for shipbuilding and Florida's numerous stands were well depleted by the time of the Civil War when the battle between the Ironclad *Moniter* and the *Merrimac* at Hampton Roads, Virginia showed the vulnerability of wooden vessels. A few of these magnificant old trees can still be seen, however. At the **Naval Live Oaks Area** in the Gulf Islands National Seashore (U.S. 98; P.O. Box 100, Gulf Breeze, FL 32561; 904-932-5302) you can walk through a 1,378-acre woodland area. The visitor center houses exhibits and audio-visual presentations.

Americans built the state's first steam sawmill in 1841 near Pensacola, which became the lumber capital of the state. By 1853 the industry had expanded to Jacksonville where there were 14 sawmills. However, the lumber industry was largely backed by Northern capital, and during the War Between the States production ceased and most of the equipment was damaged.

After the war the extension of railroad lines opened up new stands of timber, and for a few years lumbering was an important part of Florida's economy again. Prosperous lumber barons built fine homes in many Florida communities. **Pensacola's North Hill Preservation District** (Chamber of Commerce, P.O. Box 550, Pensacola, FL 32593; 904-438-4081) is filled with elegant homes reflecting the turn-of-the century heyday of the timber industry. It runs for about a dozen blocks on Palafox Street beginning at Belmont Street. The homes are generally closed to the public, but the area provides an interesting walking or driving tour. **The Dorr House** (311 S. Adams St.) a mansion in the Classic

Revival style, reflects the lumber boom in its plentiful use of high ceilings, wide pine floors, jib windows, and straight wooden staircases.

Eden State Gardens (in the panhandle off SR 24; P.O. Box 26, Point Washington, FL 32454; 904-231-4214, open daily 8 a.m. to sundown, house tours on the hour) was built in 1897 by William Henry Wesley close to his lumber company. The house was built on piers, which permitted air circulation and helped avoid flooding when the bayou or bay rose. The lumber business ended and the small community declined, but the family continued to live in the house until 1953. Ten years later it was bought by Lois Maxon who completely renovated the house and gardens.

By 1930 nearly all the good timber in Florida had been cut. Lumber mills closed or moved away, leaving millions of acres of cut-over, burned-out forest lands and thousands of people out of work. Thriving towns lost their momentum. **Cedar Key** (The Cedar Key State Museum, P.O. Box 538, Cedar Key, FL 32625; 904-543-5350) for example, experienced a boom when its particularly fine red cedar was harvested to make pencils. In 1884, lumbering swelled the population to 5,000. Fifteen years later when the cedar was all gone, the population shrank back to 1,200.

Turpentine, pitch, tar, and rosin, or "naval stores," as they were called, required particularly tedious, hard physical labor. The workers, "teppentime men" lived in isolated camps of about 160 people. They were the most poorly paid workers of the period. Many were African-American, although some Chinese were brought in as well.

Exhibits about the turpentine industry and the lives of its workers can be seen at the **Gold Head Branch State Park** (6239 SR 21, Keystone Heights, FL 32656; 904-473-4701). **St. Andrews State Recreation Area**

(4415 Thomas Drive, Panama City, FL 32408; 904-234-2522) has a reconstructed turpentine still in the park near the fishing pier. Pensacola's **Museum of Industry** (Historic Pensacola Village, 205 E. Zaragoza St., Pensacola, FL 32501; open Mon.-Sat. 10 a.m.-4:30 p.m.; 904-444-8905) includes the Piney Woods Sawmill with machinery used during West Florida's lumber boom. The **Forest Capital State Museum** (south of Perry on U.S. 19; 204 Forest Park Drive, Perry, FL 32347; 904-584-3227) also has displays on forestry, plant communities, common animals, and products made from trees. The park includes an old pioneer log house furnished from the period and hosts the Florida Forest Festival each year in October.

If you want to get a sense of the size of Florida's old trees, visit the 2,000 year old "**Fairchild Oak**" in Bulow Creek State Park off old Dixie Highway (c/o Flagler Beach SRA, 3100 AIA, Flagler Beach, Fl 32136; 904-439-2174) or "**The Senator**," a 3,000 year old bald cypress tree in a Seminole County Park near Longwood.

Cowboys and Cattle Kings

Cattle was big business in Florida in the late 1870s and 1880s just as it was in the West. In fact, cattle ranches had been flourishing on the Florida peninsula for over 250 years; both the Indians and the British developed large herds. American cattlemen moved into Florida when it became a U.S. territory, and soon began exporting to Cuba. During the Civil War, Florida was the main supplier of beef for the Confederacy, but as the war progressed distribution became more difficult and for a time after the war thousands of cattle roamed Florida woodlands and grasslands in a semi-wild state.

The lives of Florida's "Cracker Cowboys" were

similar to those of their Western counterparts. They took part in round-ups, pursued rustlers, endured long cattle drives and engaged in a fair amount of violence. They drove the cattle with whips and dogs and their own shrill cow-whoops, instead of the Western lariats which were more suited to the open range. The whips' loud musket-like cracks set the cattle in the desired direction without actually touching them.

Frederic Remington, the noted writer and painter of Western scenes, visited the ranges of Florida around Arcadia in 1895 to create "Cracker Cowboys in Florida," an illustrated article in the August 1895 *Harper's Monthly*. His words are no less descriptive than his pictures. "Two emaciated ponies pattered down the street, bearing wild-looking individuals whose hanging hair, drooping hats, and generally bedraggled appearance would remind you at once of the Spanish moss which hangs so quietly and helplessly to the limbs of the oaks."

Although the Florida cowboys dressed more simply than their Western counterparts, they were no less competent, often defeating them in rodeo competitions. One cowboy, Bone Mizell, believed to have been the model for Remington's painting, *A Cracker Cowboy*, became part of Florida's folklore. Bone could outride any cowpoke on the range, was a constant clown, and guzzled booze with the best of them. He reportedly kindled his pipe with dollar bills and branded cattle with his teeth. As head cowhand for Zibe King, a prominent rancher of the day, he carried the ranch accounts in his head even though he couldn't read, write, or do sums. The Peace River Valley Historical Society has erected a monument to Bone Mizell near the **Pioneer Park Museum** in Zolfo Springs (SR 64 & 17; 813-735-0330).

The cowboys worked for stockmen, often called

"cattle kings" because of their dominant role in Florida during the late 1800s. Zibe King was as legendary as his head cowhand, Bone Mizell. He stood six feet six in his stockings, weighed 225 pounds, could out-eat all competitors, and was not known to have ever been beaten at stud poker. Zibe didn't "rile" easily but once, so the story goes, when a wild steer attacked him, he swung a haymaker from the floor, striking the 600-pound animal near the heart and killing it instantly. One time when Manatee County couldn't pay its schoolteachers, Zibe personally provided enough gold to pay their salaries for six months.

The pioneer ranchers founded cow-country dynasties that continue, to some extent, today. The cattlemen created brands for their sons at birth and parents, friends, and relatives customarily presented children with calves as birthday and Christmas gifts. By the time boys were old enough to ride, they already had herds of their own to manage. One product of Kissimmee cow country is Hughlette Wheeler, the noted sculptor of thoroughbred horses and cow ponies. A native of Fort Christmas and the son of a cattle-raising family, Wheeler is best known for his statue of Will Rogers on horseback.

The cattlemen of the 19th century were usually paid in gold Spanish doubloons since both Cubans and Floridians distrusted Spanish bank notes and had little respect for American dollars. For about 20 years gold doubloons were more common than American money in Tampa and the cattle country. Ranchers often kept as much as $10,000 in gold in "gourd safeboxes" in their homes.

You can get a feel for the life of the Florida "cow hunter" in 1876 at **Kissimmee Cow Camp**, part of Lake Kissimmee State Park (14248 Camp Mack Road, Lake Wales, FL 33853; 813-696-1112, tours available on Sat.,

Sun., and holidays from 9:30 a.m. to 4:30 p.m.). There
you can see one of the few remaining herds of Florida
scrub cows. The Cow Camp, with a holding pen for the
cows and a crude shelter for the men, is like the camps
constructed at regular intervals along the routes of the
Spring cattle drives. The animals were rounded up
and branded, moved to Punta Rassa near Fort Myers,
and loaded aboard ships to Cuba.

In the town of **Kissimmee** (Chamber of Commerce,
320 Monument Ave., Kissimmee, FL 32741; 407-847-
3174), founded in 1878, many original buildings still
stand, including the courthouse and Makinson's Hardware Store (308 East Broadway) which claims to be the
state's first hardware store. In the early days, grass
along the town's main street was kept short by the
cattle that were allowed to wander freely in the town.
The town remains, even today, the center of a major
cattle raising area. On Wednesdays visitors can attend
the town's cattle auction at the Kissimmee Livestock
Market (Donegan Avenue; 407-847-3521). Go early.
The main action runs from about 8 a.m. to noon. If you
get to Kissimmee in late February or late June you can
take in a rodeo at the **Silver Spurs Arena** (P.O. Box
421909, Kissimmee, FL 34741; 407-847-5118). It features
professional rodeo cowboys, calf roping, steer wrestling and more.

If you miss that one, you may be able to take in the
Arcadia All-Florida Championship Rodeo (P.O. Box
1266, Arcadia, FL 33821; 813-494-2014) in July and
March at the rodeo ground, or some of the action at the
new domed 5,000 seat **Davie Rodeo Arena** near Fort
Lauderdale (Griffin Road at Davie Road in Davie, FL
33314; 305-434-7062). Davie hosts the Florida State
Championship Rodeo sponsored by the Florida Cow-
boys Association each December as well as weekly
Jackpot Rodeos.

Cattle raising is still a major industry in Florida. Fairs and Livestock shows are held throughout the state from October through May. For a list of places and dates contact the Florida Federation of Fairs and Livestock Shows, Inc., P.O. Box 11087, Tampa, Fl 33680.

Conchs in Key West

Many Key West inhabitants, referred to as "Conchs," were descendants of the English loyalists who fled from the U.S. after the American Revolution, first to British Florida and then to Eleuthera and the Great Abaco Islands in the Bahamas. They explored the waters and salvaged off the Florida Keys in the late 1700s, and in the early 1800s colonized the Keys. Salvaging became less profitable after 1850 when the first of the reef lighthouses was constructed, but it continued to be an important occupation. New businesses sprang up as well, especially sponging, which brought much wealth to the town in the 1880s and 1890s.

The Conchs pride themselves on a shrewd and stubborn individuality, and Key West, far from mainland America, was unique. Its colorful and educated inhabitants made their living primarily by salvaging goods from the many ships that went aground on the nearby reefs. Their plunder yielded exotic furnishings for their houses and formal clothes for their parties. Key West retains today the atmosphere of buoyant independence and individuality characteristic of the Conchs.

You can still see many of the unique conch houses in the old town of Key West in the blocks between Caroline and Angela and Duval and Francis. A free descriptive folder, *The Pelican Path*, published by the Old Island Restoration Foundation, is available from Hospitality House in Mallory Square. The route is marked with directional yellow signs and numbered plaques on the historic buildings. Look for **Artist House** (534 Eaton), **Eyebrow House** (1025 Fleming). **Albury House** (730 Southard), **The Bahama Houses** (703 Eaton & 408 William), and **Lowe House** (620 Southard). If you want to take some of these wonderful houses away with you, invest in the book of black and white photographs by Sharon Wells and Lawson Little, *Portraits: Wooden Houses of Key West.*

Greek Spongers

Florida's sponge industry was first located in Key West where in 1895 the sponge beds supported 1,400 men working on 300 boats. The Conchs used long poles to hook the animals from the shallow waters and when divers from Greece moved into the business with their much faster harvesting techniques, the Conchs responded with violence. The Greeks decided to move north to join other Greek divers who were settling around Tarpon Springs. They thrived there until the early 1940s when the sponge industry as a whole began to decline — a result of a red tide, a dense bloom of micro-organisms that destroyed many beds, and the introduction of synthetic sponges. Spongers still work today to meet the need for natural sponges that exist in fields like medicine.

Tarpon Springs retains a Greek flavor in its restaurants and shops. You can still see the sponge docks along Dodecanese Boulevard and **Spongerama** (510 Dodecanese Blvd., Tarpon Springs, FL 34689; 813-942-3771) has a walk-through sponge boat as well as exhibits, photos, and memorabilia from Tarpon Springs' settlement days. A movie shows how sponge is harvested. If you want to see how the divers collect the sponges, take a trip on the St. Nicholas Boat Line sponge boat (813-937-9887).

St. Nicholas Greek Orthodox Cathedral, (30 N. Pinellas Ave., Tarpon Springs, FL 34689; 813-937-3540) is a replica of Istanbul's St. Sophia and is a good example of neo-Byzantine architecture. In January you can join in the Greek Epiphany celebration when young Greeks dive into the waters of Spring Bayou for a gold cross and good luck for the coming year.

Cuban Cigar Workers

Cubans have played an important role in Florida since the early Spanish period when ships and goods moved easily between Havana and St. Augustine. The growth of the cigar industry in Key West and Tampa and the outbreak of the Ten Years' War in Cuba brought an upsurge of Cuban immigration in the late 1800s.

The work of Cuban primitive artist, **Mario Sanchez,** shows with great vividness and humor the everyday activities of early Cubans. The East Martello Gallery and Museum in Key West (S. Roosevelt Blvd., open daily 9:30 a.m.-5:30 p.m.) has many of his primitive wood carvings in its collection.

The cigar industry was particularly significant in the development of early Tampa and left historic **Ybor City** (Chamber of Commerce, 1800 E. 9th Ave., Tampa, FL 33605; 813-248-3712) as a reminder of this lively phase of Florida history. The eloquence of the Cuban revolutionaries who regularly visited the Cuban community in the U.S., coupled with America's growing economic stake in Cuba, led eventually to the Spanish-American War in 1898.

The first cigar factory was established in Key West in 1831 but not until 1868, when Vicente Martinez Ybor decided to move his famous cigar factory from Havana to Key West, did the industry really begin to boom in America. In 1886, after his factory was destroyed by the second Key West fire, Ybor accepted the offer of a free tract of land in developing Tampa and moved his business there.

Life was hard for the first workers in Tampa. Alligators crawled out on Seventh Avenue — the main street — and it was necessary to carry a lantern at night to avoid them. Snakes were numerous. After heavy rains, two large lagoons in the town often overflowed to form a lake. The first winter was especially difficult and Ybor was threatened with a mass exodus of his workers. He enticed them to stay with the promise of a huge Christmas picnic. They stayed, the picnic was a great success, and conditions gradually improved. Other factories followed quickly, set up in massive brick warehouses. As the workers rolled cigars, a reader at the front of the room read them news, poetry, and literature.

Ybor City grew into a flourishing community, peopled not only by Cubans, but also by Spaniards and Italians, and eventually Germans, Afro-Cubans, and Jews. Shop owners lived above their stores, relaxed on their balconies, and socialized in the clubs and casinos. Workers were paid adequately and lived well. The town in its early days had an exciting boom town atmosphere.

When the United States declared war on Spain in 1898 after the U.S. battleship *Maine* was blown up in Havana Harbor, Tampa and Ybor City became the staging ground for thousands of troops en route to Cuba. The short war briefly disrupted the cigar industry, but after the Republic of Cuba was established in 1902, factories reached new peaks of production.

The cigar industry and its community continued to

thrive into the 1920s, but then began to decline as a result of labor difficulties, the development of cigar-making machines, and the growing popularity of cigarettes.

One of Ybor's factories still stands today in **Ybor Square** (1901 N. 13th St., P.O. Box 384, Tampa, FL 33601; 813-247-4497) There are several other historic sites in the area. A brochure for a self guided walking tour of Ybor City can be purchased from the **Ybor City State Museum** (1818 9th Ave. Tampa, FL 33605; 813-247-6323, open Tues.-Sat., 9 a.m.-5 p.m., except lunch hour noon-1 p.m.). The museum is housed in an old Italian landmark, formerly the Ferlita Bakery. Adjoining the museum's small outdoor garden, three workers cottages (1804 E. 9th Ave., open Tues.-Fri. 10 a.m.-3 p.m.) are typical of the long, narrow "shotgun" houses built around 1895 in the southern United States. In this block, houses, stores, and factories are all clustered together, just as they always have been in Ybor City.

There are some attractive old buildings in this area. Look for the **Centro Asturiano** (1913 Nebraska Ave.; 813-229-2214). Founded in 1902, this elegant European-style theater, complete with balcony, seats 1100 persons and remains today a center for the arts in Tampa. **Centro Espanol** (7th Ave. & 15th St.) was established in 1892 to help members of the Spanish community survive hard times. **El Circulo Cubano/The Cuban Club** (9th Ave. & 13th St.; 813-248-2954) built in 1918, is one of five Ybor City historical clubs. **L'Unione Italiana/The Italian Club** (7th Ave. & 18th St.; 813-247-99012) was founded by the Italians in 1894 shortly after they were accepted into the cigar making business.

Villazon & Co. (3104 Armenia Ave.; 813-879-2291) offers guided tours of a mechanized cigar factory and demonstrates modern methods of twisting and rolling.

You can also watch craftsmen roll cigars by hand at Tampa Rico Cigars in Ybor Square (8th Ave. and 13th St.; 813-247-6738).

The Cuban presence and influence on Florida culture has continued to grow even though the cigar era is long past. **Little Havana** in downtown Miami on SW 8th Street (called Ocho) was revitalized by Cubans fleeing Castro in the early 1960's. There and throughout southern Florida, Latin music, Cuban Restaurants, and the ever present staccato of rapid Spanish remind of us Florida's historic and ongoing connections with Cuban culture. Every March in Little Havana, Cubans hold the nation's largest Hispanic festival. One of the largest collections of Cuban artwork in the U.S. is in **The Museum of Arts and Science** in Daytona (1040 Museum Way, 904-255-0285).

African-Americans

The history of African-Americans in Florida is somewhat different than in other southern states because of Florida's long Spanish history. Blacks came into Florida as soldiers with virtually every Spanish expedition. The first Black recorded to have visited Florida accompanied Narvaez on his 1527 expedition. During the British and Spanish eras Blacks lived freely in Florida and many sought its asylum from the other Southern states. Both Pensacola and St. Augustine had a tradition of intermarriage and many Blacks there became skilled artisans, learning crafts reserved elsewhere for white men. **Jullee Cottage** (210 E. Zaragoza St. in Historic Pensacola Village, Pensacola, FL 32501; 904-444-8905) was bought in 1805 by Jullee Panton, a "free woman of color," and later was owned by a succession of free Black women. It is now a museum of Black history.

African-Americans played a key role in the development of Florida from its beginnings, clearing much of
the land necessary for farming and other activities. In
addition to American Blacks, many French and British
citizens from the West Indies have settled in Florida or
worked as migrant laborers during harvest seasons.
They have brought with them the language, dance,
music, and customs of the islands.

The African-Americans got along well with the
Seminole Indians and they were close allies in times of
conflict. One of the most famous Blacks during the
Seminole Indian War period was Abraham, who
served as a translator and advisor to Chief Micanopy
and became a leader in the second Seminole War. In
spite of growing restrictions after 1840 as the state
became more closely tied to Southern plantation ideol-
ogy, many free Blacks continued to live in Florida and
own property into the early 1860s.

In the years of reconstruction after the Civil War,
nineteen African-Americans served in the state Legislature. Josiah Thomas Walls served as representative
from Florida in the U.S. Congress from 1871-1873.
Jonathan C. Gibbs, known widely as a great orator,
became Florida's secretary of state in 1868 and later
was superintendent of public instruction. After only
eighteen months in his education position, he died
suddenly of a seizure. Many suspected poisoning. It
was more than a hundred years before another Black,
Jesse J. McCrary, Jr., served in the Florida Cabinet.

But during the interim, African-American leadership was developing in other arenas. In 1892 Gallies
Hall in Tallahassee held a standing-room-only crowd
to honor Florida's first five African-American college
students as they received their diplomas from Florida
State Normal and Industrial College, now **Florida Agricultural and Mechanical University (FAMU) (904-**

599-3414). Today FAMU has more than 7,000 students, nationally acclaimed business, pharmacy, and engineering schools, and the famous Marching 100 Band, the only American band invited to perform in France's bicentennial Bastille-Day celebration. The university houses the **Black Archives Research Center and Museum** (Carnegie Library; 904-599-3020), one of the country's most extensive collections of African-American artifacts, and a research center on Black influence in history and culture. The **Foster Tanner Fine Arts Gallery**, also on the FAMU Campus, shows the works of many Black artists.

During World War I, thousands of Bahamian Blacks came to Florida to harvest crops in the "Glades." Afterwards many decided to stay. Zora Neale Hurston described the life of the Glades harvesters and of their experience during the 1928 hurricane in her novel, *Their Eyes Were Watching God.*

Hurston, a folklorist, novelist, and anthropologist, traveled throughout the Glades and turpentine camps, documenting many aspects of southern life and culture that otherwise would have been forgotten. She was born around 1901 in Eatonville, Florida, near Orlando. Incorporated in 1887, Eatonville was the nation's first incorporated Black town. Hurston was one of the leaders of the Harlem Renaissance, and spent her life trying to keep the African-American cultural heritage alive. Her work is now gaining new recognition and attention after a generation of obscurity. Two of her other books have also come back into print: *Dust Tracks on a Road: An Autobiography* and *Moses: Man of the Mountain.* All offer rich descriptions of the lives of Blacks in Florida in the first half of the 20th century. *Zora Neale Hurston: A Literary Biography* by Robert E. Hemenway gives added insight.

In Daytona Beach you can see the home of **Howard**

Thurman (641 Whitehall St., Daytona Beach, FL; 904-258-7514), a teacher and minister born in Daytona Beach in 1899, who was one of the principal American contacts for Mahatma Gandhi.

Mary McLeod Bethune, one of America's foremost educators also lived and worked in Daytona Beach. She dreamt of building a school for Black students and singlemindedly brought that dream to reality. In 1924 the school she created, the Daytona Normal and Industrial School for Girls, merged with Jacksonville's Cookman Institute for Boys to become the distinguished Bethune-Cookman College. The **Mary McLeod Bethune Foundation** (640 Second Ave., Daytona Beach, FL 32115; 904-255-1401 x372) has preserved **Mary McLeod Bethune's home** (631 Pearl St., Daytona Beach, open Mon.-Fri. 9 a.m.-4 p.m.) very much as it was when she lived there. This two-story frame structure dating from 1914 was made a National Historic Landmark in 1975.

The Martin County Black Heritage Association (P.O. Box 2279, Stuart, FL 34995) sponsors an annual **Black Heritage Festival** each year on the third Saturday of February with harmony games, art exhibits and sales, a gospel sing-out, and ethnic food booths.

CHAPTER 7

RIVERBOATS AND RAILROADS

The path of Florida's exploration widened in the late 1800s. Where Indians and Spanish conquistadors had walked single file, gangs of workers and machines cut wide swaths across the landscape. Between 1870 and 1930 the face of Florida changed radically. It was transformed from a raw frontier not too different from the wilderness faced by the first Spanish explorers to a developed, populous playground. The transition was abrupt, in many ways brutal. It was spearheaded by a rapid expansion of transportation on both water and land.

First riverboats and then railroads opened up Florida's interior and expanded the state's economy. They brought tourists from the north who came to visit and settle the Sunshine State, and entrepreneurs who wanted to get rich in Florida's boom.

Steamboats — For Tourism and Commerce

Steamboats, first put into service on the Apalachicola River in 1827, soon appeared on most inland waters. By the 1870s, steamboats dominated the commercial trade along Florida's navigable rivers and the major intercity coastal routes — from Jacksonville south to Titusville and from Cedar Key on the Gulf of Mexico to Tampa and Key West. These efficient, colorful little river boats, usually woodburning side- or stern-wheelers, could penetrate the narrow, twisting channels of the state's more scenic, spring-fed rivers. Larger models could sail with hundreds of people from Jacksonville to New York, Havana, or the Bahamas. The period 1875-1887 was the golden age of steamboat travel in Florida.

Steamboat captains were dominant figures in local life. They served as middlemen for settlers and merchants, transporting produce to market, arranging its sale, and returning with provisions. Everywhere in the state, a ship captain's signature was as good as money. Lawrence E. Will of Belle Glade, described the captains as "a tough and hardy breed," in *Okeechobee Steamboats and Their Skippers*. "Now if you're of a mind to picture the captain of one of them old smoke boats," wrote Will in Crackerese, "you'd most likely imagine him standing by his steering wheel, spare and straight, with a big white mustache acrost his lean, tanned face, with keen blue eyes, and a shock of snowy hair crowned by a battered boatman's cap."

Steamboating declined during the 1890s, primarily because of the expansion of railroads throughout the state, but they had two brief resurgences — once in 1898 when 50 steamboats assembled at Tampa for the invasion of Cuba in the Spanish-American War, and again during the 1920s real estate boom, when the railroads had more business than they could handle.

Steamboat life was colorful and profitable in Florida. Glimpses of early steamboating in the north of the state have survived in the writings of Harriet Beecher Stowe, Sidney Lanier, and other travelers. They reveal a history as lively as that on Mark Twain's Mississippi. Many small towns and cities are today delightful reminders of the period, their streets still lined with houses of "steamboat gothic" architecture.

Apalachicola on the panhandle (Chamber of Commerce, 128 Market St., Apalachicola, FL 32320; 904-653-94190), an important cotton port before the war and a major lumber port afterwards, remains one of the most charming towns in Florida, with rambling stately old homes. You can stay in one of them, **The Gibson Inn** (57 Market St., Apalachicola, FL 32320; 904-653-2191) and also visit the **David G. Raney House**, home to the area's Tourist Information Center.

At the northern end of Florida's section of the Apalachicola River, **Gregory House,** also from this period, sits high on a bluff in **Torreya State Park** (Rt. 2 Box 70, Bristol, FL 32321; 904-643-2674). It was originally built in 1849 on the other side of the Apalachicola River by a wealthy cotton planter when steamboats plied the river by the hundreds, carrying goods and supplies.

Fernandina Beach in northeast Florida (Chamber of Commerce, P.O. Box 472, Fernandina Beach, FL 32034; 904-261-3248) was a major shipping port for lumber, phosphate, and naval stores. It has streets lined with Victorian houses, preserved in a 30-block nationally registered historic district. Two are now bed-&-breakfast inns: **The Bailey House** (28 S. 7th St.; 904-261-5390) and **The Williams House** (103 S. 9th St.; 904-277-2328). If you want to really get a feeling for life at the turn of the century, you may choose to spend the night in one of them.

Ocala in central Florida (Chamber of Commerce, P.O. Box 1210, Ocala, FL 32678; 904-629-8051) also has homes from this period. The Town Square Park (NE 8th Ave. and Silver Springs Blvd.) has a replica of a domed Victorian gazebo. A few blocks away, along Fort King Avenue between 3rd and 13th streets, is an

area with over 200 homes built in styles ranging from
Gothic to Queen Anne revival. **Seven Sisters Inn** (820
SE Fort King St., Ocala, FL 32671; 904-867-1170) now a
bed-&-breakfast inn, was built in the Queen Anne
style in 1888 for the Scott Family.

DeBary in central Florida (Chamber of Commerce,
P.O. Box One, DeBary, FL 32713; 407-608-4614) was
developed as a major steamship center by Count Frederick DeBary. A millionaire born in Germany of
French ancestry, he was sent to the United States by his
family in 1840 as an agent for their exclusive cham-
pagne company franchise. He lived in New York for
many years and in the 1870s became interested first in
Florida real estate, and then in steamboats.

He commissioned an iron-hulled sidewheeler, the
Frederick DeBary, as his flagship in 1876 and dominated
waterborne trade on the St. Johns River for the rest of
the era. The *City of Jacksonville*, his second ship, was
the first coal-burner on the river. This was an important innovation because the turpentine-soaked pine
previously used for fuel was becoming scarce as heavy
boat and rail traffic throughout the state depleted resources.

DeBary's mansion, one of the most famous and
luxurious private residences on the river, was made of
cypress shipped from Georgia and surrounded by
groves of citrus and bamboo. Renovation was started
on **DeBary Hall** (210 Sunrise Blvd., DeBary; 668-5286),
in 1990 and eventually it will be open to the public.
Until it is, visitors can only get a glimpse of it from a
distance.

DeBary introduced his friend General Henry S. Sanford to the area and Sanford bought land along the
river as well. He was not well received by the locals,
however, because he had been a general in the Union
army. Since no one would work for him, he recruited

RIVERBOATS AND RAILROADS
MAP OF SITES

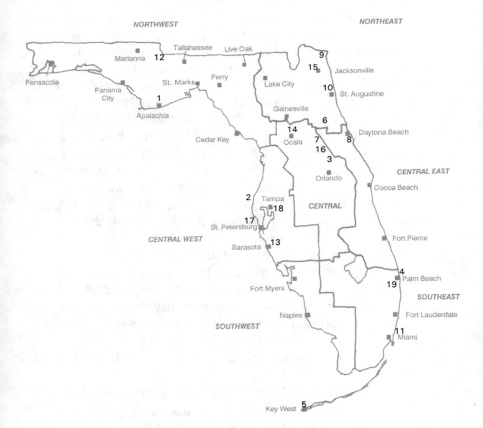

NORTHWEST

NORTHEAST

Tallahassee　Live Oak

Marianna　12

9

15

Jacksonville

Pensacola

Panama
City

Perry

St. Marks

10

St. Augustine

1

Lake City

Apalachia

Gainesville

6

Cedar Key

14

Ocala

7

16

8

Daytona Beach

3

CENTRAL EAST

Orlando

Cocoa Beach

2

Tampa

18

CENTRAL

17

St. Petersburg

13

CENTRAL WEST

Sarasota

Fort Pierce

Fort Myers

4

Palm Beach

19

SOUTHEAST

Naples

Fort Lauderdale

SOUTHWEST

11

Miami

Key West　5

RIVERBOATS AND RAILROADS

SITES TO VISIT

1. APALACHICOLA. Chamber of Commerce, 128 Market St., Apalachicola, FL. 32320; 904-653-9419.
2. BELLEVIEW BILTMORE HOTEL, 25 Belleview Blvd., Clearwater; 813-442-6171.
3. BRADLEE-MCINTYRE HOUSE, 150 W. Warren St., Longwood; 407-332-6920, open 2nd & 4th Wednesdays, 1-4.
4. BREAKERS HOTEL, 1 County Road, Palm Beach, FL; 407-665-6611.
5. CASA MARINA, 1500 Reynolds St., Key West; 305-296-3535.
6. CRESCENT CITY. Putnam County Chamber of Commerce, P.O. Box 550, Palatka, FL 32178; 904-328-5401.
7. DEBARY HALL, 210 Sunrise Blvd., DeBary, FL 407-668-5286.
8. DELAND, Chamber of Commerce, 336 N. Woodland; Deland, FL 32720; 904-734-4331.
9. FERNANDINA BEACH, Chamber of Commerce, P.O. Box 472, Fernandina Beach, FL 32034; 904-261-3248.
10. FLAGLER HOTELS, St. Augustine.
—ALCAZAR HOTEL, Lightner Museum, 75 King St., St. Augustine, FL 32084; 904-824-2874, open daily 9 a.m.-5 p.m.
—CORDOVA HOTEL, King & Cordova Sts., now St. Johns County Courthouse.
—PONCE DE LEON HOTEL, King & Cordova Sts., now Flagler College.
11. GOLD COAST RAILROAD MUSEUM, 12450 S. W. 152nd St., Miami, FL 33177; 305-253-0063.
12. GREGORY HOUSE, Torreya State Park, Rt. 2, Box 70, Bristol; 904-643-2674.
13. LIONEL TRAIN AND SHELL MUSEUM, 8184 North Tamiami Trail, Sarasota, FL 34243; 813-355-8184, open daily 9 a.m.-5 p.m.
14. OCALA, Chamber of Commerce, P.O. Box 1210, Ocala, FL 32678; 904-629-8051.
15. RAILROAD MEMORABILIA MUSEUM, Old House Museum, Pablo Park, Jacksonville; 904-246-0093, open Wed. 10 a.m.-4 p.m., Sun. 1 to 4 p.m.

16. SANFORD, Chamber of Commerce, P.O. Drawer CC, Sanford, FL 32772-0868; 407-322-2212.
17. ST. PETERSBURG MUNICIPAL PIER, 800 Second Ave. N.E., St. Petersburg, FL 33701; 813-821-6164.
18. TAMPA BAY HOTEL & HENRY PLANT MUSEUM, University of Tampa, 401 W. Kennedy Blvd. Tampa, 813-254-1891, tours Tues. & Thur. 1:30 p.m., free.
19. WHITEHALL (HENRY M. FLAGLER MUSEUM) Coconut Row & Whitehall Way, Palm Beach, FL 33480; 407-655-2833, open Tues.-Sat. 10 a.m.-5 p.m., Sun. noon-5 p.m.

Swedish, Polish and Italian laborers. Sanford (in Central Florida off I-4 on U.S. 17/92; Chamber of Commerce, P.O. Drawer CC, Sanford, FL 32772-0868; 407-322-2212) stands as a tribute to the tenacity of developers and workers alike. The Sanford enterprise grew into an important port and citrus business until a fire in 1883 destroyed all the wooden buildings downtown, and the 1894 and 1895 freezes brought a sudden end to the town's citrus production. The community switched to growing celery, which it continues to do with great success today.

It is known for its Victorian architecture, picturesque waterfront, historic downtown, and as the southern terminus for Amtrak's Auto Train. **The Seminole County Historical Museum** (300 Bush Blvd.; 407-321-2489, open Mon.-Fri. 9 a.m.-1 p.m., Sat. & Sun. 1-4 p.m., free) features steamboat and railroad memorabilia and information on the citrus industry and cattle ranching, along with rooms furnished like those in a typical steamboat-era mansion. **The Henry Shelton Sanford Memorial Museum** (520 E. First St.; 407-330-5698, open Tues.-Fri. 10 a.m.-5 p.m., Sun. 2-5 p.m., free) houses a collection of the general's books, furniture, and pictures. You can pick up a free map for an historic downtown walking tour at the Sanford Visitor Center in the City Hall (300 N. Park Ave.).

This is a good place from which to take a sightseeing cruise on the St. John's River. For a nature-oriented two-hour tour on Captain Hoy's *Riverboat Princess*, contact St. Johns River Cruises and Tours, (Sanford Boat Works next to the Osteen Bridge, SR 415, Sanford; 407-330-1612). The boat is specially designed to travel quietly and ply shallow waters where larger vessels cannot go.

Nearby **Deland** (Chamber of Commerce, 336 N. Woodland; P.O. Box 629, Deland, FL 32712-0629; 904-734-4331) also dates from the steamboat era. It is a pleasant town with old houses, big trees, and Stetson University. Further north in northeast Florida, **Crescent City** (Putnam County Chamber of Commerce, P.O. Box 550, Palatka, FL 32178; 904-328-5401) is the center of an unspoiled part of the state, full of live oak trees, pines, gently rolling pastures and old houses. **Sprague House Inn** (904-698-2430), is still functioning as an inn and restaurant, as it did in the steamboat days. There's a lazy old-Florida feeling about this area. When you walk along the street, people wave as they drive by in their cars.

North of Orlando in **Longwood**, you can visit another home from the steamboat era, the yellow and white Bradlee-McIntyre House (150 W. Warren St.; 407-332-6920, open for tours from 1-4 p.m. on the second and fourth Wed. of each month). It was built in 1885 in Altamonte Springs and moved to its present location in the early 1970s. The architecture and furnishings have been restored to the original Queen Anne style. The town has several other Victorian houses including the renovated Longwood Village Inn, built in 1885 and now an office building. Its sprawling blue-grey hulk stands immediately across the street from the Bradlee-McIntyre House.

The steamboat era was a colorful one in Florida. One way to recapture it is by taking a cruise on a restored or reproduced steamboat. Sail *Grand Romance* from Sanford, the *Empress* from Miami, *Jungle Queen* or *Paddlewheel Queen* from Fort Lauderdale, *Starlite Princess* on Tampa Bay or one of the growing number of others that ply Florida's waters.

Rails to Riches

Useful as they were, steamboats could further development only in areas easily accessible by water. Goods had to be dragged to waterways where they could be floated out to vessels, an expensive and often impossible task in the heavy tropical vegetation that swathed Florida's interior. The real key to opening up inland Florida and tying it into the rest of the United States was the railroad. Railroads expanded rapidly after the War Between the States and gave new meaning to Florida geography. The first railroads were powered by mules who pulled small cars over iron strips laid on wooden slats. In 1886 when Florida changed from narrow gauge roads to the standard gauge used by northern railroads, rail service from the North to Florida became possible. It created massive opportunities for tourism and economic development.

Several museums in Florida commemorate the railroads as well as the lives and works of great railroad magnates. Jacksonville Beach has a **1900 Railroad Memorabilia Museum**, part of the Old House Museum (Pablo Park, Beach Blvd.; 904-246-0093, open Wed. 10 a.m.-4 p.m., Sun. 1-4 p.m.). In the Tampa Bay area you can visit the **Lionel Train and Shell Museum** housed in a replica of a Victorian railroad depot (8184

North Tamiami Trail, Sarasota, FL 34243; 813-355-8184, open daily 9 a.m.-5 p.m.). In Miami visit the **Gold Coast Railroad Museum** (Metro Zoo access road at 12450 SW 152nd St., Miami, FL 33177; 305-253-0063). The museum has rows of historic trains including the *Ferdinand Magellan*, a 1942 Pullman car built exclusively for U.S. presidents, and the *Silver Crescent*, built in 1948 for the California Zephyr. You can actually ride the cars around the Metro Zoo on Sat. and Sun.

Three men emerged as state railroad giants, W.D. Chipley, Henry B. Plant, and Henry M. Flagler. William D. Chipley, a native of Georgia, became "Mr. Railroad of West Florida" as manager of the L & N properties in that region. Under Chipley's leadership the L & N invested heavily in Pensacola, helping to make it a thriving Gulf port. Today, Chipley's name is the least well-known of the three because he did not build hotels and mansions. Plant and Flagler operated on parallel lines, friends and rivals who divided the peninsula rather than wage economic war against each other. Nevertheless their competition over luxury hotels was keen.

Plant's Railroad Empire

Henry B. Plant, a native of Connecticut, eventually created a network of 2,250 miles of rail stretching from Richmond to Tampa. His railroad company maintained an agriculture and immigration bureau and a large land sales organization, all to attract settlers and provide traffic for the railroad.

Plant's **Tampa Bay Hotel** (University of Tampa, Henry Plant Museum, 401 W. Kennedy Blvd.; 813-254-1891, tours Tues. & Thur. 1:30 p.m., free) was modeled on the Alhambra, and is today considered one of the finest examples of Moorish architecture in the western hemisphere. The hotel is crowned with thirteen onion-shaped silver minarets topped by curving quarter moons (one for each of the thirteen months of the Muslim lunar year). When the hotel opened in 1891, guests arrived on private railroad tracks that ended in the hotel lobby. Its hallways were so long that visitors hired rickshaws to get around. The hotel boasted a hand-carved mahogany elevator originally powered by hydraulic force.

During the Spanish-American War, it was used as headquarters for Teddy Roosevelt and his Rough Riders and other officers commanding the Cuban Expeditionary Forces. Soon afterwards, however, the hotel fell on hard times. The city acquired it for taxes in 1905 and leased it out until the Depression dried up the tourist business. In 1933, it was taken over by the University of Tampa.

Plant also developed the **Belleview Biltmore** (25 Belleview Blvd., Belleair, Clearwater; 813-442-6171). It was built in 1897 and was said to be the world's largest frame structure, replete with clapboard and dormers. Today it has been restored to its original and unpretentious elegance with Tiffany stained-glass ceiling panels, lobby fireplaces, and brass fixtures.

Plant also had other hotels: The Seminole in Winter Park, Ocala House in Ocala, the Hotel Kissimmee, and the Port Tampa Inn, as well as inns and hotels at Punta Gorda and Fort Myers that catered to the tourists who came into Florida on his railroads. Port Tampa, ten miles from the city proper, was developed by Plant to accommodate his Plant Line steamers which sailed in the Gulf and the Caribbean.

St. Petersburg Municipal Pier, (at the foot of Second Ave.; 800 Second Ave. N.E., St. Petersburg, FL 33701; 813-821-6164) the heart of modern St. Petersburg's downtown activity, is also from the railroad days.

When it was first constructed in 1889 by the Orange Belt Railway, the pier was a large, ornate bathing pavilion with a toboggan slide and a horse-drawn flatcar to carry passengers from the boat docks two miles away. It is not as long now, but there is still a jitney service to carry you down the mile of concrete and shops. The upside-down pyramid pavilion, with craft vendors, gift shops, a restaurant lounge, an observation deck, and a small strip of sand for bathing sits out over the sparkling waters of the bay. The view from the pier is especially scenic at night.

Flagler's Empire

Henry Morrison Flagler was co-founder of the Standard Oil Co. with John D. Rockefeller. He first visited Florida in 1878 on a trip for his wife's health. The first Mrs. Flagler died in 1881 and after he remarried in 1883, he visited Florida again and decided to settle in St. Augustine and launch a new career. At first interested in hotels, Henry Flagler became involved with railroads to transport building materials and guests to his pleasure palaces. By 1896 he had pushed the railroad all the way to Miami and by 1912 he had completed the famous Overseas Railway from Miami to Key West. Meanwhile he continued to build and buy hotels. In 1908, Flagler's eight Florida hotels — the Continental in Fernandina; the Ponce de Leon, Alcazar, and Cordova in St. Augustine; the Ormond at Ormond Beach; the Royal Poinciana and Breakers at Palm Beach; and the Royal Palm in Miami — could house up to 40,000 people.

All Flagler's St. Augustine hotels as well as the Breakers and Casa Marina continue to dominate the Florida landscape, and give today's traveler some sense of the opulence and grandeur in which some tourists explored Florida from the 1890s through the 1920s.

The **Ponce de Leon Hotel** was completed in 1888 to cater to the wealthy. It remained a hotel until 1967 when it became Flagler College. It was designed to complement the sixteenth-century buildings of St. Augustine and was one of the earliest and largest cast-concrete buildings in the United States. Louis Tiffany, relatively unknown at that time, designed the windows. Of special note is the hotel's hexagonal dining room on the east side of the building and the giant marble columns in the main lobby. Visitors are welcome to wander around the gardens.

The **Alcazar Hotel**, across the street from the Ponce de Leon, was designed by the same architects for tourists of more modest means. It featured an indoor swimming pool with Roman, Russian, and Turkish baths. The hotel folded in the 1930s and stood empty until the Chicago millionaire, Otto C. Lightner, bought it and turned it into the **Lightner Museum** (King & Cordova Sts., St. Augustine, FL 32084; 904-824-2874, open daily 9 a.m.-5 p.m.). The museum includes an Antiques Mall on what was once the floor of the hotel's swimming pool. See also the Lightners' collection of brilliant period cut glass, Victorian art glass, and the stained-glass creations of Louis Tiffany, as well as other decorative arts, furnishings and costumes of the era. It also has a fine collection of music boxes. The **Cordova Hotel**, on the same square, was purchased by Flagler during the same period. It is now the St. Johns County Courthouse.

The original **Breakers** (1 County Road, Palm Beach; 407-665-6611) burned down. But it was rebuilt on the same model and is still a luxury hotel, legendary and opulent, with painted ceilings and gilded magnificence.

The **Casa Marina** of Key West (1500 Reynolds Street on the Atlantic; 305-296-3535) opened in 1922, eight years after Flagler's death. With its Spanish Renaissance design, tiled roof, arched windows, and colonnades it was to be his ultimate resort hotel. Although popular in its earliest years, its success was short-lived. The 1935 hurricane destroyed the railroad — and along with it the high volume of tourists that the hotel needed. In 1943 the government leased it for navy housing. After the war it reverted to a hotel, but was leased again by the military in 1962 during the Cuban missile crisis. For ten years after this it stood closed and empty, in a state of serious deterioration. In 1978 the Marriott chain took it over, renovating it completely and adding a new four-story wing. The old building is worth a visit for its black cypress lobby, shining pine floors, and massive fireplace reaching to the beamed ceiling.

By the time of his death at age 83 in 1913, Flagler had developed the entire east coast of Florida. The golden age of rail travel soon passed, but the Overseas Railway to Key West, badly damaged by the Labor Day hurricane of 1935, provides the base for the Overseas Highway on which we now drive through the Florida Keys. The resorts that Flagler established — St. Augustine, Daytona, Palm Beach, and Miami — remain famous today.

If you want to get a real feel for the lifestyle of the railroad magnates, visit Flagler's magnificent 55-room mansion, **Whitehall**, which he built for his wife in Palm Beach in 1901. It now houses the **Henry M. Flagler Museum** (Coconut Row & Whitehall Way; 407-655-2833, open Tues.-Sat. 10 a.m.-5 p.m., Sun. noon-5 p.m.) as well as Flagler's elegant railroad car, *The Rambler*. The mansion has a marble columned entrance and grand staircase, rooms with painted ceilings, gilt furniture, and other marks of grandeur at every turn. There's a special collection of porcelain dolls, paintings, and family treasures. Other exhibits depict the local history of the area and the building of the Florida East Coast Railway. The Palm Beach County Historical Society is housed here as well.

CHAPTER 8

PLACES IN THE SUN

A s the Florida wilderness opened up, land was cheap and abundant. Developers and entrepreneurs flocked there in hope of quick, big profits. They placed advertisements in northern papers to bring people south to buy land and fill hotels. The entrepreneurs who created Florida's railroad, real estate, and tourism boom envisioned and executed wild schemes, grand hotels, and opulent mansions. They left a legacy of buildings and gardens — American palaces that are architecturally interesting and full of antiques from all over the world. The tourists and settlers responded in droves. Florida became the winter playground of the rich, a haven for the ill, and a land of opportunity for people who wanted to start over or retire. As Florida moved into the 20th century the climate, which had been its major drawback, became its greatest resource. With the invention of insect spray and air conditioning, which was given an important boost by the early work of John Gorrie in Apalachicola (**John Gorrie State Museum**, Gorrie Square; 904-653-9347), the tropical climate became habitable year round. The magic word became development. The words conservation and environmental concern were hardly even in the state's vocabulary.

The rich and famous flocked to Florida from the 1890s through the 1920s for its warmth and the winter social season. Many settled in for long stays at grand

PLACES IN THE SUN
MAP OF SITES

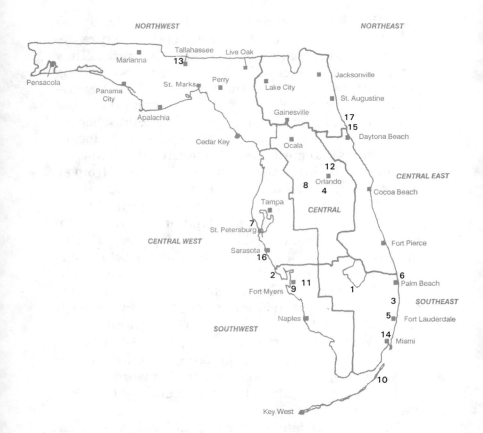

PLACES IN THE SUN

SITES TO VISIT

1. BELLE GLADE, southern end of Lake Okeechobee, 1928 Hurricane Memorial.
2. BOCA GRANDE & GASPARILLA INN (5th St., & Palm Ave., Boca Grande, FL 33921; 813-964-2201.
3. BOCA RATON, Chamber of Commerce, 1800 North Route 1; 407-395-4433, ADDISON MIZNER buildings including Boca Raton Resort and Club.
4. BOK TOWER GARDENS, Rt 27A, P.O. Drawer 3810, Lake Wales, FL 33853; 813-676-1408, open daily 8 a.m.-5:30 p.m.
5. BONNET HOUSE, 900 N. Birch Road, Fort Lauderdale; 305-563-5393, open by reservation only from April to Nov. Tue. & Thur. 10 a.m. & 1:30 p.m., Sun. 1:30 p.m.
6. CLUETT MEMORIAL GARDENS, behind Church of Bethesda By the Sea; A1A at Barton Ave., Palm Beach, FL; 407-655-4554, open daily 8 a.m.-5 p.m.
7. DON CESAR HOTEL, 3400 Gulf Blvd., St. Petersburg, FL 33706; 813-360-1881.
8. FLORIDA SOUTHERN COLLEGE, FRANK LLOYD WRIGHT BUILDINGS, Ingraham Ave., Lakeland, FL 33802; 813-680-4111, 8 a.m.-5 p.m. weekdays.
9. FORT MYERS
—FORD WINTER HOME "MANGOES," 2350 McGregor Blvd., Fort Myers, FL 33901; 813-334-3614, open with guided tours Mon.-Sat. 9 a.m.-4 p.m., Sun. 12:30-4 p.m.
—MURPHY-BURROUGHS HOME, Chamber of Commerce, P.O. Box 6109, Fort Myers, FL 33932; 813-463-6451 or 813-332-1229, tours Sun. 1-4 p.m.
—THOMAS EDISON HOME, 2350 McGregor Blvd., Fort Myers; 813-334-3614, open Mon.-Sat. 9 a.m.-4 p.m., Sun. 12:30-4 p.m.
10. ISLAMORADA, 1935 Hurricane Memorial, Mile Marker 81.5.
11. KORESHAN STATE HISTORIC SITE, US 41, P.O. Box 7, Estero, FL 33928; 813-992-0311, open 8 a.m.-sunset.
12. LEU GARDENS, 1730 N. Forest Ave., Orlando,FL 32803; 407-849-262, open daily 9 a.m.-5 p.m.
13. MACLAY STATE GARDENS, U.S. 319, off I-10; 3540

Thomasville Rd., Tallahassee, FL 32308; 904-893-4232, gardens open daily 8 a.m.-sundown, house open Jan.-April.

14. MIAMI

—ART DECO DISTRICT ("South Beach"), Old Miami Beach, Miami Preservation League, 661 Washington Ave., P.O. Box Bin L, Miami, FL 33119; 305-672-2014.

—CHARLES DEERING ESTATE, 16701 S.W. 72 Ave., South Miami, FL 33157; 305-235-1668, open Sat. & Sun. only 9 a.m.-5 p.m., canoe tours 9:30 a.m. or 1 p.m.

— FAIRCHILD TROPICAL GARDEN, 10901 Old Cutler Rd., Miami, FL 33156; 305-667-1651, open daily 9:30 a.m.-4:30 p.m.

—ORCHID JUNGLE, 26715 S.W. 157 Ave., Miami, FL 33031; 305-247-4824.

—VIZCAYA (James Deering Mansion) 3251 S. Miami Ave., Miami, FL 33129; 305-579-2708, open daily 9:30-a.m.-4:30 p.m.

15. ORMOND BEACH

—CASEMENTS and ROCKEFELLER MEMORIAL GARDENS, 25 Riverside Drive and 78 Granada Blvd., Ormond Beach, FL 32174; 904-673-4701, open Mon.-Fri. 9 a.m.-5 p.m., Sat. 9 a.m.-noon, free.

—FRED DANA MARSH MANSION, now Embry-Riddle Aeronautical University, Ormond Beach.

16. SARASOTA

—MARIE SELBY GARDENS, 811 S. Palm Ave., Sarasota; 813-366-5730, open daily 10 a.m.-5 p.m.

—RINGLING MANSION AND MUSEUMS, 5401 Bayshore Drive, P.O. Box 1838, Sarasota, FL 33578; 813-355-5101, open 10 a.m.-6 p.m., house tours 10 a.m.-3 p.m.

17. WASHINGTON OAKS STATE GARDENS, 6400 N.
Oceanshore Blvd., Palm Coast, FL 32037; 904-445-3161, open daily 8 a.m.-sunset.

---

hotels like those built by Flagler and Plant. These opulent resorts became, at least for a time, the social centers of their communities. They held jousting contests on the beach, and costume balls, and ran sightseeing trips through the jungle in horse-drawn coaches and boats. Most had private theaters and orchestras which gave daily concerts.

The burst of high-class tourism promoted by Flagler and Plant spurred other developers to build opulent hotels as well. Several still stand. **Don Cesar Hotel** (3400 Gulf Blvd., St. Petersburg Beach, FL 33706; 813-360-1881) sticks up on St. Petersburg Beach like a giant pink sandcastle, a survivor whose ongoing renovation keeps its color bright and its comfort level high. The hotel is easy to spot from a distance, at the southernmost boundary of a wall of high-rise beach hotels. It was completed in 1928, just before the stock market crash the following year, and saw dismal days during the 1930s. The army bought it during World War II to use as a hospital, and after that it suffered deterioration and neglect. A "Save the Don" committee rescued it during the 1970s and it became a hotel again in 1973, after being restored. The National Archives in Washington lists it as a historical monument.

The **Boca Raton Resort and Club** (1 Camino Real, Boca Raton, FL 33432; 407-395-3000) is an especially beautiful hotel from this period, designed in 1926 as the Cloister Inn by architect Addison Mizner. Although its style has been summed up as "Bastard-Spanish-Moorish-Romanesque-Gothic-Renaissance-Bull-Market-Damn-the-Expense," and it was forced to close after only one season, it remains a model of elegance. Today it is an extensive world-class resort. Its marble pillars, high ceilings, arched windows, pools with ornate ceramic tiles, and massive Spanish tables give it a unique old-world Floridian charm.

Wintering at the Top

Many affluent visitors to Florida returned to build their own places in the sun. John D. Rockefeller who had worked with Flagler for many years, spent his winters in central east Florida in Flagler's Ormond Hotel at Ormond Beach until 1918 when, so the story goes, he learned that he was being charged more than any other guest in the hotel. He raged out of the hotel and purchased his own mansion, **The Casements,** just a stone's throw away (25 Riverside Drive, Ormond Beach, FL 32174; 904-673-4701, open Mon.-Fri. 9 a.m.-5 p.m., Sat. 9 a.m.-noon, free).

Rockefeller spent his winters there until he died in 1937 at the age of 97. The house, named because of its many windows, was originally built in 1912. After Rockefeller's death, it was sold and eventually, like so many buildings of the period, fell into disrepair. It was finally saved and renovated in 1979 after a seven-year battle waged by local residents. Today the mansion functions as a multi-faceted cultural and civic center.

John Ringling of Ringling Brothers circus didn't spend all of his time in the "Big Top." He got into real estate too and became one of the ten richest men in America. He especially liked Florida. Ringling's mansion in Sarasota, named Ca' d'Zan, which means "House of John," is a rosy-cream stucco palazzo modeled after the Doge's Palace in Venice. Its tower and 30 rooms are built around a 2.5 story roofed court and furnished with treasures from around the world. Ringling left his art gallery, mansion, estate, art collection, and fortune to the state of Florida when he died in 1936.

The **Ringling Mansion and Museums,** Ca' d'Zan, the Museum of Art, and the Circus Museum are all open to the public (5401 Bayshore Drive, P.O. Box 1838, Sarasota, FL 33578; 813-355-5101, one admission covers all buildings; grounds open 10 a.m.-6 p.m., house tours 10 a.m.-3 p.m.).

The Museum of Art is styled after a 15th-century

Italian villa with columns, doorways, sculpture and marble brought from all the major cities of Italy. It has a fine collection of European art with a special focus on the Baroque period. Next door is the Asolo Theater (813-355-7115) which stood in a little town near Venice centuries ago. Parts of the theater was transported in boxed segments to Sarasota and reassembled. It is still used for performances. The Circus Museum is full of gilded parade wagons, calliopes, and other displays that bring back the magical moments of the circus big top.

The Bonnet House in Fort Lauderdale (off Sunrise Blvd., two blocks west of the ocean; 900 N. Birch Rd.; 305-563-5393, tours by reservation only April to November, Tue. & Thur. at 10 a.m. and 1:30 p.m., Sun. at 1:30 p.m.) has a very different style. The house nestles in a wilderness not noticed by the beachgoers who throng the public beaches just opposite. It is a plantation-style manse with 30 rooms and 35 oceanfront acres, named for the bonnet lilies that once covered the pond nearby. Frederick Clay Bartlett was given the house by his father-in-law, Hugh Taylor Birch, who also gave Fort Lauderdale a large tract of land now called the Hugh Taylor Birch State Recreation Area. Mrs. Bartlett, 100 years old in 1988, continued to live in the house after her husband's death and gave the property to a public trust for its use during the periods when she was not in residence.

The house has a fascinating Shell Room, displaying inlaid shells and a collection of paired specimens. You can also see the studio of Frederick Bartlett, with many of his original paintings on display. Swans still swim on the pond and monkeys still swing through the jungle that surrounds the house. There are horse and carriage rides, nature trails, and tours.

James Deering, International Harvester heir, also

did some building in Florida. He searched the world for the perfect climate for his winter home and finally decided on Miami, still a small town in 1914 when work started on his mansion, **Vizcaya** (3251 S. Miami Ave. Miami, FL 33129; 305-579-2708, open daily 9:30-4:30 p.m.). This gracious Italian villa on Biscayne Bay took hundreds of artisans over five years to complete. The house has superb gardens full of grottos, pools, fountains, and sculptures. There is a sound and light show weekend evenings from May 15 through September 14 at 8:30 p.m. and September 15 through May 14 at 8 p.m.

The **Charles Deering Estate** (16701 S.W. 72nd Ave., South Miami, FL 33157; 305-235-1668, open Sat. & Sun. only, 9 a.m.- 5.p.m.) was built by James Deering's brother, Charles, an industrial magnate in his own right. He began construction of his magnificent Mediterranean Revival mansion in 1918. It is attached by covered walkways to the Richmond Cottage, an 1896 home and inn which Deering retained intact. The property also contains Tequesta Indian archeological sites dating back about 1,500 years and the remains of the late-nineteenth-century town of Cutler. The property is now a county park. If you like, you can tour the 360-acre bay front estate by canoe at 9:30 a.m. or 1 p.m.

Boca Grande, on Gasparilla Island along the southeast coast, was another playground for the wealthy. Many stayed at the Gasparilla Inn (5th St. & Palm Ave., Boca Grande, FL 33921; 813-964-2201). It was built in 1912 as a stylish resort for the wealthy and still caters to the well-to-do.

One especially delightful residence is the **Thomas Edison Winter Home** in Fort Myers (2350 McGregor Blvd; 813-334-3614, open Mon.-Sat. 9 a.m.-4 p.m., Sun. 12:30-4 p.m.). Edison moved to Florida in 1885 as a widower, seriously ill at the age of 38. Doctors told him he must seek a warmer climate if he wanted to live. Florida was just what the doctors ordered. He remarried in 1886 and lived to the age of 84, wintering in Florida for over 40 years. He and his wife left a very special retreat, a mixture of the gracious style of a bygone era and the product of a highly innovative individual.

The home with its breezeway-connected guest house was prefabricated — one of the first prebuilt buildings in America. Edison drew the plans for the houses and had them built in sections at Fairfield, Maine in 1885. They were then transported to Fort Myers on four sailing schooners and erected in 1886. The buildings are encircled with large overhanging porches. Outside, in tropical gardens filled with experimental and exotic plants, is Florida's first modern swimming pool, built by Edison in 1900.

Furnished just as the Edisons left it, the house is still lit by the original carbon filament light bulbs made by Edison. The electric chandeliers were designed by Edison and hand-made of brass in his own work shop. Edison's laboratory-office, where he conducted his last major experiments, is fully set up. The estate also contains a museum, dedicated by the late Charles Edison, son of the inventor, to preserve memorabilia related to his father's life. It displays the developmental stages of the phonograph, furniture creations, and many of Edison's other inventions.

Beside the Edison home is the **Ford Winter Home "Mangoes"** (2350 McGregor Blvd., Fort Myers, FL 33901; 813-334-3614, open with guided tours Mon.-Sat., 9 a.m.-4 p.m., Sun. 12:30-4 p.m.). Henry Ford bought this quaint house in 1916 so he and his wife Clara could spend the winter months visiting the Edisons. It was opened to the public in 1990 after extensive renovation.

The **Murphy-Burroughs Home** (Chamber of Commerce, P.O. Box 6109, Fort Myers, FL 33932; 813-463-6451) was built by wealthy cattleman John Murphy in 1901 after he visited the area in the late 1890s. The architect-designed house in Georgian Revival style was highly unusual in this part of Florida at the time. The house is open to the public, although still in the process of renovation.

Not all those who built places in Florida's sun came seeking wealth or to conspicuously consume it. One group that did not was the **Koreshan community**, a utopian society founded in 1894 on the banks of the Estero River south of Fort Myers by Cyrus Reed Teed. Teed was a physician, surgeon and brain specialist in Chicago who experienced a "divine illumination" in 1869 and took the biblical name, Koresh. He formulated a detailed constitution for a new society based on communal principles: love and service to one's neighbors, communal ownership of property, and denial of monetary gain. Teed brought his followers to Florida to establish a settlement named Estero, which he believed would grow into a great city under his leadership and would promote the values of ecology and outdoor education, economic development of underdeveloped nations, and racial and sexual equality. At its peak the community had about 200 people and boasted a tropical flower garden, art gallery, printing house, university, and symphony orchestra.

Eventually the society suffered internal dissension. Some reports say the celibacy rule for church leaders was a cause for dissent, especially since Koresh and his aide, Miss Victoria Gratia claimed exemption because they had attained earthly perfection. Neighbor troubles also plagued the Koreshans. Their commitment to the equal treatment of Blacks and women provoked much hostility. In 1908, at the age of 69, Koresh died of injuries after he was stoned while speaking in Fort Myers.

The grounds and eight of the original thirty buildings of the settlement have been preserved and restored in **Koreshan State Historic Site** (on US 41 south of Estero; P.O. Box 7, Estero, FL 33928; 813-992-0311, open 8 a.m.-sunset). Tours of the grounds and gardens are available only at certain times, according to a posted schedule. Call for information.

Gardens

Some of Florida's residents, both winter and year-round, took advantage of the tropical climate and turned their creative energies to gardens.

The **Maclay State Gardens** in Tallahassee (U.S. 319, off I-10; 3540 Thomasville Rd., Tallahassee, FL 32308; 904-893-4232, grounds open daily 8 a.m.-sundown, house open Jan.-Apr.) were started in 1923 by New Yorkers, Alfred B. and Louise Maclay, who made their winter home in Florida and developed the grounds as a hobby. The gardens contain both exotic and native plants worked into a pattern of reflecting pools and avenues of stately palms. The 308-acre park, given to the state by Louise Maclay, has become one of the South's finest azalea and camellia collections. The gardens are best seen in early spring (late January to April) but there is always something blooming.

Washington Oaks State Gardens in Northeast Florida between St. Augustine and Daytona Beach (just south of Marineland; 6400 N. Oceanshore Blvd., Palm Coast, FL 32037; 904-445-3161, open daily 8 a.m.-sunset) were originally part of Belle Vista Plantation owned by General Joseph Hernandez, a Spanish Floridian who commanded troops during the Second Seminole War. A surveyor named George Washington, a relative of the first president of the United States, married Hernandez's daughter Louisa in 1844, and the couple was given this land on which they lived until 1856. In 1936 it was purchased by Mr. and Mrs. Owen D. Young. Mr. Young was chairman of the board of General Electric. They greatly expanded the gardens, groves, and plantings. Mrs. Young donated the property to the state in 1964 after her husband's death. The house has been converted into an interpretive center called Young House, which features exhibits of the park.

You can sit here on the terrace on an old-style wooden swing, enjoy the breezes, and watch the boats on the St. John's River. This is a place to relax, let cares flow away, and imagine what life must have been like in the plantation's earliest years. The formal gardens are laid out beneath a canopy of live oak trees, with exotic plants from all over the world growing beside the footpaths and reflecting pools. The gardens are well known for their azaleas, camellias and roses.

The **Ormond Rockefeller Memorial Gardens** (78 Granada Blvd., Ormond Beach, FL 32174; 904-673-4701, open weekdays 9 a.m.-5 p.m., Sat. 9 a.m.-noon) are adjacent to Rockefeller's home, The Casements. They have been restored close to their original design, with the original patio, fountain, and pond. Tours are offered every half hour between 10 a.m. and 2:30 p.m. and Saturdays 10 to 11:30 a.m.

The **Leu Botanical Gardens** in Orlando (1730 N. Forest Ave., Orlando, FL 32803; 407-849-2620, open daily 9 a.m.-5 p.m.) include over 50 acres of trees, orchids, roses, camellias, and other flowers. The best time of year for a visit is between December and March. The house on the property showcases the life-style of a wealthy turn-of-the century family.

Edward W. Bok, Dutch-born publisher and author,

The graceful sea oat anchors sand dunes with its extensive underground root system.

Panhandle beaches still offer solitude and long vistas of sand, sea, and sky.

Sunrises are well worth an early wake-up.

Boardwalks protect delicate dune areas.

Sunset or sunrise? A Florida day can be spectacular at either end.

State parks and national forests in north central Florida offer places for hiking, fishing, and quiet reflection.

Wekiwa Springs State Park is a popular swimming spot near Orlando.

Florida Citrus.
Visitors can learn how it is processed and sample the product at Donald Duck's Citrus World on Route 27, north of Lake Wales.

There is always action along the shore as birds and other wildlife seek food. Here brown pelicans wait for handouts.

Outstanding brickwork graces recently excavated Fort Zachary
Taylor in Key West.

Visitors can walk along the bastions of well-preserved Fort Clinch near Fernandina Beach on Amelia Island.

The Museum of Natural History of the Florida Keys in Marathon was dedicated on Earth Day 1990 by the Florida Keys Land and Sea Trust.

Old forts offer a glimpse of the past.

The "Junior Museum" at East Martello Museum.

Lake in Fort Cooper State Park.

Inside Kissimmee State Park.

The old well at Gamble Plantation House near Bradenton.

One of the many lakes in Florida's interior.

Wild Florida raises its own striking skyline.

Bay Port on the west coast of Florida.

Corkscrew Swamp Sanctuary near Bonita Springs in southwest
Florida.

Florida has about 3,500 species of wildflowers.

editor of *The Ladies' Home Journal*, wanted to make America more beautiful because he had lived in it. In 1929 he donated to the American people **Bok Tower Gardens** (Rt. 27A, just three miles north of Lake Wales; P.O. Drawer 3810, Lake Wales, FL 33853; 813-676-1408, open daily 8 a.m.-5 p.m.). The tower, built of pink and gray Georgia marble and coquina stone from St. Augustine, sits on Iron Mountain, the peninsula's highest point and once a sacred Indian site. Its 57 bronze bells range in weight from 17 pounds to nearly 12 tons. There are recitals daily at 3 p.m. Clock music can be heard half-hourly from 10 a.m.

The **Marie Selby Gardens** (811 S. Palm Ave. Sarasota, FL 34236; 813-366-5730, open daily 10 a.m.-5 p.m.) have, among other displays, an internationally acclaimed orchid center. The gardens encompass two landmark houses, the Selby House and the former Christy Payne Mansion, an example of Southern Colonial architecture that now serves as the Museum of Botany and the Arts.

The **Cluett Memorial Gardens** in Palm Beach (A1A at Barton Ave., FL; 407-655-4554, open daily 8 a.m.-5 p.m.) are hidden behind the Church of Bethesda By the Sea. This serene retreat has fountains, benches, and a tiled pond, in a formal setting.

Morikami Park, Museum, and Gardens (4000 Mori Kami Park Rd., Delray Beach, FL 33446; 407-495-0233, open daily except Mon. 10 a.m.-5 p.m.) pay tribute to Japanese pineapple farmers who settled the area. The 180-acre pine forest preserve includes a two acre garden done in Japanese style with a Koi pond and bonsai garden, as well as a museum devoted to Japanese folk arts.

In Miami look for **Fairchild Tropical Garden** (10901 Old Cutler Rd., Miami, FL 33156; 305-667-1651, open daily 9:30 a.m.-4:30 p.m.). The garden was conceived by winter residents Robert Montgomery and George Brett as a tribute to the plant explorer David Fairchild and as a showcase for plants that would flourish in tropical south Florida. It was landscaped by federal Civilian Conservation Corps workers during the 1930s. Today it is operated by the Metropolitan Dade County Park and Recreation Department and has one of the world's finest and largest collections of palms and cycads, 83 acres of tropical flowers and trees, and eleven lakes.

Orchid Jungle; one mile west of U.S. 1, 25 miles south of Miami, (26715 S.W. 157th Ave., Miami, FL 33031; 305-247-4824 or 800-344-2457, open daily 8:30 a.m.-5:30 p.m., admission) was developed by Lee Fennell who began his orchid business in 1888 in Kentucky and moved it and his family to Florida in 1922. The Fennells planted orchids on the huge oaks growing in 25 acres of lush hammock lands and now grow 9,000-20,000. Orchid Jungle was opened to visitors in 1923 and has paths, a waterfall and a tropical conservatory

Architectural Delights

Florida's potential challenged many architects. **Frank Lloyd Wright** left a particularly rich legacy in Central Florida east of Tampa. He designed seven of the buildings at **Florida Southern College** (Ingraham Avenue, Lakeland, FL 33802; 813-680-4111, open weekdays, 8 a.m.-5 p.m.) including a chapel with a unique steeple and the spectacular science building and planetarium. His design philosophy called for steel for strength, sand to represent Florida, and glass to bring the outdoors in. This is one of the largest concentrations of Wright's architecture in the world. The campus sits on one of the town's thirteen lakes. For a self guiding tour map of the campus, stop at the administration building.

Addison Mizner, who designed the Cloister Hotel in Palm Beach, probably never had any formal architectural training, but he nevertheless became the architect of choice for the very rich in the 1920s. Mizner was a restless eccentric man who came to Florida to die in 1918 at the age of 45. He didn't die and soon got acquainted with Paris Singer, son of the sewing machine tycoon, who commissioned him to design the Everglades Club in Palm Beach. Mizner's style caught on and despite his tendency to forget essential elements like a kitchen or a front door, he designed more than 50-million-dollars-worth of Palm Beach mansions and laid out a resort city of his own called Boca Raton. Stop by **Boca Raton's Chamber of Commerce** (1800 North Route 1; 407-395-4433) to pick up a brochure highlighting the town's buildings.

Architects had a lot of fun in the **Art Deco District** of Old Miami Beach after a new building code in the mid-1930s opened the way for innovation. Tropical Deco architecture in Old Miami Beach was originally planned to "advantageously combine an extremely modest construction cost with a heightened flashy, popular and modern appearance to specifically attract a new solidly middle-class group of tourists." The style introduced cheerful colors, whimsical or impressionistic figures in bas relief on buildings, etched glass, bold vertical forms, ziggurats (stylized stepped roofs), eyebrows (overhanging sunshades) and glass bricks.

Resort buildings went up on Miami Beach at the rate of about one hundred a year in the 1930s. The buildings were strongly geometrical, their white facades accented with tropical pastel colors. They symbolized new life and hope in an area that had suffered severely in the 1926 and 1928 hurricanes and the Depression.

Today the area has both national and local historic designations. The Art Deco District takes in about eighty square blocks — bounded roughly by the ocean, Lenox Court, and 5th and 23rd streets and containing more than 800 historic buildings — the most concentrated historic district in the nation. Known locally as **South Beach**, it is presently experiencing a grand revival as Miami's entertainment heart, with new cafes, music clubs, and restaurants opening regularly. To best absorb the deco ambience stroll Ocean Drive between 5th and 20th streets. Every block brings wonderful buildings. For a map contact the **Miami Design Preservation League** (661 Washington Avenue, P.O. Box Bin L, Miami, FL 33119; 305-672-2014). The League offers a 90-minute walking tour on Saturdays.

Another fine example of Art Deco architecture is in Ormond Beach south of Neptune Avenue on the beach — the 1929 ultramodern, streamlined mansion of **Fred Dana Marsh**, a famous artist, sculptor, muralist, and teacher. It is now owned by Embry-Riddle Aeronautical University.

After the Boom...

The 1870-1930 period in Florida was a time of expansion, roller coaster economics, optimism, and glitz. But money didn't buy everything. One thing it didn't buy was a change in the tempestuous nature of Florida's waters and climate. Hurricanes continued to roar over the land, wracking destruction without regard to class or status. Three hurricanes, in 1926, 1928 and 1935 brought this point home vividly, ending the lives and fortunes of many.

The 1926 hurricane killed nearly 400 people and destroyed and damaged thousands of buildings. The 1928 hurricane sent Lake Okeechobee roaring over its banks, killing 2,200 people. A monument to those who lost their lives in that hurricane stands in **Belle Glade,** built by a Hungarian, Ferenc Varga. Today as you circle the lake on U.S. 27 you will not see any water, just the high levees erected after that disastrous storm. The hurricane on Labor Day 1935 brought down the Flagler Overseas Railroad. Winds were recorded at over 200 miles per hour, and the barometer fell to 26.35, one of the lowest pressures ever recorded in the western hemisphere. You can see a monument to the 423 people who lost their lives in that storm in **Islamorado** at Mile Marker 81.5.

Florida's tourist trade, already in decline as a result of the end of the real estate boom in 1926 and the national economic depression of the 1930s, was further disrupted by World War II.

Although most Americans did not realize it at the time, Florida's extensive coastline (and much of the rest of the east coast) was seriously vulnerable to German submarines during the first six months after the United States entered World War II. The German U-boats prowled the waters of both the Atlantic and the Gulf and sank nearly 400 ships, some within sight of the Florida coast. The submarine threats were fought with the newly organized Civil Air Patrol, the Coastal Picket Patrol, composed of civilian small craft, blimps, and the Sub-Chaser training School in Miami. For a riveting account of this period of Florida and American history read the recent book, *Operation Drumbeat* by Michael Gannon.

The war brought a new kind of boom to Florida. World War II was a flying war, and the state's large tracts of flat, unoccupied land, high number of clear hours, and extensive pool of existing accommodations in resort hotels made it a natural for airfields and military training centers. New tenants took over the resorts of the Sunshine State. As early as April 1, 1941 the army air force was using 70,000 hotel rooms along Miami Beach and dozens of restaurants were converted to mess halls. Every major resort city in Florida turned hotels over to the armed services.

As the war began to wind down, these same hotels became hospitals, convalescent homes, and redeployment centers. Thousands of military personnel and their families discovered Florida's places in the sun, which even in wartime held the appeal that had always drawn travelers and settlers. Many of these wartime visitors flocked back to Florida after the war in new, even larger waves of tourists, and then retirees.

But there were two other forces that profoundly changed Florida's shores. Both grew out of the ingenuity of the human mind. One was the birth of the space age. The other was the creation of Disney World in Central Florida.

CHAPTER 9

FANTASTIC SPACE AND SPACEY FANTASY

The Modern Frontier — Space

During and after World War II, Florida became not so much the object of exploration as the base from which it occurred. Today naval and air force bases established during that war continue to send ships and planes all over the world. Space exploration from Cape Canaveral, one of the earliest mapped and named points in North America, opens whole new worlds to human awareness. In addition to the Kennedy Space Center on Cape Canaveral, Florida has many museums that focus on human beings' attempts to venture beyond the earth into the sea and air, and several major training bases for naval and air forces.

Museums of the Past — Training Centers for the Future

You can start your exploration of the modern frontier in northwest Florida by envisioning yourself in the pilot's seat of one of the first naval flying machines ever developed. The **National Museum of Naval Aviation** in Pensacola (Box 33104, Bldg. 3465, Naval Air Station, Pensacola, FL 32508-3104; 904-453-NAVY, open daily 9 a.m.-5 p.m., free) displays much of the history of the development of early military aviation.

**SPACE AND DISNEYWORLD
SITES TO VISIT**

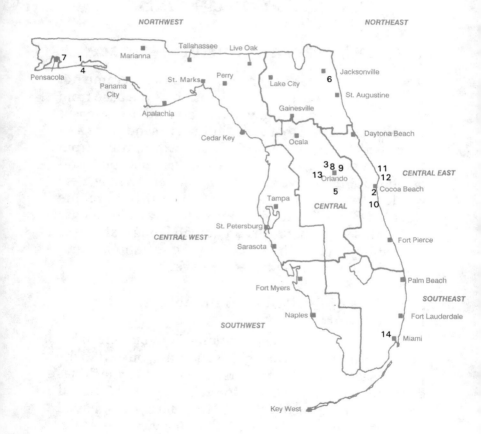

SPACE AND DISNEYWORLD

SITES TO VISIT

1. AIR FORCE ARMAMENT MUSEUM, 14 Eglin Parkway, S.E., Valparaiso, FL 32542; 904-882-4062, open daily 9:30 a.m.-4:30 p.m., free.

2. ASTRONAUT HALL OF FAME, NASA Parkway; 407-267-3184, open daily 9 a.m.-6 p.m.

3. ASTRONAUT MEMORIAL SPACE SCIENCE CENTER AND PLANETARIUM, 1519 Clearlake Road, Cocoa, FL 32922; 407-613-7889, open Mon.- Sat., call for schedule of events.

4. EGLIN AIR FORCE BASE, Fort Walton Beach, FL; 904-881-6668, tours 3 times a week, Jan-Mar., June-Aug.

5. FLYING TIGERS WARBIRD AIR MUSEUM, 231 Hoagland Blvd., Kissimmee, FL 32741; 407-933-1942, open Mon.-Sat. 9 a.m.-6 p.m., Sun. 9 a.m.-5 p.m.

6. MAYPORT NAVAL STATION, Public Affairs Office, P.O. Box 205, Mayport, FL 32228; 904-246-5226, open Sat. 10 a.m.-4 p.m., Sun. 1-4 p.m.

7. NATIONAL MUSEUM OF NAVAL AVIATION, Bldg 3465, Naval Air Station, Pensacola, FL 32508-3104; 904-453-NAVY, open daily 9 a.m.-5 p.m., free.

8. NAVAL TRAINING CENTER, NAVAL RECRUIT REVIEW, General Rees Road, Orlando; 305-646-5054, Fri. 9:45 a.m.

9. ORLANDO SCIENCE CENTER AND JOHN YOUNG PLANETARIUM, 810 E. Rollins St.,Orlando, FL 32803; 315-896-7151, open daily.

10. SPACE COAST SCIENCE CENTER, 1510 Highland Ave., Melbourne, FL 32935; 407-259-5572, open Tue.-Fri. 10 a.m,-5 p.m., Sat. 10 a.m.-4 p.m.

11. SPACEPORT USA, Kennedy Space Center, Cape Canaveral, FL 32899; 407-452-2121 or 800-432-2153 (within FL), open daily 9 a.m.-dusk, except certain launch dates, free except for bus tours and IMAX film.

12. U.S. SPACE CAMP, NASA Parkway, P.O. Box 2726, Titusville, FL 32780; 407-267-3184 or 407-268-4716, open daily 9 a.m.-6 p.m.

13. WALT DISNEY WORLD, P.O. Box 10040, Lake Buena Vista, FL 32830-0040; 407-824-4321.

14. WEEKS AIR MUSEUM, Kendall-Tamiami Airport, 14710 S.W. 128 St., Miami, FL 33186; 305-233-5197, open daily 10 a.m.-5 p.m.

Military aviation got started in Pensacola and the museum offers one of the nation's finest collections of old naval, marine, and coast guard aircraft from 1911 to the space age. Detailed exhibits cover aircraft carriers, helicopters, hands-on fighter jet and huey Helicopter cockpit trainers, and the Skylab Command Module in which a navy crew circled earth for 28 days. A film, *Great Flight* shows the first successful crossing of the Atlantic Ocean by air.

The Pensacola Naval Station is home for the famous precision flying team, the Blue Angels. They have served as the navy's official Flight Demonstration Squadron since 1946, and their trademark — the tight diamond formation, in which they fly just 36 inches apart — is recognized throughout the world. In Pensacola two airshows are scheduled annually — at Pensacola Beach in July and at Sherman Field in the fall. An aircraft carrier, the *USS Lexington*, also docks here. When it is in port, you can visit daily from 9 a.m. to 3 p.m. to get a fascinating look at how several thousand sailors spend their time at sea.

Bus tours of **Eglin Air Force Base** in Fort Walton Beach east of Pensacola, are available on Mondays, Wednesdays and Fridays during January to March and June to August. A very limited number of tickets are available at the Air Force Armament Museum at the edge of the base (904-882-4062), from The Museum Foundation (904-651-1808), and at some local chambers of commerce. You may want to get tickets ahead of time. Tours leave the Officer's Club parking lot. The base covers more than 700 square miles of land, one of the largest in the world. Doolittle's Tokyo Raiders trained here for their raid against imperial Japan, as did the Son Tay Raiders who tried to rescue Americans from North Vietnamese prison camps. The equipment that destroyed Nazi Germany's buzz-bomb launchers was created here, as well. You can also tour a climatic laboratory which can reproduce any weather condition. The **Air Force Armament Museum** (14 Eglin Parkway, S.E. Valparaiso, FL 32542; 904-882-4062, open daily 9:30 a.m.-4:30 p.m., free) displays armaments dating back to World War I.

The Sixth Fleet at the **Mayport Naval Station** near Jacksonville (Public Affairs Office, P.O. Box 205, Mayport. FL 32228) also allows the public to visit its aircraft carriers and other vessels on weekends when ships are in port. Call (904) 270-6289 for a recorded message about the vessels open for tours. They are free and no reservations are required. Hours are usually 10 a.m. to 4:30 p.m. on Saturday and 1-4 p.m. on Sunday.

If you like patriotic celebrations and military ritual try to visit the **Naval Training Center** in Orlando (General Rees Road, off Corrine Drive, north of SR 50, just before the main gate to Navy World; 305-646-5054) on Friday at 9:45 a.m. when modern navy explorers celebrate the completion of basic training at the weekly Naval Recruit Review. The center, commissioned in July 1968, is one of the largest and most modern military training facilities in the nation. Each Friday morning approximately 600 men and women pass in review in a parade that includes the Navy Band of Orlando, the Blue Jacket Chorus, a 50-state flag team, and two precision drill teams. The ceremony lasts about an hour.

At the **Flying Tigers Warbird Air Museum** (231 Hoagland Blvd. [Airport Road], Kissimmee, FL 32741; 407-933-1942, open Mon.-Sat. 9 a.m.-6 p.m., Sun. 9 a.m.-5 p.m.) you can watch Tom Reilly restore American warplanes from World War II. Planes are flown regularly but there is no set schedule. The museum sponsors a three-day flying event in December which features static and aerial demonstrations of various vintage aircraft.

In Southeast Florida, the **Weeks Air Museum** at Kendall-Tamiami airport (14710 S.W. 128 St., Miami, FL 33186; 305-233-5197, open daily 10 a.m.-5 p.m.) is dedicated to the preservation and restoration of aircraft from the beginning of flight through the end of the World War II era. This non-profit, charitable organization opened in March 1987 displays over thirty-five aircraft along with a wide variety of engines and propellers.

Space Exploration

The first American space launch took place at Cape Canaveral in central east Florida in 1958. Eleven years later NASA put a man on the moon. Today one of the biggest attractions in Florida is **Spaceport USA** (Visitors Center, Kennedy Space Center, Cape Canaveral, FL 32899; 407-452-2121 or 1-800-432-2153 [within FL], open daily 9 a.m.-dusk except certain launch dates, free except for bus tours and IMAX film).

The center runs two different bus tours. The more popular Red Tour covers the sites of current manned missions. It runs every 15 or 20 minutes, moves from launch site to launch site, and offers an opportunity to inspect a giant Saturn 5 rocket with an Apollo spacecraft displayed on its side so it can be viewed more closely. You can see the huge building where the space shuttles are assembled as well as the crawler transporters that haul the rockets to the launch site.

The Blue Tour runs just once a day to the Cape Canaveral Air Force Station, where the history of the early space program is on display. It takes visitors to Complex 19 where the Gemini flights blasted off in 1965 and 1966, and to Complex 34 where three Apollo astronauts died in a flash fire in their capsule in January 1967. Since private vehicles are not permitted on the grounds of the Kennedy Space Center unescorted, these tours are the only good way to see the center.

Check the daily schedule for these tours and get your tickets at the ticket pavilion as soon as you arrive at the center. Spaces are limited. Buses leave the visitors' center continuously from 9:15 a.m. until two hours before dark unless there is a launch in progress.

Even without the bus tour you can learn a lot about the Space Center. The 37-minute IMAX film, "The Dream is Alive," takes the viewer from astronaut training through the thundering power of a launch into the incredible vastness of space. Much of the film's footage was actually taken from space by astronauts. There is a thirty minute guided walking tour of selected exhibits conducted at regular intervals during the day along with multimedia presentations in the Galaxy Theater on various aspects of space exploration.

The Galaxy Center also features space-related displays and a space art gallery. Visitors can walk outdoors in a Rocket Garden among authentic rockets and other equipment from each stage of America's space program. A Spaceman willing to pose for pictures with visitors stops frequently at the center. If you, once again, forgot your camera, don't despair. You can check out a free camera from the information center, and purchase film at the Gift Gantry. There are also hands-on activities for children at the exploration station.

The most solemn aspect of the Space Center is the Space Mirror, commemorating the crew of the space-shuttle, *Challenger*, lost in January 1986. The Space Mirror is a wall of granite, 50 feet wide and 40 feet tall, covered with a mirror reflecting the sky. The names of the Challenger astronauts are cut through the stone like stencils. Additional mirrors direct sunlight through the holes causing the names to glow against the reflected sky.

At times when the center has "a bird on the pad," i.e., a shuttle in place in preparation for launching, access to the Space Center may be restricted. This is especially likely if the launch is a secret or military one. You can get a schedule of launchings several months in advance by calling the center. If you are on the east coast at the right time, you may want to watch one. For each blastoff, thousands of people cram the beaches and roadways around the Kennedy Space Center to watch the spacecraft's skyward flight. Those close enough can hear the deep rumble, feel the vibration, and experience the intense white light of the flame that lifts the rocket. Others farther away see the flame, the streak of white, and a few seconds later, hear the sound.

Getting a close view takes some advance planning. On a launch day, visitors who have written ahead to NASA and have obtained a pass may drive onto the causeways of the Kennedy Space Center. The roadways offer a direct view of the rocket and shuttle across six to eight miles of water. But only 1,000 passes are issued. Some of the best viewing for pass-less folks is from the mainland along U.S. 1. There are especially good spots in Titusville, directly across the Indian River from the shuttle launch sites, which offer an unobstructed view of the shuttle and its rocket from about 10 miles away.

Other good viewing points lie slightly to the south, in Jetty Park at Port Canaveral, and on Rt. A1A along the beach in Cocoa Beach or Cape Canaveral. Even from as far away as New Smyrna Beach you can see the rocket's rise and hear the delayed roar. It's not as dramatic, but still pretty awesome. Wherever you go you'll need a portable radio for updates on launch time. Don't expect it to happen exactly on schedule. Occasionally one goes off when planned, but often there are delays of hours or even days. Sometimes NASA "scrubs" a launch indefinitely. Modern space exploration is just as dependent on Florida weather as the earliest explorers were. And the weather isn't always predictable, even with all the space age technology. Binoculars are useful at a launch too, and perhaps even a portable TV, especially if you're at a distance. It's nice to be able to see closeups of all the final preparations that you can't possibly get from the outside.

Other Space Attractions

There are some other space-related sites in the area. Near the entrance to the Kennedy Space Center is the **U.S. Astronaut Hall of Fame**, opened in 1990, (NASA Parkway, P.O. Box 2726, Titusville, FL 32780; 407-267-3184, open daily 9 a.m.-6 p.m.). This non-profit facility traces the achievements of the Mercury Seven astronauts from their early days as candidates through their space missions during NASA's Mercury program. A time tunnel highlights major achievements in space through videotapes of actual flights and interviews, along with displays of personal memorabilia.

The **Orlando Science Center and John Young Planetarium** (810 E. Rollins St., Orlando, FL 32803; 315-896-7151, open daily) gives you a chance to learn your moon weight or buy freeze-dried astronaut ice cream, as well as take in a daily planetarium show. This is an especially good place for families.

In Cocoa, the **Astronaut Memorial Space Science Center and Planetarium** (1519 Clearlake Road, Cocoa,

FL 32922; 407-613-7889, open Mon.-Sat.) were built by
Brevard Community College to preserve the spirit and
tradition of the American Space Program on a personal
level. There are striking 360-degree movies which
change frequently. Call for a schedule of events.
Weather permitting, the observatory is open Friday
and Saturday nights after the show so visitors can
explore the universe through Florida's largest public
telescope.

In Melbourne, the **Space Coast Science Center** (1510
Highland Avenue, Melbourne, FL 32935; 407-259-5572,
open Tues.-Fri. 10 a.m.-5 p.m., Sat. 10 a.m.-4 p.m.) is a
dynamic participatory science and technology museum that encourages visitors to touch its fascinating
exhibits to explore computers, light, sound, gravity,
and illusions. It offers special events year-round, such
as traveling exhibits, classes, lectures, films, and field
trips for people of all ages. The science center gift shop
carries a wide selection of unusual items.

Youngsters who really want to get involved in the
space program get their chance at the **U.S. Space
Camp** (6225 Vectorspace Blvd., Titusville, FL 32780;
407-267-3184 or U.S. 800-63-SPACE). Kids in the fourth
through seventh grades can get a taste of astronaut
training and an introduction to the space program and
space science in this five-day camp, which is part of
the U.S. Astronaut Hall of Fame. They drive a lunar
rover mockup, build and launch model rockets, and
experience the difficulties and sensations of walking
in space. They can also tour NASA's Kennedy Space
Center and its visitors center, work with telescopes
and learn about astronomy at the Brevard Community
College Planetarium.

Highlights for each trainee are the simulated space
missions, using a full-scale Space Shuttle orbiter cockpit and mid-deck mockup. Trainees, in teams of

twelve, learn roles in the orbiter or mission control. The camp is operated jointly by the U.S. Space Camp Foundation and the Mercury 7 Foundation. The program accommodates 100 young people for each five-day session.

Kennedy Space Center lies in the midst of the Canaveral National Seashore which includes 24 miles of undeveloped beachfront and the Merritt Island National Wildlife Refuge. They serve as a buffer zone for the aerospace operations, but also protect one of the last pristine oceanfronts in eastern Florida. With the space center buildings and launch sites on one horizon and an uninterrupted view of Florida's waterland wilderness on the other, the seashore and wildlife refuge offer a unique perspective on the state and the planet's past and future.

Fantasyland U.S.A.

Human exploration occurs not just with the body, but also with the mind and imagination. Modern Florida's best known attraction, **Walt Disney World** (P.O. Box 10040, Lake Buena Vista, FL 32830-0040; 407-824-4321) is a tribute to the fertile imagination of Walt Disney who created some of the world's best-loved cartoon characters. For many visitors, Florida *is* Disney World. And although that is far from true, as hopefully this book illustrates, Walt Disney World is an important part of Florida. Almost everyone who comes to the state eventually visits this incredible theme park. It has transformed sleepy central Florida into one giant playground that continues to spread east and west.

The sights of Disney World are well publicized and appear in detail in many guidebooks. I would like to focus instead on the history of how Disney World came to Florida, and what Disney World taps in all of us, making it so popular.

The Beginnings of Disney World

Interest in real estate goes way back in Florida's history, but real estate in the interior of central Florida, especially in the interior pine barrens too poor for citrus or agriculture, had never garnered much interest — until 1965. Suddenly everyone around Orlando was trying to figure out who was buying up 27,500 acres outside of town. There were rumors, spies, assumed names, dummy corporations and all the ingredients of a good mystery. The company buying up the land was an outfit called Florida Ranch Lands. They were buying but would not discuss who for, in part because most of the company's brokers didn't know either. After months of negotiation and speculation, the secret was out. In November 1965 Walt Disney arrived to make the official announcement. Disney was coming to Florida.

The story of the land acquisition itself is an interesting one. It all started in 1955 back in Anaheim, California when Walt Disney created an innovative entertainment environment which he called Disneyland. But the world outside Disneyland kept invading — pollution, congestion, profit-seeking entrepreneurs. Disney decided to create his own city of tomorrow and a new theme park. Since he already had a West Coast base, he looked east, considering Washington, D.C., Niagara Falls, and St. Louis. Florida, however, was unique for its year-round climate and well-established tourist business.

But where in Florida? The Disney team considered several cities, finally deciding not to compete with a natural phenomenon like the ocean. They wanted a

self-contained environment created to their own speci-
fications. So they looked to the interior, where large
parcels of land were both plentiful and cheap. Their
attention focused on Orlando because it was centrally
located and at the confluence of major highways —
connected by I-4 to I-75 and I-95.

Then the secret wheeling and dealing began. By the
Spring of 1964, a Disney representative, working
through a Miami real estate broker, contacted three
land owners near Orlando and quietly wrangled options on 10,000 acres just off I-4 and SR 535. Traveling
under an assumed name, he made arrangements
through Florida Ranch Lands to assemble property
around the three initial tracts. One of the first tasks
was reassembling land that had been subdivided into
five-and ten-acre plots and sold from mail order cata-
logues back in 1911. County records showed that there
were 50 separate owners, scattered from New England
to California.

The hardest piece of the land puzzle to get in place
was a 37-acre tract on Bay Lake. It included an orange
grove and a cottage, but what Disney wanted most
was the 1.9 acres that bordered the lake, which he
planned to enlarge. The owner wouldn't sell. He had
pulled too many big bass from the lake, watched the
wild turkeys roam over the land, and enjoyed its peace
and serenity. "We loved the place," the owner recalls.
"It wasn't for sale." And it wasn't bought.

This owner turned down a dozen offers for the land,
even after his neighbors began to pressure him.
"You're holding back progress in central Florida," they
said. Finally he realized that he could not turn back
time. "You might as well sell," a neighbor told him.
"The place will never be the same." So he did sell —
for 25 times more than Disney had paid for the rest of
the land.

Disney died just a year after the formal announcement of his Florida plan. His idea of a futuristic city, which he dubbed EPCOT (experimental prototype community of tomorrow) never came to pass. When his successors finally did develop EPCOT, they adopted a notion of a Florida theme park that was decidedly different from Disney's original vision.

Today Walt Disney World is indeed a world unto itself. When Disney made his official announcement in 1965, the Associated Press called him "the most celebrated visitor since Ponce de Leon." To the many people who reaped the results of the economic boom he set loose on the state, he probably was. And the parallel is striking. Disney, probably more than anyone, uncovered the "fountain of eternal youth." Here adults and children alike frolic in a land of everlasting youthfulness in which the naivete of childhood remains forever fresh.

Since the opening of Walt Disney World in 1971, the entertainment complex has become the number one tourist destination in the world. Florida tourists numbered 16 million in 1965, more than twice that number in the mid-1980s.

Walt Disney World is orderly, ultra-clean, full of cornball humor and, in many ways, rather conservative. But the genius of Walt Disney shines through and touches the child in us all. As its founder hoped, it is a controlled environment, a world apart, that keeps the evils of the modern world at bay. For a few hours or a few days we can believe that the benign picture of the world we held as children is still possible. Stories have happy endings and scary things turn out not to be real. We can feel the thrill of taking risks on rides like Space Mountain, confident that the frantic swooshing and swirling will cease and that we will find light at the end of the tunnel.

Perhaps Disney World's great popularity lies in the fact that it is a giant morality play, where the difference between good and evil is clear, and good always wins. It is a lesson we yearn after and perhaps still believe, in spite of all the complexities of the modern world. For whatever reason, even the most cynical among us take our fling in Disney's Florida theme park. And most of us, sometimes in spite of ourselves, have a good time. Disney's great talent lay in taking us on that inward journey to the core where we are still children and in taking us back to a past where we played with abandon. Disney World gives us the opportunity for a different kind of exploration than in other parts of Florida. But the trip is no less authentic.

The Magical Kingdoms

The Walt Disney World Vacation Kingdom covers over 28,000 acres and includes the Magic Kingdom Park, EPCOT Center, Disney MGM Studios Theme Park, Discovery Island, Fort Wilderness recreation area and campground, three championship golf courses, a junior golf course, resort hotels, a shopping village, and a vacation community. It is entered from U.S. 192 or I-4 near Orlando in central Florida.

The Magic Kingdom starts on Main Street in the Town Square, which is lined with turn-of-the century shops. Cinderella's Castle rises in the distance. The Magic Kingdom is made up of several subkingdoms. Mickey's Birthdayland opened on the mouse's 60th birthday in 1988. There you can see Mickey's house within a playground petting farm. Mickey's friends and Mickey himself (still looking just like the young mouse we all knew and loved) greet visitors. Adventureland has several popular rides including "Pirates of the Caribbean" and "Jungle Cruise." Fantasyland has amusement park rides including "20,000 Leagues Under the Sea," a submarine voyage. In Liberty Square you get a chance to meet animated life-size figures of American leaders and can also explore the Haunted House.

Frontierland is a raucous gold-rush town whose main attraction is "Big Thunder Mountain," a runaway train rollercoaster. Depending on how you do on that one, you can decide whether to try the Magic Kingdom's ultimate rollercoaster in Tomorrowland. There "Space Mountain" challenges kids and adults alike. It is the ride that kids love to tell grandparents that they liked best, but that "Daddy wouldn't go."..or "would never go on again."

In **EPCOT Center**, the world is divided into two: World Showcase and Future World. World Showcase is a circular tour of eleven nations that includes films, live street shows, structures, goods, and foods demonstrating heritages and customs in a sort of permanent World's Fair. Future World, produced by some of the nation's leading corporations, tends to be the more popular of the two. There you can explore Kodak's "Journey into Imagination," an audio-animatronics tour through the creative process hosted by a character named Figment, and General Motors' "World of Motion." "Spaceship Earth" explores recurrent human questions: Who are we? Where do we come from? "The Land," by Kraft, gives you a glimpse into the future of food production, and "Horizons" shows how families will be living in the next century.

There are several other theme parks within the complex. *Typhoon Lagoon* (separate admission) is an aquatic park where you can snorkel among creatures of the Caribbean, such as baby sharks and parrotfish. Or you can play on the many water slides and rapids and float a tube down a 100-foot artificial mountain. In

River Country (separate admission) you can enjoy a heated swimming pool, water slides and whitewater tubing in a woodsy setting. *Discovery Island* (separate admission) gives you a nonanimated look at nature. This island zoo features more than 90 animals and 250 plant species, including rare animals such as the Galapagos tortoise.

The newest "magical Kingdom" is the **Disney-MGM Studios Theme Park**, located 2 miles south of U.S. 192. Its main street is Hollywood Boulevard. There are sound effects, sensational movie stunts, song-and-dance reviews, street comedy, and lots of cinema nostalgia. The major attraction of the new park is the "Backstage Studio Tour." It presents in dramatic detail the myriad aspects of this year's productions. Here you can get an early view of the films and shows you will be seeing next year.

Riding the Studio Tour Tram you can peek in at shooting on three state-of-the-art soundstages. There you can watch "Mickey Mouse Club" taping for the Disney Channel, see TV commercials being made, and stop at the special-effects workshop and shooting stage.

On the circle at the end of Hollywood Boulevard, a full-scale recreation of the famous Chinese Theater forms the gateway to Disney's most elaborate ride-through attraction. "The Great Moments at the Movies" ride immerses visitors in the romance, suspense, intrigue, and blazing six-shooter action of some of Hollywood's most memorable moments. In the Super-Star Television Theater members of the "audience cast" take roles beside their favorite stars in front of the cameras.

And Walt Disney World, ever changing, ever probing new dimensions of the human imagination, is already formulating plans for additional attractions.

PART III

FLORIDA'S WILDERNESS

FROM COASTS TO INTERIOR

"To be Floridian, you need not have lived long in Florida. But you must know its seasons and its wild places..."
— Gloria Jahoda, *Florida*

Part III describes major wilderness areas in the state, many preserved to look as much as possible like the Florida that the original European settlers first saw. It is good to imagine and revision the past. It is even better to explore in the present the wilderness areas of modern Florida. Through them we can learn about the state's geological underpinnings, eco-systems, vegetation, and wildlife, much of which is unique in the United States.

CHAPTER 10

SPRINGS AND SINKS

A Land of Bubbling Waters

Humans have been fascinated by springs through all of recorded history. We see them as mysterious and magical, with special healing powers. We drink from them, bath in them, and wish on them. It is no wonder the early explorers were so intrigued with Florida, so sure that it held magical qualities and great riches. Springs bubble up here with a volume and frequency almost unmatched anywhere in the world.

Ponce de Leon had the right idea when he came to Florida to look for the fountain of youth. But he must have been terribly frustrated as he searched for the right fountain. Florida has over 300 known springs, 27 of which are in the largest size category, "first magnitude" springs which flow at a rate of at least 100 cubic feet per second. No wonder the old Spanish explorer had such a hard time deciding which one held the powers of everlasting youth!

Florida springs may not promise eternal youth, but they certainly alleviate the process of aging. When we chance upon one at a quiet time, its swirling, mysterious depths bring even the most harried among us to a moment of calm and reflection. And, let's face it, springs are just plain fun. Swimmers like their naturally clear pools, snorkelers and scuba divers revel in their clarity and intriguing underwater caverns, and anglers, canoeists, and boaters enjoy the runs and rivers they create. Most developed Florida springs also offer hiking, picnicking, nature walks, or places to just sit. The geological conditions that have produced so many springs in Florida also produce sinks. Sinks result from a sudden crumbling of the earth's surface to create an indentation — in some cases a giant and very deep hole. Sinks don't have the same positive appeal that springs have, probably because they sometimes appear suddenly, swallowing up houses and property.

The state rests on layers of basal rock, limestone, and clay, as well as a unique limestone cap thousands of feet deep. Water collects and is stored below the surface at great pressure, forming underground reservoirs or aquifers. **Springs** are created when this water either seeps up or is forced up through deep well-like channels. **Sinks** occur when water dissolves the limestone, creating underground caverns that continue to enlarge until they collapse under the weight of the earth's surface. Sinkholes may be small or large, shallow or deep, wet or dry. If their drains become plugged with debris, they may fill with rainwater or underground streams to form ponds or lakes. A sink lake can become empty overnight if its plug becomes unsettled and the water drains out.

Sinks may appear with dramatic suddenness and homeowners in some areas invest in sinkhole insurance to cover unexpected holes. One famous recent sinkhole formed in May 1981 in Winter Park swallowed a house, several cars, a swimming pool and a camper into a hole 150 feet deep and 350 feet wide. The Winter Park sinkhole filled with water, but popped its plug twice only months after it appeared. One time the water level dropped 20 feet in nine minutes.

Springs and sinks can create unique biological environments as well as outstanding recreational opportunities. Many of Florida's major springs and sinks are publicly owned and protected. Others are private, but open to the public. Those described here are some of the larger ones, with either recreational facilities or historic interest. They are organized by region and alphabetically within each region. Since northwestern Florida has a large number of springs and sinks and covers such a large geographic area, I have divided it into three sections: the Panama City Area, the Tallahassee Area, and the Live Oak Area.

You may want to tour springs the way some travelers visit castles in Europe, going from one to another and comparing them. In Florida they call it "spring hopping." If the grand tour doesn't interest you, use the list to find a new place to throw in the fish line or take the grandchildren swimming. Or you may simply want an excuse to go somewhere you haven't been before. Exploring springs is a good way to get off the beaten track because so many are in unfrequented areas. A few of you may want to continue Ponce de Leon's search. Surely one of those 300 springs is the true Fountain of Youth!

The serious explorer of springs should head north. Although springs are found in 46 of the 67 counties, they are most common in northwest and central Florida, clustering especially around Gainesville, Tallahassee, and Orlando. Even the most enthusiastic explorer should find enough springs and sinks listed here to provide a good sampling of variety and size. If not, *Florida's Bubbling Springs* by Joan Lundquist Scalpone lists and describes 74 of the 175 that she has visited in a recent volume in the Mini-Day Trip series (P.O. Box 1431, Punta Gorda, Florida 33950; 813-639-5034, $5.95). If that is not enough for you, look up the U.S. Geological Survey Bulletin #31, *Springs of Florida*, by Jack Ros-

enan and others, available in the libraries. It describes
and locates all 300 known springs in the state.

Accessible Springs and Sinks

Northwest Region

Panama City Area

Blue Hole Spring is a sunny, pleasant swimming
area in **Florida Caverns State Park**. This place gives
visitors a chance to experience a spring, caverns, and
the natural bridge created by a sink, all in one park.
Although the state is riddled with underground caverns most lie under water because the state is so low.
These caverns are an exception because of slightly
higher elevation. They are Florida's only large cave
system and show evidence of use since prehistoric
times. Extremely rare specimens, including cave cray-
fish and cave salamander, still live in remote parts, so
thoroughly adapted to total darkness that they are
eyeless and ghostly white. Tours run every hour for a
small additional fee and are the only way to get inside.

General Andrew Jackson used the natural bridge
when he marched westward during his Indian campaign in 1818, unaware that the Indians he sought
were resting in the caverns beneath his feet. He refused to believe the officers of one division of his
troops, moving westward by a parallel route, who
tried to justify their late arrival by explaining they had
to construct rafts to cross a river.

Florida Caverns State Park (2701 Caverns Rd., Marianna, FL 32446; 904-482-9598) is in Jackson County,
about equally distant from Panama City or Tallahassee, located three miles north of Marianna, off SR 167.
It has facilities for picnicking, camping, swimming,

fishing, canoeing, and nature study. Stables and horse trails are available.

Falling Waters is a good place to see sinks. The hilly terrain here is honeycombed with them and several can be viewed from a wooden boardwalk that winds among them. The big attraction here is the state's only waterfall which is especially unusual because it falls into a sink. Instead of starting high on a hill and dropping to ground level, it starts at ground level and runs into a smooth-sided chimney of rock for 100 feet, where it disappears into underground cavities. You can't see all the way down because the lower 30 feet of sink is filled with debris deposited by the stream as well as hand-hewn timbers from an early grist mill that was operated here. Nevertheless it is a scenic and unique spot.

Falling Waters State Recreation Area (Rt. 5, Box 660, Chipley, FL 32438; 904-638-6130) is in Washington County near Panama City, three miles south of Chipley off SR 77A near I 10. The area has camping, picnicking, swimming, and fishing.

Ponce De Leon Springs has two flows from a limestone cavity into the Choctawhatchee River and the Gulf of Mexico which produce about 14 million gallons of crystal-clear water daily. The pool is kidney-shaped, about 100 feet by 75 feet. The day-use area has swimming, nature trails, picnicking and access to fishing. It is located in Ponce de Leon Springs State Recreation Area (Route 2 Box 1528, Ponce de Leon, FL 32455; 904-836-4281) located in Holmes County, north of Panama City, on SR 181A, off U.S. 90.

Tallahassee Area

Glen Julia Springs flows into a 200 foot by 100 foot ravine swimming pool in a county park. Above the pool is a picnic area. The springs are in Gadsden

SPRINGS AND SINKS

SPRINGS AND SINKS

Northwest - Panama City Area
1. Blue Hole Spring, Jackson County
2. Falling Waters, Washington County
3. Ponce de Leon Springs, Holmes County

Northwest - Tallahassee Area
4. Glen Julia Springs, Gadsden County
5. Indian Springs, Gadsden County
6. Natural Bridge Spring, Leon County
7. Spring Creek Springs, Wakulla County
8. St. Marks Spring, Leon County
9. Wacissa Springs Group, Jefferson County
10. Wakulla Springs, Wakulla County

Northwest - Live Oak Area
11. Alapaha Rise, Hamilton County
12. Blue Spring, Madison County
13. Blue Springs, Gilchrist County
14. Branford Springs, Suwannee County
15. Fannin Spring, Levy County
16. Ginnie Springs, Gilchrist County
17. Hart Springs, Gilchrist County
18. Manatee Springs, Levy County
19. Peacock Springs, Suwannee County
20. Troy Springs, Lafayette County
21. White Springs, Hamilton County

Northeast
22. Devil's Millhopper State Geological Site
23. Green Cove Spring, Clay County
24. Ichetucknee Springs, Columbia County
25. O'Leno State Park, Alachua County

26. Paynes Prairie, Alachua County

Central West
27. Chassahowitska Springs, Citrus County
28. Crystal River Springs, Citrus County
29. Crystal Springs, Pasco County
30. Eureka Springs, Hillsborough County
31. Homosassa Springs, Citrus County
32. Lithia Springs, Hillsborough County
33. Sulphur Springs, Hillsborough County
34. Warm Mineral Springs, Sarasota County
35. Weeki Wachee Springs, Hernando County

Central
36. Alexander Springs, Lake County
37. Juniper Springs, Marion County
38. Rock Springs, Orange County
39. Salt Springs, Marion County
40. Silver Springs, Marion County
41. Silver Glen Springs, Marion County
42. Wekiwa Springs, Orange County

Central East
43. Blue Spring, Volusia County
44. De Leon Springs, Volusia County

County, near Tallahassee, one mile southwest of
Mount Pleasant. Drive 0.7 miles southwest on SR 379
from U.S. 90. Turn right onto Glen Julia Road for about
0.2 miles to the park entrance.

Indian Springs are the focus of a privately developed recreation area open to the public for a fee. The
spring pool has diving boards and water slides. They
are in Gadsden County, near Tallahassee, located 2.5

miles southwest of Greensboro on SR 12, just 0.1 miles east of the intersection of SR 269, near the Gadsden-Liberty county line.

Natural Bridge Spring is a first magnitude spring located in Natural Bridge Battlefield State Historic Site. The park also has several sinkholes and a natural bridge where the St. Marks River disappears underground in a sinkhole and reappears some yards downstream. There is fishing, snorkeling, and scuba diving in the spring pool. The site is historic as well as scenic. It was here that the Confederates fought the Union army to keep Tallahassee the only uncaptured Confederate capital east of the Mississippi. **Natural Bridge Battlefield State Historic Site** (San Marcos de Apalachee State Historic Site, P.O. Box 27, St. Marks, FL 32355; 904-925-6216) is located in Leon County, south of Tallahassee off SR 363.

Spring Creek Springs is a first magnitude group of submarine springs (that discharge below sea level in a coastal saltwater environment), in a flat tidal marsh. Spring Creek Rise, one of the group, is usually distinguished by a pronounced boil and is visible near the old Spring Creek Hotel adjacent to the dock of the icehouse. Its reported depth is 100 feet. The group, in Wakulla County, is located 25 miles south of Tallahassee at the end of the road on Oyster Bay in a small fishing community called Spring Creek. From the intersection of U.S. 98 take SR 365 south for 4.5 miles to the end of the road.

St. Marks Spring is a first magnitude spring in the St. Marks River. It appears to be the head of the river during periods of low water, but is inundated by the river after heavy rainfall. The area has a dock on the northwest bank of the river and is used for fishing but has no public facilities. It is in Leon County, south of Tallahassee. Drive six miles east from Woodville on

Natural Bridge Road (SR 354), turn right on a sand road about 0.4 miles, then east on Old Plank Road, and go 0.7 miles to a private drive on the left. The spring is less than 0.2 miles east in the St. Marks River.

Wacissa Springs, a first magnitude group of 12 known springs along the first two miles of the Wacissa River, is a state canoe trail. The group is located in Jefferson County near Tallahassee.

Wakulla Springs in the Edward Ball Wakulla Springs State Park (1 Spring Dr., Wakulla Springs, FL 32305; 904-222-7279) is a special place. It is remarkable not only for its spring, which is one of the world's largest and deepest, but also for the Wakulla Springs Lodge, now open to the public for lodging, dining, or simply appreciation.

The spring's output is stupendous. A record peak flow was measured on April 11, 1973: 14,325 gallons per second. The spring flows from a cavern of such size that it has never been fully mapped or measured. Until the spring's source is finally located, it remains true to its Indian name, "mysterious waters."

The site has been used since prehistoric times and the springs were thought to have some mysterious curative powers by the Indians. Ponce de Leon visited the spring in 1513 and again in 1521. The first modern use of the springs was in the 1800s when tourists went onto the water with rowboats and glass-bottom buckets. The area was used in the 1930s for Tarzan movies, in the 1950s to film *Creature from the Black Lagoon*, and more recently for *Airport '77* and *Joe Panther*. Edward Ball, financier and conservationist, acquired the property in the 1930s and constructed the lodge. In 1986 the state purchased the site with funds from Florida's "Save Our Rivers" program.

Except for the small beach and observation tower at the bottom of the lodge lawn where visitors revel in the spring waters as their forebears did centuries ago, the spring is surrounded by its natural habitat and probably looks much as it did when Ponce de Leon saw it. The Wakulla River, created by the spring remains one of the last "wild rivers" in the southeast. Visitors can view the spring from glass-bottom boats and clearly see the entrance to the cavern, 120 feet below. Boat tours up the river show natural Florida in all its richness — alligators with snouts sticking out of lush water plants, snakes as thick as the tree branches they wind round, and a profusion of water birds. This remains a wilderness area in which humankind is but one part of the natural scene.

The lodge delights the eye from every vantage point. Its Spanish-style exterior, with arching windows and red tile roof, give a sense of simplicity and balance. Ceiling murals recreate the intermingling of Indian and white man's heritage. Rare Spanish tiles line the doorways, Iranian onyx urns decorate the fireplace. Everywhere there are antique furnishings and French, Italian, and Tennessee marble. The fine craftsmanship blends in so well with the general design and atmosphere that specific delights are not immediately noticeable, but are discovered one by one.

Live Oak Area

Alapaha Rise, a first magnitude spring, pumps 400 million gallons of water through its limestone walls each day, but it has not been developed because of its remote location. It remains a pleasant, quiet place to visit. The spring, with its dark tannin colored water, is in Hamilton County near the city of Live-Oak, the half way point between Tallahassee and Jacksonville. It is 12 miles northwest of SR 6, at the intersection of U.S. 90 and U.S. 129.

Blue Spring was originally a source of fresh water

for early inhabitants of the area, but now is used for swimming, snorkeling, and scuba diving. This first magnitude spring, still in its natural state, is about 25 feet across. The water is clear and blue, except when it is inundated by the Withlacoochee River during high water. It is in Madison County in the Tallahassee area, about 10 miles east of Madison. From Madison drive east on SR 6 to the river, turn south onto a road parallel to the west side of the river, and travel 0.1 mile.

Blue Springs, in Gilchrist County, fill a depression in dense forest. Clean clear water and tame fish greet swimmers. This is a scenic spot, privately owned and open to the public for a fee. The area has diving boards, picnic tables, a nature trail, and camping. The springs are located 4.5 miles west north west of High Springs. Drive west on SR 36 from U.S. 41 at the west edge of High Springs for 4.6 miles, then turn right onto Blue Springs Road and go 1.1 miles to the parking area.

Branford Springs is a popular recreation area with locals, adjacent to the Suwannee River. Its main pool is 60 feet in diameter with a maximum depth of nine feet. There is swimming, snorkeling, and scuba diving, with a dive shop and concessions on the grounds. It is located in Suwannee County, 500 feet southwest of U.S. 27 and U.S. 129 in Branford (904-776-2748).

Fannin Spring, a first magnitude spring in a town of the same name, is on privately owned land, open to the public from April to September. There are two springs here, Big Fannin and Little Fannin. Their sparkling deep blue color is striking. They are in Levy County, north of Chiefland, on U.S. 19 and U.S. 27.

Ginnie Springs, a well-known scuba and diving site, has now been privately developed as a recreation area. It has swimming, picnicking, camping, canoe and tube rental, a full- service dive center, and instruction. The spring pool is oval, 200 feet by 30 feet and about 26 feet deep with a sandy bottom. Its name has had several spellings in the past, including "Jenny." It is located in Gilchrist County (7300 N.E. Ginnie Springs Blvd., High Springs, FL 32643; 904-454-2202 or 1-800-874-8571). To get there, take either U.S. 441 or SR 47 off I-75. The area is 6.5 miles west of High Springs, off CR 340.

Hart Springs, located in Hart Spring County Park provides 600 feet of freshwater beach on the spring run and the river. It is a popular local swimming area in the summer, but is sometimes unusable in the winter when the river rises and the park floods. There is a dive platform, camping, nature trails and nearby boat launching on the Suwannee River. The park is in Gilchrist County off SR 341.

Manatee Springs in Manatee Springs State Park is a first magnitude spring which pours forth over 80,000 gallons of crystal-clear water per minute and flows through a thousand-foot-long run down to the wide Suwannee River. Swimmers can glide through the cold water of the spring head; certified divers can explore extensive underground caverns that link a chain of sinkholes in the park; children can frolic in a specially terraced shallow area. Manatee used to frolic in the area as well but today they are seen only rarely, at the mouth of the run.

The spring with its nearby abundent fish and game has been known and used by humans for centuries. William Bartram, an English naturalist, described it in 1774. You can take a boardwalk along the spring run, which passes through cypress, ash, gum, and red maple and blooms with white spider-lilies, or follow a nature trail which interprets the shady hammock and winds round past several wooded sinkholes. The area has camping, and ranger-lead activities during the summer. It is in Levy County, on SR 320, six miles west of Chiefland (Manatee Springs State Park, Route 2 Box 617, Chiefland, FL 32626; 904-493-4288).

Peacock Springs in The Peacock Springs State Recreation Area was purchased in 1987 with the help of the Florida Nature Conservancy to preserve an exemplary natural ecosystem. It has two major springs, a major spring run, and numerous sinks which are in nearly pristine condition. One of the longest underwater cave systems in the continental United States lies within the park. There is swimming, picnicking, and diving. The area is 16 miles southwest of Live Oak on SR 51, two miles east of Luraville on Peacock Springs Road (Ichetucknee Springs State Park, Rt. 2 Box 108, Fort White, FL 32038; 904-497-2511).

Troy Springs has no public facilities, but locals swim and scuba dive in this deep, first magnitude spring. It contains the submerged hull of the steamboat *Madison*, reportedly either a gunboat or supply boat of the Confederate army which was trapped on the Suwannee River and run aground and scuttled by its captain to avoid capture by Federal Forces. The spring is in Lafayette County 6 miles northwest of Branford on the southwest side of the Suwannee River. From Branford drive 4.8 miles northwest on U.S. 27 to SR 20. Turn right and go 1.2 miles, then turn right again onto a sand road for 0.6 miles. The spring is beyond the end of the road.

White Springs, or White Sulphur Springs are sulphur springs once considered sacred by the Indians who believed their warriors were impervious to attack while recuperating here. The area still holds the hint of spirits. Towering oaks and cypress, eerily draped with moss, line the river. The town of White Springs was once a health resort. You can still see the foundations of the old springhouse. The springs are now part of the

Stephen Foster State Folk Culture Center. They still flow, but there is no swimming. The center covers 250 acres of wooded land beside the Suwannee River which the composer immortalized in his song "Old Folks at Home." There is a museum, carillon tower, and hiking. Narrated sightseeing trips on the Suwannee are offered on a replica of an early riverboat. The springs are located in Hamilton County 15 miles east of Live Oak on SR 136 (Stephen Foster State Folk Culture Center, P.O. Drawer G, White Springs, FL 32096; 904-397-2733).

Northeast Region

In **Devils Millhopper State Geological Site,** an interesting site near Gainesville, you get a sense of how long the sink phenomenon has existed in Florida. Just a short walk down a boardwalk brings you to an ancient sink with plants and animals that do not exist elsewhere in the world and some that are usually found only north of the Appalachians. This site was acquired and restored in 1974. There is a interpretative display at the top of the sink and a pleasant picnic area. It is located in Alachua County, two miles northwest of Gainesville, on SR 232 (4732 N.W. 53rd Ave., Gainesville, FL 32601; 904-336-2008).

Located in Spring Park in the town of Green Cove Spring, **Green Cove Spring** swirls down 31 feet in an irregularly shaped funnel. It feeds a nearby swimming pool enclosed by a chainlink fence and then flows on to the St. John's River. The town was a fashionable spa in the late 1870s and 1880s. Steamers from Charleston and Savannah landed passengers, including President Grover Cleveland, at the resort piers; band concerts were held daily during winter months. But with the coming of the railroads, visitors preferred to travel further south. Today there is little remaining in the quiet riverside park to remind you of those busy, elegant days. Green Cove is in Clay County, on SR 16 west of the St Johns River.

Ichetucknee Spring, a first magnitude spring in Ichetucknee Springs State Park,, gets its flow, at least in part, from Alligator Lake and Rose Creek which vanish into sink holes further north and re-emerge here in a gush. The spring pours forth nearly 30 million gallons of water a day, at a temperature around 73 degrees fahrenheit. Steps, an irregular stone wall, and a grassy sunbathing area enclose it. There is a homey, sunny feeling about the spot, like a local town beach.

If this spring isn't enough, the park has eight others: Blue Hole, Coffee Spring, Roaring Springs and Singing Springs (sometimes referred to together as Mission Springs, in honor of the old Spanish mission that used to be nearby), Boiling Springs, Grassy Hole Spring, Mill Pond Spring, and Cedar Head Spring. Most can be seen only from the river.

Blue Hole Spring is one of the few that can be seen from a trail. it is just a short walk beyond Ichetucknee, but it has a different quality — mysterious and eerie — a blue hole framed by ancient cypress trees. It wells up from its center without a gurgle or bubble, spreading out in irregular patterns toward the rim. The silent, perpetual motion is almost hypnotic. A swimming platform with a bench extends along the side and the urge to jump in for a swim is almost irresistible.

Ichetucknee Springs was established as a park in 1970, but the river and its spring have long attracted visitors, settlers, and wildlife. Richard Adams swam the river many times and used it for a scene in his book, *The Girl in a Swing*.

It is considered by many to be the best inner-tube float in the world. Visitors can tube down the river year round. The clear water cuts a path between hanging vines and flower-draped trees, flowing languidly past other springs, through wilderness otherwise inaccessible to visitors. The peak season is May 1 to September 30, when shuttle buses run daily from the south end of the park back to the north entrance. Then the area takes on a carnival atmosphere. Use of the upper and more fragile section of the river has been restricted in recent years to preserve the natural environment. Weekend service is available in April and October and at other times arrangements for transportation can usually be made at the time of tube or canoe rental. Off searon, it is so still that a small snake can sun undisturbed on the empty wooden tube and canoe launching platforms along the river while only natural tubers — seedpods and leaves — float the river.

Ichetucknee Springs (Rt. 2, Box 108, Fort White, FL 32038; 904-497-2511) is in Columbia County, within an hour's drive of Gainesville, and easily accessible from I-75. It is a delightful place to picnic, walk, or swim any time of the year. Tubing on a warm off-season day may be especially rewarding to the visitor who seeks the quiet beauty still to be found in natural Florida.

O'Leno State Park's most striking feature is the disappearance of the Santa Fe River into a sink hole. The river gives no hint that it is about to vanish as it flows calmly past the park's main picnic area. Its dark water, soft with tannins from surrounding swamps and pine forests, sloshes noisily around stands of cypress. The river seems too substantial to disappear just a few hundred yards downstream. But it does, its flow diverted to a hundred rivulets that ooze away in sinks and swamp while the main stream narrows and finally swirls slowly underground. And it is too substantial to stay submerged for long. After collecting itself, the river flows through its subterranean channel for three miles, then rushes forth in a big boil. The Santa Fe has washed out through its sink for as long as we have records, providing a natural bridge for man and beast.

O'Leno is one spot to recapture the broodingly mysterious quality of the original Florida, a place of dark, quiet rivers, and rich vegetation. Its black ghost of a river casts a spell that is hard to throw off as one walks along one side of the river and finds oneself back on the other side without ever crossing a bridge. It is in Alachua County north of Gainesville on SR 441 off I 75 (Rt. 2, Box 1010, High Springs, FL 32643; 904-454-1853).

Paynes Prairie is an 18,000 acre state preserve encompassing the gigantic Alachua Sink. It is one of the most significant natural and historical areas in Florida. The basin, today covered by marsh and wet prairie vegetation, has at times been a lake, most recently in 1871. Paddlewheel steamers plied the waters carrying oranges, vegetables, and supplies as well as pleasure travelers. Then one day in 1891 the sink plug opened. Within a few hours the steamers were stranded on the drying bottom of the prairie. It is in Alachua County just outside of Gainesville (Paynes Prairie State Preserve, Rt. 2 Box 41, Micanopy, FL 32667; 904-466-3397).

Central West Region

Chassahowitzka Springs, of first magnitude, form the headwaters of the Chassahowitzka (Chassa-witzka) River, one of the most scenic and unspoiled rivers in Florida. Its waters are ideal for canoeing. The freshwater creeks which feed it support one of the best (and least known) largemouth bass populations in the area. The banks are lined with cypress and hardwood forest at the headwaters, and with sawgrass and mangrove where the river joins the Gulf. There is a boat harbor for pleasure and fishing boats, as well as swimming and snorkeling. The several springs flow into a main pool, which is nearly circular and about 150 feet in diameter. The area is located in Citrus County, south of Homosassa Springs. Go 6 miles south of Homosassa Springs on U.S. 19, then turn west on SR 480 and go 1.7 miles to the end of the road.

Crystal River Springs, a first magnitude group of thirty springs clusters, form the mouth of the Crystal River. Divers find the clear water good for investigating underwater life and Crystal Spring or "Big Hole," on the south side of Banana Island, is reported to be one of the finest fresh-water dive sites in Florida, owing to the excellent visibility, size, convenience of access and potential for underwater photography. It is 65 feet deep, 200 feet in diameter, and on calm days at low tide shows a slight boil or slick. The Crystal River archeological site is here too, with a temple and burial grounds built by Indians 1,600 years ago. As many as 450 Indian burial grounds have been uncovered since 1903. The area is in Citrus County, off U.S. 19.

Crystal Springs, in Pasco County, are privately owned and operated as a park and recreation area. The pool, partly lined with concrete, is 400 feet by 150 feet and has many vents in the bottom. The area offers swimming, canoeing, fishing and nature trails four miles south of Zephyrhills off Highway 39 on Crystal Springs Road.

Eureka Springs are part of a county park featuring a botanical garden of tropical plants from around the world. Tropical fish farms were once abundant in this area. They were raised in shallow pools fed by the river flowing from wells that tapped the same aquifer as the springs. The site is located in Hillsborough County, three miles east of Tampa. Go East on I-4, turn left (north) onto U.S. 301, then go 1.5 miles to Hamilton Road, turn right (east) and go 0.6 miles to Eureka

Springs Road, turn right (south) to go 0.5 miles to springs.

Homossassa Springs, a first magnitude spring and the headwater of the Homossassa River, has been a tourist attraction since the early 1900s when trains stopped to let passengers rest there. It was a commercial park for many years but in 1984 was purchased for protection as an environmentally-sensitive area. It is now the Homossassa Springs State Wildlife Park. The spring, for unknown reasons, is inhabited by thousands of both salt and freshwater fish. You can see them, as well as manatees, from a unique floating observatory, "Nature's Fish Bowl." This is one of the only places in the world where manatees may be observed at close range year-round. The springs are located in Citrus County, on the Gulf coast on U.S. 19, about two miles from the town of Homossassa (9225 West Fishbowl Drive, Homossassa, FL 32646; 904-628-2311).

Lithia Springs consists of two pools, Major and Minor, each with runs flowing to the river. The maximum depth is 16 feet. The size and shape of the pools vary with changes in the river height. They are in the 300 acre Hillsborough County Park on the Alafia River. There is camping here and a 4-hour tubing trip with put-in at Alderman's Ford on SR 39. The springs are 20 miles southeast of Tampa off SR 640. Go 0.6 miles southeast from the Alafia River bridge on Pinehurst-Lithia Road. Turn right (west) onto a paved road and go 1.4 miles to the springs (813-689-2139)

Sulphur Springs is owned and operated by the City of Tampa as a recreational facility. It includes a 50-foot circular swimming pool with concrete walls and a maximum depth of 30 feet. The area is in Hillsborough County seven miles north of downtown Tampa, just southwest of the intersection of U.S. 41 and Sitka Street.

Warm Mineral Springs is so unusual that it has been put on the National Registry of Historic Places. Animal and human remains removed from the spring have been radiocarbon age-dated as around 10,000 years old. The water is salty with a sulfurous odor and taste and the spring is also known as "Warm Salt Spring,," "Salt Spring," and "Big Salt Spring." Its pool is 250 feet in diameter. It slopes to 17 feet, then drops off sharply to 124 feet or more. There is a cave with stalactites which underlies a 43-foot ledge. This is a privately developed swimming and resort area. There is considerable variation in the pool's visibility. It is clearest at night or after extended periods of heavy rainfall. It is in Sarasota County southeast of Venice, one mile north of U.S. 41 (813-426-1692). **Little Salt Spring**, two miles east, also has yielded human skeletons and artifacts dating back 12,000 years. Owned by the University of Miami since 1982, it is now being explored with the help of a grant from The National Geographic Society.

Weeki Wachee, a first magnitude commercial spring, is over 130 feet deep. Daily shows feature shimmering fanciful mermaids whom ancient mariners once believed were transformed manatee. The professional underwater shows are viewed through an underwater amphitheater. This tourist attraction is in Hernando County near Tampa, 13 miles west of Brooksville on U.S. 19 and SR 50 (800-342-0297).

Central Region

Alexander Springs, a first magnitude spring, boils up in a sunny swimming area, fringed by a sandy beach on one side and a semi tropical rain forest on the other. Canoes are available; canoe trips on Alexander Spring Creek last from one and a half to four hours, depending on the take-out point. There is an interpretative nature trail near the spring with signs explaining how early man used the natural environment for his survival. The springs, with a full range of recreational opportunities, are located along with Juniper Springs and Salt Springs in the 380,000-acre Ocala National Forest off SR 445 (904-669-3522).

Juniper Springs rises in a beautiful clear pool in a basin carved out of natural rock by the Civilian Conservation Corps in the 1930s. When swimmers tire of the water they can sunbathe on the stone terrace that surrounds the pool. There is a shallow fenced-off area where children can wade safely. Nonswimmers can watch the action from the nearby shaded wooden deck with picnic tables. At one end of the pool in an old mill house that once generated electricity for the campground, is a visitor center that displays the history of the springs' development. Canoeists can rent craft on site and take a four-hour trip down Juniper Creek. There is also an excellent nature trail along the spring run. The spring is part of Ocala National Forest in Marion County (east of Ocala off SR 4; 904-625-3147).

Rock Springs, located in a wooded ravine, has no well-defined pool. It flows from a cavern only partly submerged and feeds Rock Springs Run, one of the state's most popular canoe trails. It is adjacent to Rock Springs Run State Reserve in Orange County, northwest of Orlando, located near Sorrento, on SR 46 via SR 433 (Route 1, Box 365D, Sorrento, FL 32776; 904-383-3311).

In a state full of fresh-water springs, **Salt Springs** is somewhat unusual. These springs rise from the deposits of an ancient underground seacoast. The pool is nearly round, about 110 feet in diameter and four feet deep throughout except in the vicinity of the spring orifices, the deepest of which is 19.5 feet. There is a

pleasant swimming area with a cement retaining wall
and a railing on three sides, sloping grass lawns, and a
picnic area under ancient trees. The area, within the
Ocala National Forest, has a wide range of facilities
and services for both the day user and the camper. It is
located in Marion County off SR 19 and 315 near Lake
George.

Silver Springs are perhaps the best known springs
in northern Florida. The commercially developed springs are just outside of Ocala (5656 N.E. Silver Springs Blvd., P.O. Box 370, Silver Springs, FL 32688;
904-236-2121; or 800-342-0297). They are estimated to
be 100,000 years old. Fossilized remains of mastodons
and manatees indicate that it was a watering place for
prehistoric animals. The springs were developed early
and include over 100 acres of landscaped park and
gardens. Visitors can ride the world famous Glass Bottom Boat or engage in a variety of other activities — a
jungle cruise, a reptile show, or a walk through the
deer park where children can touch, feed, and walk
with friendly animals. There are outdoor dining areas
and gift shops, a giant pool, volleyball, and miniature
golf. Silver Springs is just down the road from Juniper
Springs and some travelers might want to visit both to
contrast the natural and developed settings.

Silver Glen Springs, a first magnitude spring which
for many years was privately owned, is now under
public management. The site has become so popular
that federal and state officials are concerned about its
rapidly deteriorating condition and may close it for a
period to allow for rejuvenation and redevelopment.
The pool, bounded by semi-tropical forest, has a maximum depth of 21 feet and shows a strong boil on its
surface over the spring. The large snail shell mounds
near the springs have yielded many Indian remains
and artifacts. The spring is located in Marion County,

nine miles northwest of Astor. Drive west on SR 40 for
8.1 miles from the bridge over the St. John's River at
Astor, then turn north onto SR 19. Go 6 miles, turn east
onto a paved road and continue 0.3 miles to the spring
pool. For information about its status contact the Ocala
National Forest (904-625-2520).

Wekiwa Springs in Wekiwa Springs State Park provides resources for understanding both sinks and
springs. The springs, headwaters of the Wekiwa River,
flow into a kidney-shaped pool about 200 feet by 100
feet and the 6,400-acre park also has numerous sink
holes. Like so many of Florida's state parks, Wekiwa
bears the aesthetic touches of the Civilian Conservation Corps, who constructed a naturalistic pool and
stone banked grassy terraces. The springs are located
on Wekiwa Springs Road, off SR 434 or 436 near
Apopka (1800 Wekiwa Circle, Apopka, FL 32712; 407-
889-9920).

Central East Region

Blue Spring, a first magnitude spring in Blue Spring
State Park flows from a steep-sloped springhead. It is
a cloudy bluish green circle surrounded by lowland
hammock trees and has a slight hydrogen sulfide odor.
Visitors can swim in the spring or downstream at a
dock. The park provides a warm water lair for the
manatee during winter months when river and ocean
waters are too cold.

There is a self-guiding nature trail, and canoeing is
available either alone or on ranger-guided tours into
undeveloped swamp forests that look much as they
did when John Bartram canoed through them in 1766.
The old Thursby House, which played a key role in the
St. John's River traffic around 1861, stands promi-
nently in the park. The park is in Volusia County two

miles west of Orange City, off I-4 and U.S. 17-92 (2100 West French Ave., Orange City, FL 32763; 904-775-3663).

DeLeon Springs, sometimes referred to as Ponce De Leon Springs, is located in newly developed De Leon Springs State Recreation Area in an area known for many years as Spring Garden. Its history is long. According to local traditions, the Spaniards built a sugar mill here prior to 1763 and additions were made by the British when the region was ceded to them in 1763. Planter William Williams of New Smyrna grew cotton, corn and sugarcane on the fertile ground surrounding the spring around 1804. Major Joseph Woodruff acquired the property in 1823 and built a water-wheel for a gristmill. Colonel Orlando Rees, the next owner, modified the mill for sugar cane by connecting the wheel to heavy rollers to crush juice out of the cane stocks.

John James Audubon, who visited Colonel Rees in 1832, described the spring: "This spring presents a circular basin, having a diameter of about sixty feet, from the centre of which the water is thrown up with great force...a kind of whirlpool is formed, on the edges of which are deposited vast quantities of shells...The water is quite transparent, although of a dark color, but so impregnated with sulphur that it emits an odour which to me was highly nauseous." The mineral content has apparently decreased in recent years; there is no longer a "nauseous" odor. But the spring's reputed healthful qualities gained fame in the late 1800s when the railroad arrived. Its name was changed to De Leon Springs, and its waters were touted as "impregnated with a deliciously healthy combination of sods and sulphur." Advertisements appealing to retired northerners claimed that the spring was a fountain of youth.

Although the name Spring Garden is gone and the
plantation era is long over, remnants of the past remain. Sugar kettles, cane-crushing rollers, and other
mill machinery left near the spring remind us of the
brief era when sugar plantations dominated Florida's
economy.

Today the spring may not lengthen our lives but it
can enhance their quality as we swim in its 76 degree
fahrenheit waters, walk along its peaceful nature trail,
or canoe through the 18,000 acres of nearby Lake
Woodruff National Wildlife Refuge. Fishing enthusiasts can find bass and bream in the spring run and
certified scuba divers can explore the caves below. The
park is located in Volusia County near the town of De
Leon Springs off U.S. 17 (P.O. Box 1338, De Leon
Springs, FL 32030; 904-985-4212).

CHAPTER 11

WETLANDS AND WOODLANDS

When the Spanish first saw the Florida peninsula, it was an expanse of wetlands and woodlands. Swamps and marshes spread along the coasts and river mouths and even fanned out through large areas of the interior. The rest of the land was heavily forested with great stands of live oak, mahogany, cypress, cedar, and pine. Extensive development and four centuries of lumbering and swamp draining have taken their toll. But segments of the original wetlands and woodlands remain today, thanks to farsighted and hardworking conservationists who have fought for the preservation of at least some part of Florida's natural environment. The modern explorer who wants to experience Florida as it was when the first Europeans arrived still has a chance to do that in an accessible network of state, national, and local parks, refuges, preserves, and wilderness areas.

From Picnicking to Primitive Camping

There are several different kinds of natural areas in Florida. Most offer fishing, swimming, hiking, boating or canoeing, interpretative activities, birdwatching, camping, and picnicking, and have at least basic facili-

ties for visitors such as restrooms and developed picnic areas and campgrounds. Some parks provide even
more, like playing fields or tennis courts. **City and
County Parks,** for example, usually allocate most of
their space to recreational facilities with less devoted
to natural settings. State Recreation Areas have a
roughly 50/50 allocation.

State Parks have even more land in natural areas —
usually 80 percent or more of their total acreage. The
Florida state parks are outstanding in their effort to
preserve samples of the original landscape in its natural condition, just "as the first Europeans saw it."
Parks give residents and visitors alike rich opportunities to see "the other Florida." A park may commemorate a historical event or some unusual geological
phenomenon, but a large portion of its area is devoted
to natural land and it usually has rich animal and
birdlife and varied plant life. State parks offer easy
access for people of all ages and abilities to some of the
finest, most authentic natural areas throughout Florida. Most offer ranger-led and interpretative activities,
including museums and exhibits. Facilities are clean
and well maintained, and accessible to the handicapped.

State and National Forests are active, working forests containing thousands of acres of woods, most of
which are under cultivation for timber production.
They also sometimes allow other uses, such as cattle
grazing, oil wells, or mining. Recreational areas in the
public forests range from highly developed, popular
campgrounds to remote primitive sites with few or no
facilities. Most forests offer naturalist programs or
ranger-led activities.

National Wildlife and Bird Refuges are managed
primarily for the preservation of wildlife and birds
and their natural habitats. The outdoor recreation they

offer must be compatible with these goals; they do not permit camping and often provide only minimal facilities for visitors. **National Parks and National Seashores** are dedicated to preserving an outstanding natural area while encouraging compatible outdoor recreation. A few sections of a national park may be highly developed and may even contain motels and restaurants, but most of its land will be natural or pure wilderness. Florida's national parks have excellent exhibits, talks, trails, and naturalist-led interpretative programs.

State Preserves are large undeveloped areas, generally 10 to 30 thousand acres, that are set aside to maintain a living portion of Florida's original environment, free from major human disturbance. In order to maintain the diverse and fragile balance of nature in these areas there are few, if any, visitor facilities. Preserves sometimes permit hiking, boating access, or primitive camp sites, and are often used for scientific study. Florida's newly created **Ecological Reserves** are even more protective of the natural environment and prohibit visitors altogether, except for occasional guided environmental classes.

Some state parks, preserves, national forests, and national parks have specially designated wilderness areas, that are closed to motorized vehicles and offer the opportunity to hike or canoe in a region virtually untouched by human activities. Most wilderness areas in Florida permit primitive camping from canoe or backpack, but often restrict the number of visitors.

Wetlands and woodlands are all over Florida. The main natural areas are described here, listed alphabetically within each of the state's seven geographic regions. A full list of state parks and their facilities is available from the **Department of Natural Resources** (Division of Recreation and Parks, 3900 Commonwealth Blvd., Tallahassee, FL 32399-3000). You can also get more detailed information from the individual parks you want to visit.

Even if you never expect to camp, you may want to get *Florida Parks: A Guide to Camping in Nature* by Gerald Grow (Long Leaf Publications). It is a highly informative conservationist-oriented guide to all of Florida's parks by someone who knows them intimately. I have relied on it, in its several editions, in my own exploration of Florida over the years.

Northwest Region

Apalachicola National Forest, with one-half million acres of varied terrain, is the largest national forest in the state and really enables people to get away from it all. It offers swamps, sandhills, flatwoods, hardwoods, and through it run two rivers — the green, swampy, and sometimes swift Ochlackonee River and the large, pure Apalachicola. Most of the forest is remote and unpopulated. Within it is the Bradwell Bay Wilderness Area, a huge, dense swamp in which it is easy to get lost. Apalachicola National Forest is located southwest of Tallahassee between the Apalachicola River and U.S. 319/SR 369 in Wakulla, Liberty, and Leon counties. (USDA Forest Service, 227 N. Bronough St., Tallahassee, FL 32301; 904-681-7265). The forest is administered in two sections. The headquarters of the East Section is on Hwy. 319, 2.3 miles north of Crawfordville (904-926-3561) and the headquarters for the West Section is on Hwy. 20 in Bristol (904-643-2282).

Apalachee Savannahs Scenic Byway is a 32-mile-long picturesque road located in the Apalachicola National Forest. It has been designated as the first National Forest Scenic Byway in Florida. It passes through forested landscapes characterized by cypress swamps, grasslands (savannahs), and numerous creeks and sloughs featuring unusual plant communities with spectacular seasonal wildflower displays. The route is made up of portions of SR 65 and CR 12 and 379, starting from the north near Bristol and continuing south through Sumatra and Fort Gadsden State Park to Buck Siding.

Big Lagoon State Recreation Area, just off SR 292 before the bridge to Perdido Key provides shelter for numerous birds and animals in its long stretches of salt marshes and sandy beaches. Picnic tables right beside the water offer delightful spots to relax and take in a landscape created by interwoven colors and textures as sky, beach, water, birds, and waving grasses come together. You can get a panoramic view of Big Lagoon and Gulf islands from the observation tower or a close-up view of the park's ecology from three miles of boardwalks and nature trails. There is swimming, fishing, boating with access onto both Big Lagoon and the Intracoastal Waterway, camping, and picnicking. Big Lagoon is located about 10 miles southwest of Pensacola on SR 292 (Gulf Beach Highway). Contact Big Lagoon State Recreation Area (12301 Gulf Beach Highway, Pensacola, FL 32507; 904-492-1595, open year around).

Blackwater River State Forest, with 180,000 acres, has forests of longleaf pine trees and famous canoe trails. The 21-mile Andrew Jackson Red Ground Trail traces an early trade route which Jackson took on his historic trip to the Florida Territory during the Seminole Indian Wars in 1818. The trail from Karick Lake to the Red Rock Picnic Area, now part of the Florida Trail System, is marked with red paintmarks on the trees. This park is best in the spring and fall and has miles of dirt road for walking and driving. But get a forest map, before you start — the area can be confusing. Within

WETLANDS AND WOODLANDS

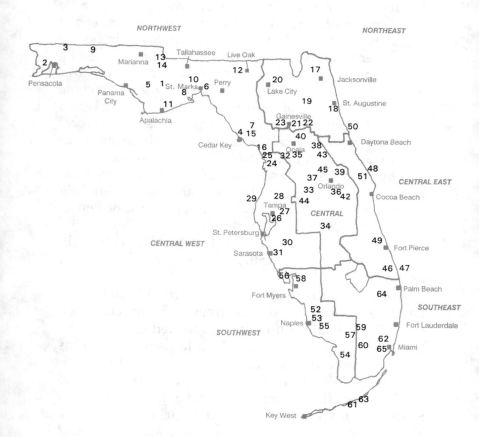

WETLANDS AND WOODLANDS

Northwest

1. Apalachicola National Forest
2. Big Lagoon State Recreation Area
3. Blackwater River State Forest and State Park
4. Cedar Keys Wildlife Refuge
5. Dead Lakes State Recreation Area
6. Econfina River
7. Lower Suwannee River National Wildlife Refuge
8. Ochlockonee River State Park
9. Rocky Bayou (Fred Ganon) State Recreation Area
10. St. Marks National Wildlife Refuge
11. St. Vincent National Wildlife Refuge
12. Suwannee River State Park
13. Three Rivers State Recreation Area
14. Torreya State Park
15. Waccasassa Bay State Preserve
16. Yankeetown County Park

Northeast

17. Cary State Forest
18. Faver-Dykes State Park
19. Gold Head Branch State Park
20. Osceola National Forest

21. Morningside Nature Center
22. Paynes Prairie State Preserve
23. San Felasco Hammock State Preserve

Central West

24. Chassahowitzka National Wildlife Refuge
25. Crystal River National Wildlife Refuge
26. Egmont Key National Wildlife Refuge
27. Hillsborough County Parks
28. Hillsborough River State Park
29. Moccasin Lake Nature Park
30. Myakka River State Park
31. Oscar Scherer State Recreation Area
32. Withlacoochee State Forest

Central

33. Green Swamp Flood Detention Area
34. Highlands Hammock State Park
35. Lake Griffin State Recreation Area
36. Lake Kissimmee State Park
37. Lake Louisa State Park
38. Lake Woodruff National Wildlife Refuge
39. Moss Park

40. Ocala National Forest
41. Prairie Lakes State Preserve
42. Reedy Creek Environmental Study Center
43. Seminole County Parks
44. Tenoroc State Reserve
45. Wekiva River State Preserve

Central East

46. Hobe Sound National Wildlife Refuge
47. Jonathan Dickinson State Park
48. Merritt Island National Wildlife Refuge
49. Savannas Recreation Area
50. Tomoka State Park
51. Tosohatchee State Reserve

Southwest

52. Big Cypress National Preserve
53. Briggs Nature Center, Conservancy Nature Center

54. Collier-Seminole State Park
55. Corkscrew Swamp Sanctuary
56. Ding Darling National Wildlife Refuge
57. Fakahatchee Strand State Preserve
58. Nature Center Museum and Planetarium

Southeast

59. Chekika State Recreation Area
60. Everglades National Park
61. Key Deer National Wildlife Refuge
62. Larry and Penny Thompson Park
63. Lignumvitae Key State Botanical Site
64. Loxahatchee National Wildlife Reserve
65. Oleta River State Park

---

the state forest is Coldwater Recreation Area, developed primarily for horseback riding and hunting-dog field trials. Coldwater is reached either by SR 191, where there is a marked turnoff a few miles south of Munson, or by SR 4 from a turnoff 13 miles west of Munson. Blackwater River State Forest touches on the Alabama border north of Pensacola. Headquarters are near Munson, on SR 191, just south of SR 4 (Rt. 1, Box 77, Milton, FL 32570; 904-957-4111).

Blackwater River State Park is just below the state forest. The river is not only one of the cleanest in America, it is one of the most eerily beautiful, with its virtually black water reflecting the snow-white sandbars at each bend. There is swimming off a wide sandbar in the river and good canoeing for novices. Camping is excellent, with campfire programs, nature study, and guided walks by rangers. There is a wealth of wildlife. Blackwater River State Park is located 15 miles northeast of Milton, three miles off U.S. 90(Rt. 1, Box 47-C, Holt, FL 32564; 904-623-2363).

Cedar Keys Wildlife Refuge covers several off-shore islands five miles from the town of Cedar Key. It is accessible only by boat and even that can be difficult because the islands are surrounded by shallow sand and mud flats. Primarily a study area, only its beaches are open to the public and there are no facilities. Swimming is good off the beach at Seahorse Key, but don't venture too far inland. The island is known for its large population of poisonous cottonmouth snakes. Charter boats for the refuge leave daily from the dock at Cedar Key. For information contact the Refuge Manager (Chassahowitzka National Wildlife Refuge, Rt. 2, Box 44, Homossassa, FL 32646; 904-382-2201)

Dead Lakes State Recreation Area presents an unusual sight. It is a flooded forest, where the bleached skeletons of thousands of dead trees rise above the still water. Most people come here to fish, but the area has some nature trails as well. The park is located west of the Apalachicola River on SR 71, two miles north of Wewahitchka (P.O. Box 989, Wewahitchka, FL 32465; 904-639-2702)

Econfina River is a 4000-acre tract on the Gulf of Mexico that was recently acquired for public use and is currently operated as a public-private enterprise. Unimproved hiking and horse trails wander by salt-

water marshes and estuaries, through pine islands and
cabbage palm forests. Boat ramps and camping are
available. For directions and more information call
904-925-6216.

Lower Suwannee River National Wildlife Refuge
includes 40,000 acres of varied terrain, with 26 miles
fronting on the Gulf of Mexico. It is rich in wildlife; 258
species of birds have been reported. The main part of
the refuge, the Ocala Tract at the mouth of the river, is
accessible by boat only. The Suwannee River, 235 miles
long, winds through two states and eleven counties,
yet still flows through Florida in near pristine condition. The refuge is located 17 miles south of Chiefland,
off SR 347 (904-493-0238).

Ochlockonee River State Park (pronounced
o'CLOCK-nee) is an example of the pine flatwoods of
unspoiled northern Florida. Its scenic drive and nature
trail has lots of wild flowers in the warm months. The
park is located south of Sopchoppy, off U.S. 319 (Box 5,
Sopchoppy, FL 32358; 904-962-2771).

Rocky Bayou (Fred Ganon) State Recreation Area is
located within Eglin Air Force Base on the shore of a
gentle bayou off sprawling Choctawhatchee Bay. It has
a nature trail along the border of Puddin Head Lake
and a picnic area with fine views of the bay. There is
both salt and freshwater fishing. Rocky Bayou is located three miles east of Niceville, north of SR 20 (P.O.
Box 597, Niceville, FL 32578; 904-897-3222).

St. Marks National Wildlife Refuge is Florida's only
wintering area for Canadian geese. But that's only part
of its charm. It has a much wider range of facilities
than many wildlife refuges — including a visitor center with interpretive displays, boat ramps on the bay,
an observation tower, crabbing and fishing, a picnic
area with restrooms and drinking water, and one of the
oldest lighthouses in the southeast, constructed in

1831 of stones from the old Fort San Marcos de Apalache. This is a place where you want to get out of your car and walk — or cycle, or canoe, or sea kayak. Marked trails stretch for miles, through some of the most diverse habitats in Florida.

You can see freshwater springs boiling to the surface both in the refuge and just offshore. One of these, Spring Creek, may have an average daily discharge higher than any spring in the United States. There are also many prehistoric Indian sites in the refuge. St. Marks has the usual guided nature trails, but it also has many miles of primitive walking trails (try the 5-mile trail to High Ridge or the 13 mile trail to Stoney Bayou) and 45 miles of the Florida Trail, which has recently been made part of the National Scenic Trail. It also has a 16-mile bike trail which connects the park with Tallahassee on a former railroad bed. If you do go exploring, especially by water, be sure to take a compass and maps, and always, of course, water or fluids.

This 64,000-acre refuge is a typical coastal area with wide sweeping salt marshes, low tidal flats and creek estuaries, pine woods, hardwood swamps, and oak-palm-cedar hammocks. It is a good place to see birds and wildlife, especially in the winter months. St. Marks is located south of Tallahassee, three miles south of U.S. 98 on SR 59, across the St. Marks River from Newport. It is open during daylight hours (Box 68, St. Marks, FL 32355 904-925-6121).

St. Vincent National Wildlife Refuge, near Apalachicola, is accessible only by boat over nine miles of water and has no visitor facilities or drinking water. The 12,000-acre barrier island remains remarkably preserved in its native state. It supports a small herd of enormous Sambur deer, imported from Asia early in the century, some bald and golden eagles, and rare peregrine falcons. There are occasional tours for organized groups with a special interest in nature. For information contact P.O. Box 447, Apalachicola, FL 32320; 904-653-8808.

Suwannee River State Park stands at what was once a busy point of commerce, where the Withlacooche River (one of two rivers by that name in Florida) flows from Georgia into the Suwannee River. This was the town of Columbus, Florida, made prosperous by a railroad bridge across the Suwannee, a ferry landing, and a large sawmill. Steamboats toured up and down the rivers, carrying visitors, cotton, and supplies. George Drew the sawmill operator, who became governor of Florida in 1876, had a stately mansion near where the rivers joined. That's all gone now. Only the town graveyard remains, and the earthworks thrown up by the Confederates during the Civil War to protect the railroad bridge. It was this bridge that Union troops were attempting to capture when they were turned back in the Battle of Olustee in 1864. Standing in the town's stead is an especially lovely state park, one of the less traveled in Florida, and "as real a Florida Park as you will find." The rustic overlook provides a panoramic view of the rivers and the surrounding wooded uplands. The park is located 13 miles west of Live Oak, on U.S. 90 (Box 297, Rt. 8, Live Oak, FL 32060; 904-362-2746).

Three Rivers State Recreation Area, formerly the Jim Woodruff State Park, is on Lake Seminole and the rivers Chattahoochee, Flint, and Apalachicola. The park is somewhat hilly, located in dense northern Florida woods in one of Florida's most rural counties. It is a place of winding roads, little towns, and friendly people, where the pioneer past still seems close. Lake Seminole is popular for fishing and water sports. It is located off SR 271, one mile north of Sneads (Rt 1, Box 15A, Sneads, FL 32460; 904-593-6565).

Torreya State Park is a special place that looks less like Florida than someplace in the North. It has steep bluffs and ravines and contains certain flowers, plants, and animals found nowhere else in the world. If you get homesick for a northern fall head for Torreya. It offers Florida's prettiest autumn display. The park was named for the Florida torreya, a rare tree that grows on the bluffs of the river. The only other species of this tree in North America is found in the Sierra Nevada of central California. Also called "stinking cedar," it leaves a pungent odor when crushed.

The unusual plants and animals are left from when the last ice age pushed northern trees and animals into the South about 12,000 years ago. When the ice receded, a few pockets of northern ecology remained. High bluffs and deep ravines carved by the Apalachicola River divide the park into three land areas: river swamp, hardwood hammock, and high pineland. Each community has a different set of shrubs, wildflowers, and trees. The park also contains Gregory House, a plantation house from the 1840s, originally built across the river. The park is located between Bristol and Greensboro on SR 271, off SR 12 (Star Rt. Bristol FL 32321; 904-643-2674, open 8 a.m.-sunset, year round).

Waccasassa Bay State Preserve contains over 30,000 acres, most of which are salt marsh dotted by picturesque wooded islands. This is only a small remnant of the once vast hardwood Gulf Hammock. The extensive salt marsh and tidal creeks are breeding and nursery areas for saltwater fish, crabs, and shellfish. Thousands of migratory waterfowl, shorebirds, and wading birds feed here. Although salt marshes are not especially hospitable to human beings, they are one of the most important ecological habitats in the world. They absorb the shock of waves and protect the land from storm and sea, and they also spread out the nutrients carried down to the mouths of arriving rivers, so they can be absorbed and utilized more fully. One of their greatest values in our polluted age is their ability to filter out fertilizers, agricultural runoff, and other water contaminants. Florida has lost a high percentage of its salt marsh land over the past century and this poses a serious threat to the ecology of the whole state.

Waccasassa has few recreational activities beyond fishing out of fishcamps near the Gulf Hammock, a primitive campsite on the Waccasasa River, and occasional ranger-led canoe trips. Its main purpose is to support life and ecological systems elsewhere. Boat entrances to Waccassassa Bay are located near Cedar Key and Gulf Hammock (P.O. Box 187, Cedar Key, FL 32625; 904-543-5567).

Yankeetown County Park has a saltwater beach, restrooms, picnic tables, and primitive campsites. It is located on the Gulf at the mouth of the Withlacoochee River, at the west end of CR 40 (904-447-9465 or-2907).

Northeast Region

Cary State Forest has 3,400 acres open to the general public for day use only. There is a nature-study trail with a good guidebook. It is located northeast of Jacksonville on U.S. 301, halfway between Callahan and Baldwin (District Forester, FDF, 8719 Beaver, Jacksonville, FL 32220; 904-781-1434).

Faver-Dykes State Park was donated by Hiram Hall Faver in memory of his parents, with the stipulation that it be kept in as natural a state as possible. The special quality of this 750-acre park is simply the tranquil beauty of Old Florida, just as it has been for the past 100 years — pine woods and old dirt roads. It is 15 miles south of St. Augustine, off U.S. 1 (RFD 4, Box 213-J-I, St. Augustine, FL 32084; 904-794-0997).

Gold Head Branch State Park, developed by the Civilian Conservation Corps during the 1930s, has a wide diversity of terrain, including four lakes and a marsh. Its most dramatic feature is a ravine where water gushes and the rare needle pine grows. There is good swimming and diving in a small deep lake. Gold Head is located 6 miles northeast of Keystone Heights on SR 21, about halfway between Gainesville and Jacksonville (6239 SR 21, Keystone Heights, FL 32656; 904-473-4701).

Osceola National Forest with 157,000 acres of mostly pine flatwoods, has one distinctive and outstanding area, Big Gum Swamp, a thick, varied, wet area of great beauty. For several years this was an area of controversy. Companies holding mineral leases to about a third of the forest wanted to begin strip-mining for phosphate ore, which would have devastated the plant and animal communities. Strip mining in the forest was finally restricted by the passage of the Florida Wilderness Bill. The forest is located west and north of Lake City, off U.S. 90. Leave I-10 for U.S. 90 at the Lake City or Sanderson exits (District Ranger, U.S. 90, P.O. Box 70, Olustee, FL 32072; 904-752-2577).

Morningside Nature Center, a 278-acre sanctuary of longleaf pine savannahs, offers a program of guided walks, courses, workshops, and periodic surveys of birds and wildflowers (3540 East University Ave., Gainesville, FL 32601; 904-374-2170).

Paynes Prairie State Preserve, with 18,000 acres, has been inhabited by humans for almost 10,000 years. Part of the area was a lake for a time in the late 1800s. There is an observation platform and an overlook off Rt. 441. Look for the buffalo and also the sandhill cranes that nest here from November through February. There is a new nature exhibit at Lake Wauberg. Call for information about the monthly ranger-led

hikes — one goes nine miles to a primitive site overlooking the prairie basin and the other goes 1.3 miles
along the trails walked by English naturalist William
Bartram in 1774. Paynes Prairie is located off U.S. 441,
immediately south of Gainesville (Rt. 1, Box 41, Micanopy, FL 32667; 904-466-3397).

San Felasco Hammock State Preserve is a 5,500-acre
wild and natural region on the edge of a major metropolitan area. It was recently acquired as part of the
Environmentally Endangered Lands purchase. The
hammock is one of the largest remaining examples of
Florida climax forest — the mesic hammock. The area
is full of small springs, steep ravines, rocky hills, and
sinks. There is a day-use nature trail at the parking lot
on SR 232. Ranger-led walks and guided nature-study
trips can be arranged. It is located northwest of
Gainesville, on SR 232 (Devil's Millhopper, 4732 N.W.
53rd Ave., Gainesville, FL 32601; 904-336-2008).

Central West Region

Chassahowitzka National Wildlife Refuge (pronounced Chaz-wits-ka), with 30,000 acres, is one of the
finest waterfowl areas in Florida. Over 250 species of
birds have been recorded here. Fishing is excellent.
Although the main body of the refuge is accessible
only by boat from the Homosassa and Chassahowitzka
rivers or Mason Creek, there is a one-half mile, self-
guided nature trail starting from the refuge headquarters on U.S. 19, four miles south of Homosassa Springs
(Rt. 2, Box 44, Homosassa, FL 32646; 904-382-2201).

Crystal River National Wildlife Refuge is a popular
place for divers to see endangered manatees. During
winter weekends as many as a thousand divers visit
the springs and the nearby dive shops. If you do dive,
check the rules carefully. Some areas are closed. The

refuge is located in Kings Bay (contact through Chassahowitzka NWR, Rt .2 Box 44, Homosassa, FL 32646; 904-382-2201).

Egmont Key National Wildlife Refuge, located in Tampa Bay, was established because of its wildlife and its archaeological sites. Although it is accessible by boat only, its beaches swarm with visitors during the summer. An excursion boat, *Miss Cortez* goes there Tuesday and Thursday afternoons (Cortez Rd., Cortez: 813-794-1223).

Hillsborough County has several fine parks that bear exploration. Most have full recreational facilities in addition to their special features. For more information contact P.O. Box 1110 Courthouse, Tampa, FL 33601; 813-681-7990. The parks are open sunrise to dark. They are listed here with brief descriptions.

1. Alderman's Ford (on SR 39, south of SR 60 in east Hillsborough County) is one of the most popular canoe spots in the state.

2. Edward Medard Park, (6 miles east of Brandon on Turkey Creek Road) was formerly known as Pleasant Grove. It is located on an 800-acre reservoir made from abandoned mine-pits and operated by the Southwest Florida Water Management District, as a popular freshwater fishing spot.

3. E. G. Simmons Park (19th St., N.W.; 813-645-3836) has 469 acres for camping with a waterfront view.

4. Eureka Springs Park (on Eureka Springs Road north of I-4, near the junction with U.S. 301) has a botanical garden of rare and unusual plants with a greenhouse, trellised walks, interpretative trails, and a picnic area.

5. Lake Park (North Dale Mabry at Van Dyke Road (813-961-4226) is a 600-acre park with five lakes, a bicycle motorcross track, an archery range, and equestrian facilities for handicapped citizens.

6. Lettuce Lake Park, northeast of the Fletcher Avenue bridge, just west of I-75 is a 240-acre park, with an observation tower.

7. Lithia Springs Park, (Lithia Springs Road southeast of Brandon (813-689-2139) has a natual spring pool.

8. Upper Tampa Bay Park, (8001 Double Branch Rd., off SR 580)

was slated at one time to become a housing project, but growing concern about the preservation of coastal wetlands led to its development as a park instead. The park has fresh-water ponds, pine flatwoods, salt marshes, a chain of one-table roofed pavilions with names like Maple and Oak, long benches overlooking the estuary, and an environmental study center operated jointly with the Hillsborough Community College.

9. Wilderness Park includes five sites which give access to 17,000 acres of forest, being developed cooperatively between Hillsborough County and the Southwest Florida Water Management District. The access points are at Flint Creek (Stacy Road and U.S. 301), Morris Bridge (Morris Bridge and Hillsborough River), Dead River (Dead River Road and U.S. 301), Tis A Wee (on U.S. 301, south of SR 574), and Flatwoods, (Morris Bridge, one mile north of Hillsborough River). All offer picnicking, fishing, boating, canoeing, and hiking. For more information call 813-986-2172.

Hillsborough River State Park runs along a stretch of the river in which limestone rocks jut out to form rapids, highly unusual in this part of the state. Two footbridges built by the Civilian Conservation Corps in the 1930s cross the river. There is a nature trail along with camping, picnicking in a large shady grove, swimming, fishing, canoeing (good primitive trails), and bicycling. Fort Foster, dating from the Seminole Indian wars is also located here. The park lids 6 miles south of Zephyrhills, off U.S. 301, (Rt. 4, Box 250-L, Zephyrhills, FL 33599; 813-986-1020).

Moccasin Lake Nature Park is a 51-acre nature preserve which includes a five-acre lake, nature trails, animal, plant, and energy exhibits, an interpretive center, and a multi-purpose pavilion. A 30-foot pier extending out over Moccasin Lake allows for the observation of aquatic life. The park is located at 2750 Park Trail Lane, Clearwater (P.O. Box 4748, Clearwater, FL 34618-4748, 813-462-6024, open Tue.-Fri., 9 a.m.-5 p.m., Sat. & Sun. 10 a.m.-6 p.m., closed Mon.)

Myakka River State Park is one of Florida's largest and oldest state parks, famous for its scenic panoramas of lakes, river, marshes, hammocks, and prairies, and for its abundant wildlife populations. In 1934 the sons of Mrs. Potter Palmer donated a large tract of this land in memory of their mother. The state acquired additional lands and in 1935 the Civilian Conservation Corps created the park for public use. Part of the park is a 7,500-acre wilderness preserve with limited access. There is an interpretative center and ranger-guided walks and campfire programs, including a winter program on birdwatching for beginners. The park boasts the world's largest airboat, a seventy-passenger enclosed "Gator Gal" which offers a scenic lake cruise, as well as a "tram safari" land tour which goes off the paved roads into remote areas. Both tours last approximately one hour and fill up early, especially on weekends and in the winter. Sign up at the entrance as soon as you enter the park. It is located 17 miles east of Sarasota on SR 72 (Rt. 1, Box 72, Sarasota, FL 33583; 813-924-1027).

Oscar Scherer State Recreation Area consists of 462 acres of pine and scrubby flatwoods on the banks of a small tidal creek. The park is noted for its population of Florida scrub jays, which are a threatened species. The land was bequeathed to the state by Mrs. Elsa Scherer Burrows in memory of her father, Oscar Scherer. It is two miles south of Osprey on US 41 (P.O. Box 398, Osprey, FL 33559; 813-966-3154).

Withlacoochee State Forest consists of three separate areas: Croom, Citrus, and Richloam. All have excellent hiking and nature trails, with good self-guiding brochures. The Withlacoochee, called "the long and winding river" by the Indians, runs from south to north through the Croom section, which is the main visitor area. One small corner of Croom is devoted to

Buttgenbaugh Motorcycle Area, in which old mine pits have been converted into a motorcycle park. A permit is required to use it and violators of its rules lose their permits. The entrance to this area is by the Holiday Inn at SR 50, just west of I-75.

The Citrus Section of Withlacoochee State Forest is dry, with no running streams. It includes a horse stable camp (also known as Tillis Hill) developed for horseback riding and dog field-trials. The Richloam District, the wettest, is used primarily for hunting and fishing. Withlacoochee is located off I-75 near Brooksville. Forest headquarters are located on U.S. 41 at SR 476 (7255 U.S. 41, North Brooksville, FL 33512; 904-796-4958).

Central Region

The Green Swamp Flood Detention Area is a new area of 50,000 acres that has been opened to hiking and primitive camping between Clermont and Lakeland. Contact Florida Trail or SW Florida Water Management District for information (904-796-7211).

Highlands Hammock State Park was opened to the public in 1931 and was one of the four original parks in Florida's State Park System, created in 1935. Much of it was developed by the Civilian Conservation Corps with hand-constructed stone walks and native stone fireplaces. The park's 3,800 acres preserve a magnificent hardwood forest. This park really does look the way it did when the Spanish conquistadors first arrived. Some trees are over a thousand years old. A nature trail gives easy access to the hammock and its immense oaks, hickories, sweetgums, and cabbage palms. Be sure to ask for a guide to the nature trail at the entrance station.

A good way to get an overview of the park is to take a tram tour, which runs every day except Monday.

Highlands Hammock is located 6 miles west of Sebring, off U.S. 27. Turn west at the sign onto SR 634 (Rt. 1, Box 310, Sebring, FL 33870; 813-385-0011).

Lake Griffin State Recreation Area is locally famous for its occasional "floating islands," blocks of peat that break loose from the marshes and float out into the lake. It is located north of Leesburg, its entrance is on U.S. 27-441 (P.O. Box 608, Fruitland Park, FL 32731;904-787-7402).

Lake Kissimmee State Park consists of 5,030 acres bordered by Lakes Kissimmee, Tiger, and Rosalie, part of a wide flat area called the Osceola Plain which was partly covered by the sea during one of the ice ages. The plain was created by the action of endless waves sweeping over it to crash against a beach that was several miles inland. To see the edge of this ancient seashore, drive five miles west on Camp Mack Road to where the highway rises sharply and then dips up and down over rolling ground that was once a series of sand dunes paralleling the ancient coast. You can get good views of Lake Kissimmee and the park from the observation platform at the picnic area. The lake and a chain of smaller lakes around it, are the headwaters of the Florida Everglades and water from the lake is carried by a canal (that was once the Kissimmee River) to Lake Okeechobee. The park includes a wilderness preserve and the historical Kissimmee Cow Camp. Contact Lake Kissimmee State Park, (14248 Camp Mack Road, Lake Wales, FL 33853; 813-696-1112).

Lake Louisa State Park lies in the vast Green Swamp, a large, wild area. Its 1,790 acres, with two and a half miles of shoreline along Lake Louise, contain ten distinct biological communities. This is a day-use only area. It is located south of Clermont on Lake Nellie Road, 2.5 miles off SR 561 (Rt. 1, Box 107-AA Clermont, FL 32711; 904-394-2280).

Lake Woodruff National Wildlife Refuge has shallow freshwater marshes, and an enormous list of birds (over 200 species) and animals. The winter migratory season, from November through February, is an especially good time to visit. The area is open for fishing all year, but there is no camping or picnicking. Drinking water and restrooms are available at the refuge headquarters. The refuge is located northwest of DeLand, with the entrance near DeLeon Springs (Refuge Manager, Lake Woodruff NWR, P.O. Box 488, DeLeon Springs, FL 32028; 904-985-4673).

Moss Park (Orange County) has 1550 acres, one of the largest county parks in the state. It is located on a long spit of land between Lake Hart and Lake Mary Jane, 25 miles southeast of Orlando. Take SR 15, go left at 15-A and then left on Moss Park Road (Orange County Parks, 118 W. Kaley Ave. Orlando, FL 32806; 305-273-2327).

Ocala National Forest is the oldest national forest east of the Mississippi River and the southernmost in the nation. It is a very popular recreation area and its largemouth bass fishing is world renowned. The park's main feature is the "Big Scrub," an ancient, immense spread of sand pine, unique in the world, that covers the central and western sections of the forest. This austere yet beautiful scrub once stretched from southern California across Texas, northern Mexico, and into Florida. Climatic changes that made the world warmer and moister 9,000 years ago isolated the Florida scrub from its western counterparts and confined it to the sand ridges where water drains through the soil nearly as fast as it falls, to create a dry environment in a moist land. Scrub provides some of the most important aquifer recharge areas in the peninsula. Its plant and animal life is adapted to the tough, hardy existence of heat and dryness captured so well by Marjorie Rawlings in *The Yearling*.

Ocala National Forest has nine major recreation areas. The Ocala National Recreation Trail crosses the forest with over 66 miles of hiking through some of its most scenic and secluded areas. This is part of the Florida National Scenic Trail which will eventually run the length of Florida. Ocala also has some especially fine canoe trails, horseback riding on the Ocala One Hundred Mile Horse Trail, and logging roads for off-the-road vehicles (ORV). A good route for exploring this huge area by car is a loop that begins north on SR 314, then goes south on SR 19, out of the forest toward Mount Dora. For information contact Ocala National Forest Supervisor (227 N. Bronough Street, Suite 4061, Tallahassee, FL 32301; 904-681-7265) or the ranger for the section you want to visit (Lake George District Ranger, Rt. 2, Box 701, Silver Springs, FL 32688; 904-625-2520; or, Seminole District Ranger, 1551 Umatilla Rd., Eustis, FL 32726; 904-357-3721).

Prairie Lakes State Preserve was recently acquired and is still being restored to its natural condition. This 8,000-acre preserve is open for hiking, picnicking, nature study, and fishing. There are twelve miles of trails in two loops over flat terrain, with minimal facilities. Three lakes border the preserve. The most unusual community found on the preserve is the dry prairie, a vast expanse of low saw palmetto dotted with cabbage palms and an occasional small marsh or hammock. The preserve is located on SR 523 (Canoe Creek Road) nine miles north of Kenansville (P.O. Box 220, Kenansville, FL 32739; 305-436-1626).

Reedy Creek Environmental Study Center has a 2,000-foot-long boardwalk along the large Reedy Creek Swamp past a dozen virgin bald cypress trees. The center is part of the Osceola District Schools, but is open to the public Saturdays from 10 a.m. to 5 p.m. and Sundays noon to 5 p.m., free. It is at South Poinciana Blvd., Kissimmee, FL 32758.

Seminole County has several parks with wilderness areas. Soldier's Creek Park includes 315 acres in the Spring Hammock area with fishing and picnicking and an Environmental Studies Center (1 mile east of U.S. 17 on SR 419; 407-323-9615). Mullet Lake Park has 151 acres with primitive camping. It is located 8 miles east of U.S. 17 on SR 46 (407-323-9615).

Tenoroc State Reserve is a new 6,000-acre park that centers around lakes created by the reclamation of stripmined land. It permits day use only, with picnicking, excellent bass fishing, and boat ramps. The reserve is experimenting with different largemouth bass management strategies so each lake is managed under its own set of regulations. Anglers must make reservations and specify which lake they wish to visit. Each fisherman is required to return a completed creel information sheet and daily permit upon check-out. For information or reservations call Thursday through Sunday noon until 4 p.m., 813-665-8270. To get to the reserve take U.S. 92 from Lakeland east to Combee Road, then go north to Tenoroc Mine Road and turn east.

Wekiva River State Preserve is a recent purchase of 3,500 acres made with funds from the Environmentally Endangered Lands Bond, that provided $200 million for the purchase of rare and vanishing segments of natural Florida. It has not yet been developed for public access. It consists of dense, beautiful swamp and probably will be open for primitive canoe camping, hiking, and ranger-led activities. The park is located near Wekiwa Springs State Park (407-322-7587).

Central East

Hobe Sound National Wildlife Refuge is a small preserve donated by residents of Jupiter Island to save one of the last examples of its native habitat. There is a small strip of beach off SR 708 on the north end of Jupiter Island and a nature trail over high dunes. It is located 4 miles north of Jupiter, off U.S. 1, (South Florida Refuges, Box 510, Big Pine Key, FL 33043; 407-546-6141).

Jonathan Dickinson State Park was named for a Quaker who was shipwrecked nearby in 1696, discovered by Indians, and survived all sorts of adventures before getting his wife and baby safely back to Philadelphia. His journal gives valuable insight into early Florida (Jonathan Dickinson's Journal, Valentine Books, P.O Box 777, Pr Salerno, FL 33492). The park includes five miles of the Loxahatchee River, called the last wild river in the south east. The Loxahatchee winds from a completely freshwater environment, through a blend of temperate and tropical vegetation, to the saltwater mangrove community, one of the few rivers in the United States that can boast such a diversity of plant and animal life.

In addition to the river, the park includes 10,000 acres of native woodlands, three nature trails, and the Trapper Nelson Interpretive site, the frontier home and lands of a New Jersey man who came to live in the area in the 1930s and became known as the Wild Man of the Loxahatchee. You can hike to Trapper Nelson's or take the *Loxahatchee Queen.* Be sure to call the park for reservations if you plan to take the boat because it doesn't run every day. Jonathan Dickinson is located 13 miles south of Stuart on U.S. 1 (14800 SE Federal Highway, Hobe Sound, FL 33455; 407-546-2771).

Merritt Island National Wildlife Refuge, near Cape Canaveral, captures the extremes of history in Florida. You can see birds in their 140,000 acres of natural and ancient habitat against the background of space shuttle launching pads. The wildlife doesn't seem to mind the 20th-century activity, although recent tests show that some creatures suffer hearing loss. Merritt Island is, in fact, one of the best waterfowl sites in Florida, supporting 19 wildlife species listed as endangered or threatened, more than any other refuge in the United States.

There are several nature trails, a photo blind, and a visitor center, four miles east of Titusville on SR 402. Drinking water is available only at the visitor center. The area may be closed around shuttle launch times. It is on SR 402, off SR 406 (P.O. Box 6504, Titusville, FL 32780; 305-867-0667).

Savannas Recreation Area used to be an old city water reservoir. When it became obsolete for that purpose, it was allowed to return to its natural state. Now it is a beautiful wilderness area within the city limits of Fort Pierce. The 550-acre area, developed in 1963, includes a botanical garden and a petting farm, as well as attractive campgrounds and freshwater fishing. It is located at 1400 East Midway Road, between U.S. 1 and Indian River Drive (St. Lucie County Recreation and Parks, P.O. Box 760, Fort Pierce, FL 34954; 407-464-7855 and 407-464-8594).

Tomoka State Park is one of the finest coastal hammocks in Florida, famous from the earliest written records. John James Audubon came here to paint birds. The park, although covering only 900 acres, has some magnificent trees. It has good camping, rental canoes, and fine picnic areas along the Tomoka River. There is fishing, but note the warning signs: the surrounding waters have reportedly been contaminated by inadequate municipal and private sewage disposal systems. So don't eat the fish and don't swim.

The Tomoka State Museum displays natural and local history as well as spunky and often humorous works of art by the late Fred Dana Marsh. Tomoka is located 3 miles north of Ormond Beach, on North Beach Street (P.O. Box 695, Ormond Beach, FL 32074; 904-677-3931).

Tosohatchee State Reserve preserves 30,000 acres of unspoiled marshlands, including several thousand acres of virgin cypress swamp. There are only three or four known places in the U.S. where this can still be seen. The reserve also has a tract of 40 acres of native slash pine in its virgin habitat — unlogged and unplanted. The Tosohatchee hiking trail, developed and maintained by the Florida Trail Association passes through many of these areas. A visitor center may be built in the old Bee Head Ranch House, a fine example of early Cracker architecture. The area also has camping for youth groups, and horse trails. It is located between Orlando and Titusville, crossed by Highways 520 and 50, and the Beeline Expressway. The entrance is near Christmas off SR 50 (3365 Taylor Creek Road, Christmas, FL 32709; 305-568-5893).

Southwest Region

Big Cypress National Preserve is a 500,000-acre preserve, with minimal public access at this time, although the Florida Trail goes through a portion of it and a visitor center is planned for the future. It was acquired for the purpose of protecting the water-flow to Everglades National Park and may never be extensively developed for recreation. It is crossed by U.S. 41

and SR 94 around Monroe Station. For information contact 813-695-2000, or Oasis Station 813-6995-4111.

Briggs Nature Center at the Rookery Bay National Estuarine Sanctuary between Naples and Marco Island, is one of two centers maintained by the Collier County Conservancy. There is a small museum, a boardwalk into the sanctuary and an observation platform on the edge of Duck Lake; as well as guided boat, canoe, and hiking tours by reservation during the winter. Visitors can borrow binoculars if they leave their car keys (401 Shell Island Road, Naples, FL 33962; 813-775-8569, open Mon.-Sat. 9 a.m.-5 p.m., Sun. 1-5 p.m., with some variation by season).

The **Conservancy Nature Center** in Naples houses a large exhibit hall where visitors can learn about south Florida habitats from the shallow Gulf to the Atlantic's coral reefs. The Shell Game exhibit lets participants match shell names with descriptions and one particularly nice diorama portrays life in the Everglades. There is an Animal Rehabilitation Center, open to the public on Tuesdays and Thursdays. The Naples Center (14th Ave. N., off Goodlette Rd., Naples, FL 33942; 813-262-0304) is open 9 a.m. to 5 p.m. Monday through Saturday, except May through October when it is closed on weekends.

Collier-Seminole State Park, south of Naples, is one of only three places in America where you can see the royal palm in its natural setting. In the 1920s this land was part of the holdings of Barron Collier who owned a million acres of land in the surrounding region. He offered a small hardwood forest, known as the Royal Palm Hammock, plus other lands to the federal government for a park to be designated the Lincoln-Lee National Park. When the federal government did not accept it, the land was turned over to the county and then, in 1947, to the state. A white-pillared memorial to Barron Collier stands in the middle of that grove.

Almost 4,800 of Collier-Seminole's 6,500 acres are maintained as wilderness preserve. It is a place of convergence and extremes, where there are only two seasons — wet and dry — and tropical and temperate zones mix together. The water here is alternately salt and fresh. Salt-tolerant grasses are the dominant plants. The hammock trees have adapted to the limits of their environment. Their leaves have a thick waxy coating to prevent water loss during the dry season and a pointed tip to channel drainage during the rainy season.

There is a fine nature trail, with boardwalks through a tropical hammock and mangrove area and a salt marsh lookout from which you can see the northern edge of the great mangrove forest of southern Florida, one of the world's largest. If you are quiet you can hear the tiny sounds of the marsh — the rubbing of one grass leaf against another, the single tiny chirp of a small bird, and the clickings and clatterings of the wind blowing high in the trees. The further out you look on the marsh, the lighter, more delicate it appears, like silk.

The area has boat docks, a picnic area, and camping (reservations recommended). A 13-mile canoe trail spans the wilderness preserve, but registration is necessary. Winter (the dry season) is an especially good time to visit. The bugs are fierce in summer. Collier-Seminole is located 17 miles south of Naples, on U.S. 41 (Marco, FL 33937; 813-394-3397).

In **Corkscrew Swamp Sanctuary** managed by the Audubon Society, southeast of Fort Myers, immense 500-year old trees arch 130 feet or more into the sky, as they once did all over Florida. This large preserve is an extraordinary place with sights, smells, and sounds worth many trips in every season. Winter is the peak season for birds but June brings acres of wild red hibiscus and nesting wood storks. The sancutary is home to the largest colony of wood storks in the country, but in recent years their numbers have been declining. They are prehistoric-looking white birds with a homely wrinkled head and elegant wings trimmed in black. Corkscrew has a visitor center, a two-mile boardwalk trail with occasional benches and covered shelters. There is an excellent guidebook and a naturalist on duty in the preserve. Wheelchairs are available for those who need them. There are occasional interpretative programs. The park is open 9 a.m. to 5 p.m. daily. It can be reached off I-75 by taking SR 846 (exit 17) 15 miles east (Rt 6, Box 1875-A, Naples, FL 33964; 813-657-3771).

Ding Darling National Wildlife Refuge, on Sanibel Island, near Fort Myers (1 Wildlife Dr., Sanibel, FL 33957; 813-472-1100) is named for the Pulitzer prize-winning political cartoonist who was an ardent conservationist before anyone ever heard of the word ecology. It is at the southern end of the Atlantic flyway for migrating ducks. Viewing is best in the winter, and at sunrise or sunset. Nevertheless this is a special place any time of year. Although you can drive, bike, or walk, the best way to see the area is by canoe along the Commodore Creek Canoe Trail. Contact Canoe Adventures (813-472-5218) for guided canoe trips or Tarpon Bay Marina (813-472-8900) for rental canoes, guides or group tours. Tarpon Bay, located within the preserve, also rents bicycles. The Ding Darling visitor's center runs a continuous video about birds currently in residence and is well worth viewing before you go through the refuge. There are walks and viewing points along the way, interpretive signs and a good guide book. Nearby is Sanibel Island Conservation

Foundation (813-472-2329) with a network of walking trails. It is dedicated to conservation of natural resources on and around the islands and provides tours, workshops, exhibits and classes.

Fakahatchee Strand State Preserve, along U.S. 41, is a narrow elongated swamp forest in the southwestern portion of the Big Cypress Swamp. The Big Cypress Swamp is basically a flat, gently sloping limestone plain. During the rainy season (June through September) water flows slowly southward over this plain into the mangrove swamps bordering the Gulf of Mexico. In places, the flow of water has cut channels into the limestone. These channels, or drainage sloughs, hold tall, dense, elongated swamp forests (called strands) that stand out on the horizon in contrast to the open terrain that borders them. The Fakahatchee Strand is approximately 20 miles long and three to five miles wide. It encompasses the largest strand of native royal palms, along with the largest concentration and variety of orchids in North America.

You can explore it either on foot, along the 2,000-foot boardwalk that leads into the preserve at the rear of the Indian village at Big Cypress Bend on U.S. 41 (seven miles west of the intersection with SR 29) or along the 20-mile Janes Scenic Drive near Copeland (which has a nice picnic area after seven miles). If you want to explore this area in depth, inquire about the special ranger-led wades (P.O. Box 548, Copeland, FL 33962; 813-695-4593).

The Nature Center Museum and Planetarium is a 105-acre site in Fort Myers with a museum, planetarium, two miles of nature trails and boardwalks, and several pavilions for special activities. The Audubon Aviary rehabilitates injured birds on site and returns them to the wild whenever possible. The nature center is at 3450 Ortiz Avenue, just north of Colonial Blvd.

near I-70, exit 22 (P.O. Box 06023, Fort Myers, FL 33906; 813-275-3435, open 9 a.m.-4 p.m. Tue.-Sat., Sun. 11 a.m.-4:30 p.m.).

Southeast Region

Chekika State Recreation Area (formerly Grossman Hammock) is a high use area with 640 acres. A slightly sulphurous, cool, pleasant lake spills from an artesian fountain created during unsuccessful oil drilling in the 1940s. There is a nature trail with an excellent guide-book. A small museum houses exhibits on the Ever-glades, and rangers offer special programs during the winter season. It is located 11 miles northwest of Homestead. Follow the signs off SR 27 (P.O. Box 1313, Homestead, FL 33030; 305-253-0950).

Everglades National Park has two seasons — Sum-mer and Winter. Summer is hot, muggy, and very buggy. There are torrential downpours, lightning storms, temperatures in the high 80s and 90s, and abundant insects. Winter is mild, very dry, and the wildlife is concentrated in areas where it can more easily be seen. The major visitor season is from mid-December through mid-April, and it's not just because there is snow in the north. Especially if you plan to stay any length of time, take one of the sightseeing cruises, or do a lot of hiking, try to plan your trip between November 1 and April 30 when everything is open and conditions are more habitable for humans. On the other hand, don't pass up a chance to see this extraordinary area if your only chance is in the sum-mer. Stock up on insect repellant, put on your long pants and long shirt, drive down the park road at least part of the way, and explore one or more of the nature walks.

The Everglades is a highly complex and unique environment where tropical and temperate species blend. It has been designated as an International Biosphere Reserve and a World Heritage Site. It is not dramatic, but an experience that slowly seeps into your being. The longer you look and listen, the more you see and hear. This is an enormous area and I cannot begin to do it justice here. There are numerous books on the park, well worth perusing.

The national park's 1.4 million acres are only a part of what we call The Everglades. You're actually in the Everglades' ecosystems when you're in Corkscrew Swamp Sanctuary, Collier Seminole State Park, the Loxahatchee National Wildlife Refuge, the Chekika State Recreation Area, and the Fakahatchee Strand State Preserve. The Everglades starts far to the north of the park's boundaries.

The Everglades is the southern portion of the larger drainage system which includes Lake Okeechobee and the Kissimmee River and reaches all the way up to Orlando. These marshlands slope southward almost imperceptibly (three inches per mile) slowly draining water from the Okeechobee Basin into Florida Bay. Today the Everglades and the many species which depend on them for survival are in grave danger as the free flow of water essential to their health are being restricted by drainage and construction projects and water diversion to the north.

The Everglades National Park's main visitor center is 10.8 miles southwest of Homestead on Rt. 9336. A short introductory film is shown regularly and you can pick up trail maps and other literature. You can also get insect repellent, a wise move especially if you are visiting in the summer. Mosquitoes are part of the food chain — and in this environment so are you. The main park road begins at the visitor center and ends 38 miles later at Flamingo. Many walking trails take off from this road and several more begin at Flamingo. If you want to really experience the Everglades, you can stay overnight at the **Flamingo Lodge Marina and Outpost Resort**, where you can rent a houseboat or stay in a cottage or motel.

Several naturalist-guided sightseeing tours leave from Flamingo. The Backcountry Cruise on the pontoon *Pelican* leaves twice a day for a three-hour exploration of the maze of mangrove islands and waterways at the heart of the park. The Florida Bay cruise gives you an hour and a half when during low tides you can watch herons, terns and shore birds feeding on the mud flats, and at high tides you can view the mangrove islands of the Florida Bay keys. Sunset and low tide cruises are especially recommended.

The Snake Bight/Wilderness Tram Tour chugs for two hours through a dense tropical forest dripping with vines, air plants, and climbing cacti. Guided canoe trips of one and a half hours explore shallow water areas full of marine and wildlife. There is also a day trip to Cape Sable on the *Nomad*, a steel hulled, diesel powered motor sailing ship, as well as overnight, guided canoe trips. For information contact **Flamingo Lodge Marina & Outpost Resort** (P.O. Box 428, Flamingo, FL 33030; 305-253-2241 or 813-695-3101).

The "Understanding the Everglades" program based in Homestead sponsors five-hour programs given by ranger-naturalists on special topics. The programs usually run from 10 a.m. until 3 p.m., although most bird walks begin earlier and start at various places in the park, depending on the topic. Each program is limited to 30 people and reservations are important. Contact **"Understanding the Everglades"** (Box 279, Homestead, FL 33030; 305-247-6211, ext. 220) for information about times, topics, places, and reservations.

You can also get into Everglades National Park from its northern edge, near Everglades, Florida. National Park Service Scenic Boat Tours depart from park docks on Chokoloskee Causeway on Rt. 29 daily. **The Mangrove Wilderness Trip** takes you inland up Turner's River, named in honor of a pioneer homesteader of the 1870s, past ancient Indian shell mounds, into Half-Way Creek and through twisting mangrove tunnels back to the docks. The Ten Thousand Island Boat Trips take you among the outer mangrove islands bordering the Gulf of Mexico. For information about these trips contact **Everglades National Park Boat Tours,** P.O. Box 119, Everglades, FL 33929; 813-695-2591.

Shark Valley Tram Tours start on U.S. 41, 30 miles west of Miami. These two-hour tours stop along the way to spot birds or alligators and for discussions on the park's hydrology, geology, vegetation, and wildlife. You also have time to climb the 65-foot observation tower, which provides views of the vast wetlands. Explorers may also travel the tram road on foot or bicycles, which can be rented at the entrance.

If you really want to get a feel for the size of the Everglades you may want to view it from the air. Stop at the Everglades City Airport and hop aboard Happy Harry's Scenic Airplane Rides (813-695-4211) or Everglades Aviation (813-695-3174).

For information about Everglades National Park contact Homestead, Fl 33030; 305-247-6211. Disabled explorers will find a full range of barrier-free activities available, including a unique four-hour canoe and camping trip to the Pearl Bay backcountry site.

Key Deer National Wildlife Refuge protects the miniature white tail deer found only in the Keys. They have survived from thousands of years ago, stranded as the earth thawed out after the last ice age and ocean levels rose. They depend for fresh water on unusual pockets of limestone on the lower keys which catch and hold rainwater. The reason for their small stature is still a matter of debate. The herd had diminished to around 50 animals by 1947 due to overhunting, poaching, and the widespread destruction of their habitat as cars, roads, and houses took over the wild scrub which they depended on for their livelihood. After 25 years of protection in the refuge, the herd grew to more than 400 animals, but it is believed to be on the decrease again.

Today the greatest cause of deer deaths is collisions with cars on U.S. 1 and Key Deer Boulevard. Speed limits are posted and strictly enforced in Key deer areas and speeders get absolutely no sympathy when they are stopped. Drive slowly and carefully and take a few minutes to go through the refuge in hopes of catching sight of one of these lovely small animals. The refuge is located on SR 940 off U.S. 1 (Refuge Manager, P.O. Box 510, Big Pine Key, FL 33043; 305-872-2239).

Larry and Penny Thompson Park (Dade County) is a 275-acre park with campgrounds, 5 miles of bike and walking paths, 2.5 miles of bridle paths, a 22-acre man-made lake for swimming, boating, and fishing, and some areas for nature study. It is heavily used. Note that there are two Thompson Parks in Dade County. This one is adjacent to the new zoo, (12451 SW 184th St. at 125th Ave.; 305-233-8231).

Lignumvitae Key State Botanical Site is still in its natural state, with virgin tropical forest that thrives here as it once did on most of Florida's upper keys. Because it is not sprayed for bugs you can see a profusion of butterflies (26 species). The site, accessible only by boat, was scheduled to be sold and cleared for a housing development when the Nature Conservancy secured the land until the state park system could take it over in 1971. One-hour guided walks are given at 10:30 a.m., 1 and 2:30 p.m. Thursday through Monday. A three-hour round-trip boat tour to the key departs from Indian Key Fill on U.S. 1 at 1:30 p.m. Thursday through Monday. Be sure to make reservations. There have to be at least four people for a tour. Take bug repellant; mosquitoes can be bad, especially in the summer. Lignumvitae Key is located one mile west of U.S. 1 at Mile Marker 78.5 (P.O. Box 776, Long Key, FL 33001; 305-664-4815).

Loxahatchee National Wildlife Reserve is a 220-square-mile segment of the Everglades. A visitor center at the headquarters has programs, a boardwalk nature trail, and calendar of events. For airboat tours and boat rentals call 407-426-2474. The reserve has three entrances: Twenty Mile Bend is 18 miles west of Lake Worth on U.S. 98; Hillsboro Recreation Area is on SR 827 about 10 miles west of Deerfield Beach; and Refuge Headquarters is on U.S. 441 between SR 804 and 806. The reserve is a day-use area only and permits fishing, boating, bird watching, and regulated waterfowl hunting in season. It is located inland, west of Lake Worth (Rt. 1, Box 278, Boynton Beach, FL 33437; 407-734-8303).

The Museum of Natural History of the Florida Keys and the **Florida Keys Children's Museum,** recently opened by the Florida Keys Land and Sea Trust, interpret the unique eco-system of the Keys. The Children's Museum, housed in a restored 1910 Flagler Railroad house, includes interactive exhibits, marine touch tanks, archeological excavation, and a salt water lagoon. Exhibits should continue to expand as the Trust undertakes acquisition of endangered lands in the keys (P.O. Box 536, Marathon FL, 33050; 305-743-3900).

Oleta River State Park has 900 acres of brackish water with an interesting canoe route. It is located across from Haulover Beach and Florida International University (NE 151st Street; 305-947-6357).

PART IV

SEARCH FOR THE PERFECT BEACH

Florida is, after all, synonymous with beaches. It is one of the best places in the world to engage in that most delightful of all outdoor explorations — the search for the perfect beach. The final decision is always, of course, in the eye of the beholder — or should I say the toe of the tester. But it doesn't really matter whether anyone else agrees with our choice. The search is what is important. That can take a long time in Florida. It has more beach than any other state in the country — over 8,000 miles of tidal shoreline. Not all of that is sandy beach, but an incredible amount is. Beaches stretch in an almost uninterrupted ribbon along the Atlantic coast on the east side and out along the Florida Keys. They start again on the Gulf coast, just above Everglades National Park, fade out above Tarpon Springs, and reappear in particularly pristine beauty along Florida's panhandle. There are also delightful sandy beaches around innumerable lakes in the state's interior, that would win praise on their own in any other environment. It's impossible to find yourself far from a good beach in Florida. One of the nicest aspects of Florida's beaches, especially for walkers, is their miles of public access. Roman law decreed the seashore and sea as "common to all," a concept that carried over into English law, and ultimately into American law, which gives control of the tidelands to the states as a public trust. Florida legally separates private and public portions of its beaches at the mean high-tide line averaged over a 19-year period. This stretch of shoreline is often called the "wet sand" area. Florida is now actively attempting to open up more of the "dry sand" area for public use as well.

In 1983 the state began the acquisition of beaches for preservation and public use through the "Save Our Coast" program. This program also helps local governments get easements across private property so that they can improve, increase, and post public access. As a result, legitimate beach access is provided about every half-mile in many parts of Florida, even in residential areas. Watch for public roads or paths that lead to the beach, usually marked with a "beach access" sign. But do keep to the public space and respect private property. And remember that on the beach, the public area is limited to the sand below the high tide mark. Residences and hotels that restrict access to their pools, beach chairs, dune walkovers, and other amenities are within their rights.

Many of Florida's finest beaches are on barrier islands, long, thin, delicate shifting islands (or spits) of sand that protect the mainland. With a few exceptions like Miami Beach, most of these have remained relatively unpopulated until recently. Not only were they inaccessible, except by boat, but they were inhospitable in severe storms and hurricanes. Barrier islands take the full impact of a storm, protecting the mainland. Their dunes act like a dike preventing the storm surge, which can be 10 to 13 feet above normal tide in an average hurricane, from being forced ashore to flood inland areas. Early settlers who moved to the barrier islands, like the Spanish in Pensacola, often relocated back to the mainland after losing large segments of their populations in severe weather.

Sandy beaches look durable and in many ways they are. Sea oat-held dunes have survived hurricanes that obliterated reinforced concrete buildings nearby. But they are part of a very delicate ecosystem, one that has been severely stressed in Florida and elsewhere by rapid and often environmentally unconcerned growth. Beaches are by nature dynamic, ever shifting, growing, and eroding. They are subject to continuing change by factors such as wave action, offshore slope, sea-level rise, climatic conditions, and type and source of sand. Construction which destroys sand dunes and manmade structures like seawalls, intensify and change wave action, accelerating erosion. As polar ice caps melt, seas throughout the world are rising, bringing even greater concern about the beaches of Florida.

Some fabled wide beaches of a generation ago would be almost gone today without beach restoration — a process of finding, transporting, and replacing acceptable sand back along the shoreline. A major restoration of Miami Beach was undertaken in 1978-1979 by the Army Corps of Engineers, at a cost of over 62 million dollars. The project dumped 13.5 million cubic yards of sand on the city's 9.3 miles of shoreline to create a new beach 310 feet wide. But restoration cannot stop erosion. Miami Beach needs 211,000 cubic yards of sand annually just to maintain its desired width.

The high cost of initial and ongoing restoration is stimulating the development of more preventative measures for beach protection and rejuvenation. Central to these measures are sand dunes — the very heart of the shoreline. Efforts are now being made throughout Florida to protect and stabilize existing dunes and encourage the formation of new ones. Beach visitors can help by always using the protective walkovers across the dunes and never climbing through them. Even "footprints" damage dunes. It's equally important to leave dune grasses and other vegetation undisturbed. Sea oats, for example, are vital to dune stabilization and growth. They are unique plants. They not only tolerate wind-driven salt spray and sand, they thrive on them. As sand strikes the grass blade and drops, it gradually accumulates, stimulating the growth of the grass and reshaping and expanding the dune. Other plants on the dune's leeside also work to keep it in place. Their roots probe deep for fresh water. The roots entwine around sand grains bonding them together, stabilizing the dune so it can withstand strong winds and waves. These plants also protect and provide food for a variety of wildlife — animals, small snakes, and birds that make the shore such an aesthetically pleasing and interesting environment.

After all this talk about preservation and protection, it seems like a contradiction to mention motorized vehicles on the beach. But people do drive here, and it's important to be aware of it. Otherwise you might be in for a rude awakening after an early morning snooze on the sand, finding yourself in the middle of a road at rush hour. In counties which permit drive-on beaches, the beaches are legally considered county roads. Everything — and I do mean everything — that is allowed on a county road may be allowed on the beach. That translates into big trucks, campers, trailers, motorcycles, zippy little motor scooters, and anything else that can drive down the ramp. Some local areas attempt to control traffic by restricting size and collecting either one-time or annual fees at toll booths at each beach access point. But the fees are usually too low to deter drivers and the booths are not usually occupied round the clock.

There is growing controversy about beach driving. People who favor it say that it gives them almost unlimited access to the whole shoreline, as well as close proximity to the shelter of their vehicle and freedom from having to haul mounds of beach and picnic equipment over seeming miles of scorching sand. Another argument, not inconsequential in a state dedicated to public access to shoreline, is that the right to drive on the beach is a long standing tradition in Florida which goes as far back as cars.

Conservationists and beachcombers without wheels may be less enthusiastic about the practice. Some days the beach resembles a long narrow parking lot. And beach enthusiasts who want to doze in the sun, or even just sit awhile may feel more than a little insecure without their own iron fortresses beside them to signal their presence and provide a buffer against oncoming traffic. Sitting beside the pool of an expensive resort watching the beach traffic roar by may not be one's idea of the perfect beach day either.

If you've always wanted your own vehicle by the sea and want to give beach driving a try yourself, make sure you are in an area where it is allowed. The beach should be smooth, hard, and wide. Most Florida beaches are not suitable for driving. Those that are tend to be concentrated on the northern end of the east coast, primarily around Ponte Verde Beach, St. Augustine Beach, Ormond Beach, and Daytona Beach. If you can, use an older car. Salt spray and sand can corrode and damage vehicles; incoming tides do even worse.

If the very thought of wheels on the seashore sends exhaust tremors through your brain, either plan to get in your beach activities early in the day before the vehicle traffic gets heavy, visit drive-on beaches during the week and out of season when traffic is minimal, or search out one of the many beaches where driving is forbidden.

Chapter 12, "Beaches I: Gulf Beaches" covers Florida's west coast and its northern panhandle. Chapter 13, "Beaches II: Ocean and Keys" describes the east coast beaches and the Florida Keys. Both chapters start with northern shorelines and move south.

Because of the extensive public access, individual beaches sometimes seem to merge into one another and it is hard to be sure where one beach technically ends and the next one begins. Unless you're trying to meet someone at a pre-arranged spot or find your way back to your car, it probably doesn't matter.

For beachcombers who want the full experience of exploring Florida beaches, one by one, I strongly recommend *Florida's Sandy Beaches: An Access Guide*, published by the Office of Coastal Studies and the University of West Florida Press (University Presses of Florida, 15 NW 15th Street, Gainesville, FL 32603) available by mail or in many Florida bookstores. This excellent guide gives the name of every Florida beach and shows access points. It also includes a wealth of information about Florida's shoreline ecology.

CHAPTER 12

BEACHES I

GULF COAST

Northwest Region: The Panhandle

Florida's panhandle is a beach lovers delight. Emerald green water curls along white beaches with sand so fine it looks like it has been put through a sifter. The beaches stretch mile after mile — many of them still empty. The Emerald Coast is unusual for the composition of its sand, which is almost pure quartz, washed down in rivers from the Appalachian mountains 5,000 to 10,000 years ago. It is the quartz that gives these beaches their fine texture and lustrous whiteness.

The barrier islands along this coast are especially active, responding to dynamic coastal processes that constantly flatten and rebuild them as the sands move from east to west. At times they are dramatically reshaped by the severe storms and hurricanes generated in the Gulf of Mexico and the Caribbean Sea. It's useful to think about the panhandle beaches in three segments. The western segment around Pensacola runs from the Alabama border to Fort Walton Beach; the central segment stretches to just southeast of Panama City; and the eastern segment runs from the Tyndall Air Force Base to St. George Island, south of Eastpoint.

The two major cities along the coast, Pensacola and

Panama City, offer a variety of cultural and recreational activities. Both have a good supply of excellent and reasonably priced accommodations and restaurants. Visitors who want the carnival atmosphere of a busy resort can find it in Panama City Beach. Those who seek isolation, good fishing, scuba diving, camping, hiking, or boating can find all those activities too. Here the peak tourist season is March to September, rather than winter as it is in southern Florida.

If you can go to the panhandle off-season, do it! Spring and fall are often especially beautiful and offer the opportunity for outstanding bargains in accommodations. The Gulf in October and November is warmer than the water ever gets in the middle of the summer in most places in the United States. The climate here may not be tropical, but this is still one of the southernmost areas in the country.

The panhandle is growing in popularity as a diving and snorkeling area. The warm crystal clear waters of the Gulf are home to a tremendous variety of sea life and visibility is excellent, sometimes up to 100 feet. In the 1970s the Panama City Marine Institute began a program of artificial reef-building and it now monitors over 50 sites from 19 to almost 200 feet, offering conditions for all levels of diving skill.

The beaches are so good all along the coast that it is hard to choose one over another. Although the Pensacola and Panama City areas may get crowded in the summer and over big weekends, the press of population doesn't come close to that of southern Florida. In most areas parking is easy and free. Major beaches have life guards in the summer, but not off-season. The panhandle's distinction is its long miles of pristine, undeveloped shoreline, but those who prefer developed beaches shouldn't have any trouble finding them at state parks, the national seashore, and county and municipal access points.

Western Panhandle Beaches (Pensacola Area)

The Pensacola area has one of the two national seashores in Florida. **Gulf Islands National Seashore,** authorized in 1971 at the urging of citizens from Florida and Mississippi who were working to save deteriorating historic forts along the coast, includes 150 miles of beach in the two states. Gulf Islands is the largest and the most frequently visited of the national seashores, its temperate climate drawing people year-round. There are no fees and these beaches are very popular. Parking can be a problem, especially in the summer.

In Florida the Gulf Islands National Seashore includes six distinct sections. Four are beaches — Perdido Key, the Fort Pickens area of Santa Rosa Island, the Santa Rosa area near Navarre Beach, and a small Okaloosa area east of Fort Walton Beach. Two other sections are primarily historic sites — the Historic Forts section (Fort Barrancas) on the Pensacola Naval Air Station and the Naval Live Oaks area, east of Gulf Breeze. Park headquarters and an attractive visitor's center with displays, a bookstore, and free literature on the seashore are located in the Naval Live Oaks area, just off U.S. 98.

There is a nature walk through the Live Oaks grove as well as picnicking and a beach. But the beach here is not in the same class as most of the others in the area. If you want to do more than get your toes wet, it's worth pressing on to one of the others. For information about any of the national seashore beaches contact: Superintendent, Florida District, Gulf Islands National Seashore, (1801 Gulf Breeze Parkway, Gulf Breeze, FL 32561; 904-932-9994).

The most westerly national seashore beach, and thus the furthest removed for visitors coming from other parts of Florida, is **Perdido Key: Johnson Beach.** It is at the mouth of the Perdido River which divides Florida from Alabama. Johnson Beach has a concession area with parking, restrooms, picnic shelters, and lifeguards from Memorial Day to Labor Day. At its eastern end it is sand, sun, sky, and sea — pure *beach* in all its vastness and simplicity. If you go off-season or during the week, you can park along the road that runs along the ridge of the island and walk toward the water making new tracks in the wind-rippled sand. When you get across this expanse of beach (one of the widest I've come across in Florida) you look out and see nothing but the Gulf and perhaps a pair of great blue herons with whom you share the water's edge.

Those who are interested in viewing remnants of the island's early coastal defenses can hike six miles to the end of the key to see three old batteries and the site of Fort McRee, built on the tip of the key and now underwater. There are no trees here and it can get hot, so if you plan any walking be sure to carry plenty of water.

Perdido Key State Recreation Area, at the western end of the key, was recently ranked the third best beach in the nation in a rating of 650 U.S. beaches by geologist Dr. Stephen Leatherman, director of the University of Maryland's Laboratory for Coastal Research. It lies right along the road, in two sections separated by a segment of private land. It has parking, restrooms, and picnic areas. For information contact Perdido Key SRA, Big Lagoon State Recreation Area, (12301 Gulf Beach Highway, Pensacola, FL 32507; 904-492-1595).

To get to either beach, travel 15 miles southwest

from Pensacola on SR 292 which leads into SR 293. To reach the national seashore, turn left as soon as you cross the bridge onto the key. Stay right for the state recreation area and drive west on SR 292 until you see the park.

Perdido Key provides a good example of the way barrier islands protect the mainland. In hurricane Frederick in September 1979, the island took the full brunt of the storm which sheared off its 15-foot-high dunes and flooded the island with six feet of water. Had it not been there, the storm could have devastated heavily populated subdivisions along Big Lagoon.

Fort Pickens and Langdon Beach southwest of Pensacola on Santa Rosa Island is a second part of the Gulf Island Seashore. In addition to the 17 miles of beaches, visitors can tour the old fort, visit museums, and inspect some late-nineteenth and early-twentieth-century concrete batteries still in place. This area is easily accessible from Pensacola over a short toll bridge from Gulf Breeze and has a full range of accommodations and restaurants nearby. The area has a visitor center, bicycle trail, several nature trails, a large campground, a fishing pier, and scuba diving. To get there turn west after the bridge and drive for three miles along Fort Pickens Road.

Beaches stretch along this coast one after another. The third national seashore area, the **Santa Rosa Area Beach**, is ten miles east of Pensacola Beach on SR 399 on both Santa Rosa Sound and the Gulf of Mexico. It has restrooms, picnic areas, an exhibit room open year-round, and concession stands open during the spring and summer. Just east of it is **Navarre Beach**, which is also easily accessible by toll bridge from U.S. 98, 19 miles east of Gulf Breeze. Its fishing pier is at 8525 Gulf Blvd. This is a delightfully quiet spot on the Gulf, bordered by the national seashore on the west and

Eglin Air Force base to the east. Its main concern is to maintain the natural beauty of the area. The Shoreline Park, a small community recreation area on Santa Rose Sound, lies on both sides of the Navarre Beach Bridge. Except for a section of shoreline from Navarre Beach to Fort Walton Beach closed off by Eglin Air Force Base, the stretch of beaches continues eastward unabated. A fourth national seashore area beach, **Choctawhatchee Bay**, is 26 miles east of the Santa Rosa beach, past Eglin Air Force Base and Fort Walton Beach along U.S. 89. It is on Choctawhatchee Bay rather than the Gulf and has restrooms, outdoor showers, and a picnic area.

Central Panhandle & Panama City

The South Walton area beaches are characterized by high, wind-sculpted sand dunes, the largest in the state. They are especially scenic, with a string of lakes running along the shoreline, their dark stillness accenting the white dunes. These beaches are unpretentious and family oriented, with most accommodations privately owned. East of them stretches the highly developed Panama City Beach area.

Henderson Beach State Recreation Area (2 miles east of Destin on U.S. 98; 904-234-3751) has snow-white sand and crystal-clear water. Purchased in 1983, it was the state's first acquisition under its "Save Our Coast" program. Nearby is the **Silver Beach Wayside Park**.

Walton County has recently developed a series of beach access points with excellent facilities and you can find beaches here at regular intervals. If you have a bent for beaches with dunes you may want to spend some extra time here. Look for the turn-offs from U.S. 98 to Miramar Beach and Four Mile Village, near the large resort of Sandestin. An especially scenic stretch of beaches is on the coastal road SR 30A, off U.S. 98.

Dune Allen Beach has lakes and sand dunes; **Ed Walline Park,** at the junction of SR 30A and SR C393, includes a park with picnic shelters, showers, attractive green-trimmed restrooms and bathhouses, and an observation tower. **Gulfview Heights Access** is not well marked — turn at Great Feathers Raw Bar and look for a new development, Gulf Dunes. **Blue Mountain Beach,** at the intersection of SR 83 and 30A, has high dunes and blue-white sand.

Grayton Beach State Recreation Area is exceptional. Ranked as number 2 in Dr. Leatherman's recent rating of U.S. beaches, the broad beach backed by high dunes and bordered by turquoise water is only part of what this area has to offer. The park's 336 acres include part of brackish Western Lake and an extensive salt marsh, abundant in fish and birds. The tops of an almost-buried pine forest look just like scrbby bushes. The area has a nature trail, camping with campfire interpretive programs, hiking, swimming, surf fishing and boating with a boat ramp on Western Lake. It is on SR 30-A, near the junction of C283 (Rt. 2, Box 790-1, Santa Rosa Beach, FL 32459; 904-231-4210).

Just east of the park is the town of **Grayton Beach** first homesteaded in 1880. One of the early houses, a dark green clapboard which came to be called "Washaway" because it stood in the path of several hurricanes, can still be seen. This small sleepy community with its beach, weathered cypress houses, and sand streets has several good restaurants and an art gallery that specializes in photographs and paintings of the area.

Seaside stands in sharp contrast to other communities along 30A. It is a new, planned community that has won all sorts of architectural awards for its New England Victorian style and its people-oriented scale. It sits like a multi-colored pastel fairyland atop the high dunes. Some people love it, some people hate it. But it is growing rapidly and is clearly here to stay. And at its one public beach, it offers some special amenities that are rare in these parts. Just below Per-spi-cas-ity, a delightful, aesthetically pleasing Mediterranean-style outdoor boutique, it is close to several good restaurants (including one with take-out service), a bookstore, a playground, a lookout platform with chairs, and a concession that rents beach chairs, umbrellas, Hobie cats, and 3-wheel ocean bikes. And if you have a craving for a delectable beach picnic, you can satisfy it at the gourmet grocery store and deli just across the road.

Seagrove Beach, at the junction of C395 is the second oldest community in the South Walton area. It was initially developed in 1939 and carefully planned as a family residential beach community, with the slogan, "Where Nature Did Its Best." Today, in spite of some new development, it retains that casual, residential character. You can find beach access paths down almost any of the little roads leading to the Gulf, but there is no satisfactory parking — better to respect the privacy and property of local residents and head for one of the areas with developed parking. A little further east is **Phillips Inlet Area** where the situation is similar. Many of the communities in this area were homesteaded as part of a federal government program for veterans after World War II.

Panama City Beach is the resort city of the panhandle. In the past it was known for its honky-tonk and colorful strip, referred to by some as the "Redneck Riviera." Today it bills itself as a beach designed for families and with an ample supply of excellent and reasonably priced beachfront accommodations and restaurants, along with many family oriented activities, it really is. If it's razzle-dazzle you want, you can still find it here with a little looking. If what you are after is a well-equipped resort community with wonderful beaches and all the water activities you could possibly think of, you've got it here — miles of it.

In case you are wondering, the city was named by its original developer during the construction of the Panama Canal because it is on a direct line from Chicago to the Panama City in the Canal Zone. During World War II, the city was a major ship-building and armaments center as well as a temporary home for thousands of war workers. Today a series of beach access points and community beaches start well west of the city and continue at regular intervals to the east side of Panama City. They all have full day-use facilities. The Dan Russell City Pier built in 1978 is an area landmark and reportedly the longest fishing pier in the Gulf of Mexico.

A little further west is **St. Andrews State Recreation Area**, located off SR 392 (4415 Thomas Drive, Panama City, FL 32408; 904-234-2522). In addition to the main area, easily accessible by road, there is a primitive section on the western third of Shell Island, accessible only by boat. St. Andrews has 1,063 acres, bounded by the Gulf of Mexico, the Grand Lagoon, and the ship channel. If you tire of the beach and want a bit of history, check out the reconstructed Cracker turpentine still near the fishing pier. Note also, along one shoreline of the park, the stumps of an ancient forest — now submerged by the rise in sealevel. The park's waterfront camping sites are particularly popular. This park gets very busy in the summer.

Eastern Panhandle (Apalachicola Area)

The sometimes-congested, sometimes-boring stretch of U.S. 98 around Panama City and Tyndall Air

Force Base divides the eastern part of the panhandle's Gulf coast from its central and western ends. It takes about an hour in the best of conditions and there really is no alternative route. **Mexico Beach** on the eastern edge of this great divide has good beaches and numerous access points. The Mexico Beach Canal Park includes a canal with ample docking facilities, a short jetty, and beach access to the west. This is a pleasant area with interesting activity along the canal, picnic tables, and restrooms back toward the road. The only thing lacking here is shade. The city also has a fishing pier on 37th Street and a Beach Front Public Park with a good-sized parking area. The town is heavily residential with small cinder block cottages, mobile homes, and some townhouses.

Further east in Gulf County there are a series of beaches, none particularly outstanding except for **T. H. Stone Memorial St. Joseph Peninsula State Park** off SR 30-E, off U.S. 98, near Port St. Joe (Star Rt. 1 Box 200, Port St. Joe, FL 32456; 904-227-1327). Beaches here have coarser sand than those further west, better for shelling. Here the water is more blue than green. On a calm day the coast looks like a pastel painting with every shade of blue and aqua imaginable, and waves make the slightest white scallop along the shore. Some of the bath houses, which look quite ordinary on the outside, have spiffy new white tile dressing rooms and toilet stalls with natural wood finished doors. The park, surrounded by water, has 20 miles of white-sand beaches, freshwater ponds, and salt marshes, with striking dune formations.

If you have a boat you may want to visit the beaches on **St. Vincent National Wildlife Refuge**, off St. Vincent Sound, just east of St. Joseph Peninsula. There are boat launch sites at Indian Pass, 21 miles west of Apalachicola on SR 30B, and at Apalachicola.

Apalachicola doesn't have beaches of its own, but is within easy reach of both St. Joseph Peninsula and St. George Island. It is a lovely small town, its streets lined with Victorian houses, a good place to stay or explore. This is a place for great seafood — over 90% of the state's oysters are harvested around the Apalachicola Bay area. The tourist information center here, housed in the David G. Raney House has an especially good collection of literature about regional attractions.

St. George Island is one of the best examples of Florida's Gulf coast barrier islands. It has 29 miles of near-primitive beaches bordered by the Gulf of Mexico on the south and Apalachicola Bay on the north. The island is linked to the mainland off U.S. 98 at Eastpoint, by a bridge and causeway 4.2 miles long. **Dr. Julian G. Bruce St. George Island State Park** (Box 62, Eastpoint, FL 32328; 904-670-2111) occupies 1,883 acres at the eastern end of the island. This is a wonderful park with camping, hiking, nature study, and shelling as well as miles of white beaches.

A little further along is **Carrabelle Beach** located one mile west of Carrabelle on U.S. 98/319. It has a gradual sloping beach on St. George Sound. Nearby **Dog Island**, available by a toll ferry, has isolated white-sand beaches just off the coast of Carrabelle.

There aren't many beaches along Florida's Big Bend where the west coast bends down toward the peninsula. The explorer who fantasizes wonderful, undiscovered sandy shores at the end of the roads that wind through swampland out to the Gulf of Mexico will be sorely disappointed. They are simply not there, even when the end-point has the word beach in the name. Mud flats roll out for miles in some places. Boaters and anglers find this a wonderful place. Its very lack of beaches has saved it from major development and it is a good place to see Old Florida. If you enjoy exploring

out-of-the-way places, like to get away from the commercial world, and don't really care whether you find
a beach or not, this area is worth a visit.

Central West Region

Although the beaches don't really begin again until
around Tarpon Springs, there is one spot west of Crystal River. **Fort Island Gulf Beach** has natural, fine
white sand, parking, shower facilities, and outstanding sunsets. It is located at the western end of Route 44.
Around Bay Port and Pine Island, **Alfred A. Mc-
Kethan County Park** maintains a small, sandy beach,
picnic shelters, restrooms, and a parking area.

From Tarpon Springs south, sandy beaches stretch
down the coast in an almost uninterrupted ribbon of
white to the Everglades. Pinellas County has 28 miles
of them in offshore barrier islands which remain in
their natural state alongside major beach resorts. This
area has been heavily developed and is close to the
large population centers of Tampa and St. Petersburg.
Every beach activity one could imagine can be found
here along with a glittering nightlife, extensive shopping, good restaurants, and luxury accommodations.

Anclote Key State Preserve (Caladesi Island State
Park, #1 Causeway Blvd., Dunedin, FL 34698; 813-443-
5903) is the northernmost island in the 320-mile-long
barrier island system of west peninsular Florida. It is
believed by scientists to be about 1,000 years old and
in an era when much attention is being focused on the
erosion of beaches, it has grown about 30% in size
since 1957. In addition to its beautiful four-mile beach
and picturesque 1887 lighthouse, the park supports six
distinct biological communities and dozens of species
of birdlife including the rare red cockaded wood-
pecker, bald eagle, and piping plover. There is nothing

on this island except nature. It is accessible only by boat; visitors who wish to camp or swim must bring all their water and supplies and carry all their litter home.

Other beaches in Tarpon Springs include **Howard County Park,** a fully developed beach connected to the mainland by a mile-long causeway, one half mile north of Keystone Road. (SR 582) on Florida Avenue N., and **Sunset Beach,** with a municipal pier located at the end of Gulf Road.

Two of the outstanding beaches in this area, where you really can have your own space, especially if you go off season or during the week, are **Honeymoon Island State Recreation Area** (#1 Causeway Blvd., Dunedin, FL 34698; 813-734-4255) and **Caladesi Island State Park** (#1 Causeway Blvd., Dunedin, FL 34698; 813-443-5903). These two islands were one before 1921, when a hurricane carved out Hurricane Pass between them. Honeymoon Island used to be called Hog Island until a New York developer constructed 50 palm-thatched "honeymoon" bungalows for couples who won a contest sponsored by major northern department stores in 1939. The bungalows are gone, but the honeymoon feeling is still there, and it's much nicer to write home about "Honeymoon Island" than "Hog Island."

The island has mangrove swamps, tidal flats, and a stand of virgin slash pine. Most important to the beachcomber, it has over 10,000 feet of beachfront with dune walkovers, picnic areas, and group facilities. The park is north of Dunedin, across the Dunedin causeway at the extreme west end of SR 586. Caladesi Island, accessible only by boat, is a 20-minute ferry ride from Honeymoon Island Park. The ferry departs hourly on weekdays from 10 a.m. to 5 p.m. and every half hour on weekends and holidays from 10 a.m. to 6 p.m., with reduced service from December through

February. The maximum time allowed on the island is four hours. Round trip fare is $3.75 for adults and $2.10 for children. For information about ferry service call 813-734-5263. Private boaters may utilize the 99-slip bayside marina or anchor offshore. Overnight docking is limited to 20 vessels from March through Labor Day. Caladesi has two miles of developed beach, picnic shelters, nature trails, and a small concession stand. Don't expect to buy extensive supplies there, however. You will do best to take most of your picnic with you, as well as extra clothes, rain gear, and the like. There really isn't much except sun, sand, and sea, but what else could a beachcomber ask?

As you work your way down the coast you come to **Clearwater Beach Island** which lies between Clearwater Beach and the Gulf of Mexico. It is connected to the Clearwater central business district by Memorial Causeway (SR 60) and has several beaches, all developed, lifeguarded areas with a full range of activities.

Beaches string along the barrier islands like a necklace. If you are really into a beach survey you may want to check them out one by one. Several are Pinellas County parks, noted for their especially attractive landscaping. Others are municipal beaches. **Indian Rocks Beach** is really made up of seven individual communities: Belleair Bluffs, Belleair Beach, Indian Shores, Indian Rocks Beach, North Redington Beach, Redington Shores, and Redington Beach. **Madeira Beach**, an informal fishing village, with nearby John's Pass Beach and Park, is a center for anglers. Especially well known is the **Treasure Island Beach**, once a hideout for pirates. **St. Petersburg Beach** has over seven and a half miles of sand and a full range of accommodations. At the southern end is **Pass-a-Grille Beach Park**, a popular gathering place for young sunbathers in an area of quaint homes and low-rise buildings.

Fort De Soto Park (St. Petersburg County Bldg., 150 5th Street, North, Room 63, St. Petersburg; 813-866-2662) is built on five islands with seven miles of waterfront and almost three miles of fine swimming beaches. Ponce de Leon anchored here in 1513 to clean his ship of barnacles. During the Civil War the park was used as a coastal defense point and visitors today can still explore the fort. Access is via the Pinellas Bayway (SR 679), a tollway. This is a well-developed recreation area with camping, fishing, and bicycle facilities, as well as abundant bird, plant, and animal life.

Tampa has only one salt-water beach. It is **Ben T. Davis Municipal Beach**, a stretch of sand lying along the Courtney Campbell Causeway, the nine-mile drive linking Tampa and Clearwater. It is well landscaped and the sand is soft and white. This gets crowded, however. You may want to travel further afield.

Manatee County has 20 miles of beaches. All the county's beaches may be reached from I-75 or U.S. 41 by taking either Manatee Avenue (SR 64) or Cortez Road (SR 684) to Longboat and Anna Maria Keys. They all run along the Gulf side of the keys and have a small-town, easy-going character. Access is provided at some street ends, but parking is a problem. **Palm Sola Causeway**, the Manatee Avenue causeway across Palm Sola Bay, has a long sandy beach fronting the bay with boat ramps, a dock, and picnic tables. **Greer Island**, at the north end of Longboat Key, is a secluded peninsula with a wide beach and excellent shelling. It is accessible by boat or North Shore Blvd.

Egmont Key National Wildlife Refuge at the mouth of Tampa Bay, accessible only by boat, is a two-and-a-half-mile-long stretch of sand and sea oats with a rather violent history. You can still see the crumbling ruins of Fort Dade, built in 1900 during the Spanish

American War. If you don't have your own boat you can take the *Miss Cortez*, an excursion craft leaving every Tuesday and Thursday afternoon from Cortez, a fishing village just west of Bradenton on SR 684 and the Intracoastal Waterway. For reservations and information call 813-794-1223.

The **Sarasota** area shoreline is a chain of peninsulas and barrier islands with soft white sands. Although many private homes, clubs, and condominiums on the beach minimize public access, there are still several good public beaches and plenty to do, no matter what the weather. **Lido Key** offers great beach areas, all accessible from Sarasota on SR 789. **South Lido Beach,** is a county park with a wide range of recreational opportunities. A plus for this area on a hot day is that much of the parking is shaded.

Siesta Key, a large barrier island, has numerous public beaches with good facilities. The sand here is especially fine and white, the water is clear, and there is still an offbeat character about the place. This is the home of John MacDonald, creator of that ingenious Florida adventurer, Travis McGee, and there is a substantial colony of writers and artists here. However these very attributes make it especially popular and often crowded. **Siesta Public Beach** located mid-island off Beach Road, is visited by as many as 18,000 people on a weekend. **Crescent Beach,** just south, is the location of Point of Rocks, where snorkelers can see sea sponges, small fish, and other underwater wonders. The view at this crescent shaped-beach is breathtaking either below or above water. **Turtle Beach,** smaller, and less crowded, is toward the southern end of the island.

The most remote beaches in this area are on the next island down, **Casey Key,** reachable from SR 789. **North Jetty Park,** at the south end of Casey Key Road is one of the Gulf's best surfing beaches and a favorite with anglers.

The City of Venice, patterned after its namesake in Italy, has a large well-maintained public beach and a long concrete fishing pier. **Venice Municipal Beach,** 600 feet long, is developed and has lifeguards. **Caspersen Park Beach** is considered the best shelling beach in the Venice area and fossil sharks' teeth are often found here. It has two miles of virtually untouched beachfront which remain relatively uncrowded throughout the year. There are picnic tables in shaded wooded areas and a boardwalk. Further south, Manasota Key has three public beaches along its long stretch of private homes. All are accessible from SR 775. **Manasota Beach,** at the west end of Manasota Bridge, has lifeguards year-round. It is at the west end of Manasota Bridge. **Blind Pass Beach,** 2,000 feet long is undeveloped and especially nice. **Indian Mounds Park,** named for a historic Indian mound, is along Lemon Bay.

Southwest Region

Charlotte County is named for Charlotte Harbor, which intrudes into the mainland and is the largest indentation in the southwest Florida coast. Although the county is only 17 miles long, north to south, it has over 120 miles of coastline. Punta Gorda, the lovely county seat, sits directly on Charlotte Harbor. Towering palms line its streets and the waterfront district combines shopping, boating, and park complexes to serve many needs. This is a prime fishing area, but the range of beaches is very limited because the islands off the coast are undeveloped and inaccessible by land. The beaches that are here, however, are pleasant. Look for **Englewood Beach** (access via SR 776 from the mainland) and **Port Charlotte Beach Park**, at the southern end of Manasota Key (accessible from SR 776). **Don Pedro Island State Recreation Area** (Cayo Costa State Park, P.O. Box 1150, Boca Grande, FL 33921; 813-964-0375) is on a barrier island between Knight Island and Little Gasparilla Island, reachable only by boat.

Lee County includes 51.5 miles of sandy beach, mostly located on the Gulf side of its many barrier islands. The northernmost island, Gasparilla, accessible from Charlotte County via the Boca Grande (toll) Causeway at CR 775 and Placida, has a colorful history and remains relatively unspoiled. Legend has it that the infamous pirate Jose Gaspar settled on the island in the 1700s and hid his treasure here. There is no sign of pirates today — or of the treasure, unfortunately — but Boca Grande, founded by the wealthy DuPont family at the turn of the century, has wonderful old houses, a bicycle path running the entire length of the island, an enchanting street lined with tangle-limbed banyan trees, and a lazy tropical feel about it. Gasparilla is also a world-famous spot for sport fishing, notably for tarpon.

The **Gasparilla Island State Recreation Area** (Cayo Costa State Park, P.O. Box 1150, Boca Grande, FL 33921; 813-964-0375) allows everyone to enjoy this area's beaches. The park offers picnicking, swimming, fishing, nature study, and shelling. There are several other beach access points on the island. The **Boca Grande Beach Park** provides a white sandy beach and plenty of shade trees, with picnicking, restrooms, and fishing. Turn right at the four-way stop after you cross the causeway. There is a $1.00 fee. **Boca Grande Lighthouse Park**, along SR 771 at the southern end of Gasparilla Island, has fishing, picnicking, and a beach, but swimming is not recommended because of the strong current.

Cayo Costa and Upper Captiva, the next two barrier islands, are mostly owned by the county and state, which intend to preserve their natural condition. **Cayo Costa State Park** (P.O. Box 1150, Boca Grande, FL 33921; 813-964-0375) is accessible only by private boat or ferry from Punta Gorda (813-639-0969) or Pine Island (813-283-0015). It has unique vegetation, Indian mounds, colorful birds, and shelling. The island has a camping area and twelve rustic cabins at its northern end. There are no stores and no electricity. No reservations are needed for tent camping. For cabins call 813-966-3594; Monday to Friday.

Sanibel Island and more remote **Captiva Island** are world famous for their shelling beaches. More varieties are found here than anywhere else on the continent. They can be reached from the mainland by a toll Causeway (SR 867). Even if you don't get excited about shelling, you may want to spend some time here. The islands offer a noncommercial atmosphere —viewed as a model of thoughtful environmental planning and controlled development. There are no high rise buildings and several public and private nature preserves, including the J. N. "Ding" Darling National Wildlife Refuge, which has a third of the world's population of roseate spoonbills, a rare and endangered pink wading bird. It was on Captiva that Anne Morrow Lindberg wrote *A Gift From the Sea*. The island is like a tropical paradise, its main road a narrow tunnel through lacy Australian pines, crowded on each side by lush vegetation from private estates. Much of the island is either privately owned or controlled by South Seas Plantation, an exclusive resort closed to all but its guests.

You may feel that you could spend all your time

right here on Sanibel Island, but before you make that decision you should know that there are more than 100 barrier islands on this part of the coast. If you want to explore them you can take a shelling charter, sign up for a cruise, or rent a boat on your own. The Island Visitor's Center, to the right just as you come off the causeway, has brochures for several marinas, tours, and guides. If you really get hooked on shelling, you may want to visit in early March during the annual Sanibel Shell Fair, which draws participants from around the world. Regardless of when you are there, you may want to invest in one or both of two recent island publications available in many stores: *The Sanibel Captiva Handbook* by John and Helma Reynolds (Jonathan Summer Pub., P.O. Box 1084, Captiva Island, FL 33924) or *The Best of Sanibel and Captiva Islands* (ed.) Joan S. Hooper (Landmark Pub. Inc., Box 929, Sanibel Island, FL 33957). Both are full of historic tidbits, information about local shops and restaurants, and great enthusiasm for life on these special islands.

All of the island beaches open up long expanses of sand and sea. **Turner Beach**, situated at Blind Pass between Sanibel and Captiva islands off SR 867 is prime shelling territory and gives good access to Captiva, which has almost no public parking. It is also a great place to view the west coast sunsets. Parking is limited, however, and dangerous currents limit swimming. You may find more space at **Bowman's Beach** a nicely developed country park on Sanibel with a $2 parking fee. **Gulfside City Park**, located off Casa Ybel Road offers free parking, swimming, and picnicking in lovely shaded areas. **Tarpon Bay Road** also offers beach access and parking. **Sanibel Lighthouse Park**, near the historic lighthouse on the southern tip, has swimming, picnicking, pier fishing, and free parking.

This is a popular spot for boats to anchor just off-shore for fishing and swimming.

Estero Island, frequently referred to as **Fort Myers Beach** is heavily developed, but still retains a residential, easy going atmosphere with low buildings and plenty of foliage. The area has a gentle slope and absence of riptides, it is a good site for a family vacation. There is beach access at regular intervals. **Lynn Hall Memorial Park,** a county park located next to the fishing pier at the northern end of the island, has swimming, picnicking, restrooms, showers, a playground and limited, metered parking. Beware, traffic patterns around the bridge and county park are crazy. Don't despair if it takes two or three times around the block to get where you want to go.

Below Estero Island on CR 865 is a lovely long stretch of sea and sky, **Lover's Key State Recreation Area** (Delnor-Wiggins Pass State Recreation Area, 11100 Gulf Shore Drive North, Naples, FL 33963; 813-597-6196). It is undeveloped at this time and has limited facilities. **Carl Johnson Park,** however, is developed and covers three small islands — Lover's Key, Inner Key and Black Island. There are picnic tables along the road and good spots for fishing. Beach-goers ride a tram across wooden bridges and down sandy paths through the area's unique mangrove ecosystem to a secluded beach and picnic area. Admission is $1.50 for adults, and 75 cents for children. South of Carl Johnson Park, **Bonita Beach Park** rises in a stand of condos, but below that the profile is low, with a sense of quiet and space. It is especially noted for its good surf fishing. Admission is free. Just below it is **Barefoot Beach,** a shelly spread of sand with little vegetation and an unsophisticated air about it. It has a picnic area and volleyball.

Below Barefoot Beach is the **Delnor-Wiggins Pass**

State Recreation Area (11100 Gulf Shore Drive North, Naples, FL 33963; 813-597-6196) on a narrow barrier island, separated from the mainland by mangrove swamps and tidal creeks. There is Gulf-front swimming, fishing, and boating in a lush setting of sea oats, sea grapes, cabbage palms and mangroves. Shaded picnic tables face the Gulf. There are bicycle racks, beach front bath houses, and an observation tower that gives a good view of the area. Below that is **Vanderbilt Beach** which provides walkway access to two miles of undeveloped beach along Gulf Shore Boulevard. It is also accessible by road at the west end of Vanderbilt Beach Road.

Clam Pass Collier County Park is at the intersection of Gulf Shore Boulevard N. and Park Shore Drive in Naples. There is a small fee for parking and the beach is reached by riding a continually circling electric tram or walking the three-quarter-mile-long boardwalk through lush mangrove forests, lagoons, and tidal creeks. Sands in this part of Florida are very white quartz mixed with shell fragments that have been carried southward by rivers and shore currents from Alabama, through Georgia and northern Florida. Sunglasses are an absolute necessity. The small tidal range of three feet minimizes beach erosion. Although this is the second largest county in land area in Florida, it is relatively unpopulated and over 70% of its land area is under preservation. The main city in this area is Naples, an affluent community with clusters of specialty boutiques and good seafood restaurants along the river in picturesque Tin City. **Naples Municipal Beach** has frequent street-end access to the Gulf of Mexico with metered parking areas (25¢ for 20 minutes) and a fishing pier at 12th Avenue South. **Lowdermilk Park**, a shady city park with fine wide sand and volleyball nets. The latter tends to be crowded, with lots of teenagers on weekends.

Marco Island has the most southerly beach along the west coast. It sits right along the Gulf Stream and on the map it looks like it should be isolated and remote. But be prepared. It has been discovered and developed with hundreds of condominiums. **Tigertail Beach,** in a suburban area on the outskirts of town, is nevertheless a marvelous beach. It has full facilities including a children's playground and a pleasant outdoor restaurant and is reached by a system of wooden walkovers from Hernando Drive. To the left you can walk with unobstructed views along unoccupied dunes. At low tide it is easy to get to an offshore sand bar, which is full of nesting and baby birds in June. The sight of thousands of tiny legs darting thither and yon along the water's edge leaves one quite dizzy.

CHAPTER 13

BEACHES II

OCEAN AND KEYS

Northeast Region

Visitors who drive past Florida's northeastern shore in their eagerness to get further south are missing some of the nicest beaches and towns in the state. Amelia Island, just over the border from Georgia has thirteen miles of unspoiled beach. Its main town, historical Fernandina Beach, possesses blocks of Victorian houses and several good restaurants. **Fort Clinch State Park** (2601 Atlantic Ave., Fernandina Beach, FL 32034; 904-261-4212) on the northern end of the island, provides excellent swimming, camping by the sea, a fishing pier, and a well-preserved fort which you can tour. This is a good place to look for prehistoric shark's teeth, which can really put your life in perspective. The darker, fossilized ones are 15-25 million years old!

You will find this a hospitable place if you ride horseback. It is one of the few locations in Florida where you can still ride on the beach. Contact Sea Horse Stable (U.S. A1A, 904-261-4878) at the south end of the island for rental.

The lack of high-rise buildings and the predominately residential character of the island gives it a sense of openness, although recent development is changing the landscape of its southern tip. On land that was once designated for strip mining, Amelia Island Plantation sprawls over 1,240 acres, bounded on one side by four miles of pristine beach and on the other by carefully preserved tidal marshlands. The resort was designed to fit into the natural environment and has won accolades for its success. Next to it, **Amelia Island State Recreation Area** (Fort Clinch State Park, 2601 Atlantic Ave., Fernandina Beach, FL 32034; 904-261-4212) opens 200 acres of beach to the public.

For a special excursion from Amelia Island, make reservations to take a National Park Service ferry over to **Cumberland Island National Seashore** from nearby St. Marys, Georgia (nine miles east of I-95, just north of the Florida-Georgia border). Cumberland Island is the longest undeveloped beach along the east coast, a retreat of the Carnegie family from the 1880s until the mid-20th century. There you can explore the ruins of Dungeness, Lucy Carnegie's own mansion, see Plum Orchard, a mansion built for one of the Carnegie children, and enjoy a natural area with long beaches, hiking trails, good fishing, camping, wildlife preserves, and historic sites.

Only a limited number of visitors are allowed on the island at any one time so stop by or call ahead for reservations (912-882-4335, 10 a.m.-2 p.m. Mon.-Fri.). The ferries leave St. Marys at 11:45 a.m. and return at 5:30 p.m. daily during the summer and every day but Tuesday and Wednesday the rest of the year. There are no supplies, other than water, on the island so take along food and whatever else you might need. If you want to stay overnight, you have a choice between camping and the privately-owned Greyfield Inn, one of the four original Carnegie homes.

There are several other beaches close to Jacksonville, each with its own special atmosphere. **Little Talbot Island State Park** (12157 Heckscher Dr., Fort

George, FL 32226; 904-251-3231) encompasses an unspoiled barrier island, one of a chain of unique islands
off the northeast coast of Florida. Its size and shape
have changed drastically over the years, sculpted by
wind, sea, and the natural movement of sand. It has 5.5
miles of glistening sandy beach along the Atlantic
Ocean, as well as a maze of salt marsh and tidal creeks
to the west, which are good for observing migratory
birds and other estuary life. The long stretch of relatively unused beach in the middle of the island is
especially appealing to the beachcomber who seeks
solitude. Little Talbot Island has some good waves for
body surfing. It is 17 miles northeast of Jacksonville on
A1A.

Big Talbot Island (c/o Little Talbot Island State Park,
12157 Heckscher Dr., Fort George, FL 32226; 904-251-
3231) just to the north is now a state park also. It is
undeveloped, but has several miles of beach along
with a picnic area and some trails. **Huguenot Memorial Park** (10980 Heckscher Dr., Jacksonville, FL 32226)
is a Jacksonville city park just below Little Talbot Island State Park at the southern tip of Fort George
Island. It has two miles of beach, with boating facilities, fishing, picnicking, and camping. Huguenot is the
only park in the area where you can drive on the
beach, but four-wheel drive is recommended

Further south is **Hanna Park** (500 Wonderland Dr.,
Atlantic Beach, FL 32233; 904-249-2316), a city and
county park with one and a half miles of unspoiled
beach. This nicely laid out, well-maintained park with
clean, hard sand is able to handle large crowds in the
summer. It has footpaths and nature trails, separate
(and shady) areas for tent and primitive camping, a
convenience store, concession stands, picnic areas, and
freshwater fishing. There are good restaurants in
nearby Atlantic Beach and Mayport.

Jacksonville Beach (JAX Beach), just twelve miles from the downtown area, is white, hard sand and good surf, extremely popular with local people. It is more crowded than the more residential, middle class **Neptune Beach** and **Atlantic Beach**. If you like your beach surrounded by commercial hubbub, head for Jacksonville Beach. It has a casual atmosphere, a variety of people, and is the center of the area's tourist trade. A little further down the coast, in St. John's County, are **Ponte Verde Beach** and **South Ponte Verde Beach**. These provide miles of mostly primitive ocean beach. The former is in a town of old money manses, near the new-money mansions of the town of Sawgrass.

St. Augustine has history, color, interesting accommodations, and wonderful beaches a few minutes away. The beaches are firm-packed and wide and motor vehicles are permitted on almost all of them. Some have very strong tides, run-outs, and under-tows so it's important to be cautious. Here, in particular, avoid swimming alone. If you do get caught in a strong tide, swim parallel to the shore until you find a place where you can swim safely back in. If a raft or toy is swept out, let it go! If you enjoy shelling, look for sand dollars, moon snails, olive and scallop shells, jack-knife clam shells, angel wings, and pen shells. During certain times of the year, you can also see beds of "periwinkles," tiny multi-colored mollusks that surface above the sand as water flows over them, then disappear as the waves flow back.

Guana River State Park (2690 South Ponte Vedra Blvd. Ponte Vedra Beach, FL 32082; 904-825-5071), on the Intracoastal waterway five miles north of St. Augustine off SR A1A, encompasses several miles of beach on the Atlantic with grainy sand, lots of shells and a wild untamed feeling.

On the coast south of St. Augustine there is a long

stretch of beaches with firm white sand. **Anastasia State Recreation Area** (5 Anastasia Park Dr., St. Augustine, FL 32085; 904-471-3033)) offers a fully developed beach and some of the best swimming close to the city. It is also one of the busiest parks in Florida. Reservations are a must for camping. When wind and waves are high along the ocean, try Salt Run Lagoon, which offers more protection. Anastasia is a drive-on beach; access is 2,000 feet north of Pope Road.

St. Augustine Beach extends along SR A1A from Pope Road south to St. Augustine-by-the-Sea. Vehicles are permitted on the beach from here south to Matanzas Inlet. Three beaches with easy access from A1A to the whole shoreline are **Unnamed Beach, Frank B. Butler Park**, which fronts on both the ocean and the Intracoastal Waterway and has full facilities and **Crescent Beach**.

Matanzas Beach, three miles in length, lies within the boundary of the Fort Matanzas National Monument, where the Spanish murdered the French Huguenots who founded Fort Caroline. Further down the coast, **Marineland Acres** has a beach with swimming and fishing.

There is a fairly long stretch of minimally developed coastline below Marineland until you reach Palm Coast, the area's newest community. Planning started in 1969, and when completed the town will include 42,000 acres of homes, shopping centers, industrial parks, and various amenities. Just south of it is **Flagler Beach**, an old community which strings out for a mile or so along a relatively treeless shoreline ridge. The beach here is soft, brown grainy sand. Below it, the **Flagler Beach State Recreation Area** (3100 South A1A, Flagler Beach, FL 32136; 904-439-2474) is a popular camping area, booked solid most of the year. The campsites overlook the Atlantic Ocean, but the lack of trees make them rather warm. The park extends across the barrier island to the Intracoastal Waterway on the western side where there is an excellent boat basin, picnic area, and nature trail.

Central East Region

Whether your taste runs toward wild undeveloped beaches or busy commercial ones, you can find what you want along the central east shore of Florida. This coastline with its long string of barrier islands, is separated from the interior central region by miles of sawgrass and palmetto, with few roads and fewer towns. There is a lot of shoreline here to keep the beachcomber occupied. At its northern end, there are other attractions as well. In fact, the problem in this section of Florida is that the concentration of tourist attractions is so overwhelming that it may be hard to find time for the beach. Not only is there Daytona Beach with its fascinating history of auto racing, there is also inland Orlando which has a growing list of cultural and recreational activities. The top attraction of the area is, of course, Walt Disney World with the Kennedy Space Center running a close second.

North of Daytona Beach, **Ormond-by-the Sea** and **Ormond Beach** are long established residential communities with good public access to their beaches. In the 1800s, the Ormond Beach area became known as "Millionaire's Colony," frequented by Vanderbilts, Astors, and Rockefellers. To see how these folks lived, visit The Casements, former winter home of John D. Rockefeller, and the adjacent Rockefeller Gardens. Don't be intimidated by the moneyed atmosphere, however. There are many public beach access points for you here if you find this area, with softer sand and mainly local users to your taste.

For many of us, **Daytona Beach** is synonymous with auto racing. And from the early 1900s until the late 1950s, races were held on the Daytona Raceway, 23 miles of wide, firm white quartz sandy beach. When the International Raceway was constructed a few miles inland, the action moved there. But don't let anyone fool you; the speed limit may have dropped to 10 miles an hour on the beach, but the cars are still there. Lots of them. This is a drive-on beach par excellence. Daytona Beach is also a popular Spring break spot for college students and families.

If it's action you want, this may be the place you are looking for. Daytona probably has the most varied entertainment along this part of the coast. Check out The Boardwalk, directly north of the Main Street Pier and south of the bandshell. A stroll takes in approximately 1,700 feet of amusements, rides, and food. It is open daily from 9:00 a.m. to approximately 2:00 a.m. The recently refurbished Bandshell, which seats 800, features many outdoor concerts and special events. The Seaside Music Theater (904-252-6200) mounts productions year-round.

If you want to avoid the vehicles, head for areas either north or south of Daytona Beach itself, which are less crowded. And get up and out early, before the rest of the world gets its wheels on the sand. For beach walking, you can't find a better place. After all, what makes these hard-packed stretches so good for cars, also makes them good for mile upon mile of walking or running by the sea.

South of Daytona Beach, **Daytona Beach Shores** and **Wilbur-by-the Sea** are less developed. **Ponce Inlet Park** (Lighthouse Point Park) (904-756-4958 or 904-254-2981) at the end of Atlantic Avenue has one of the prime beauty spots in the area. At one time part of the state park system, the beach is now administered by

Volusia County. It remains relatively undeveloped, but there are restrooms and lovely walkovers to the beach with roofed picnic tables and stunningly beautiful vistas of the ocean and inlet. The park is open 8 a.m. to 7:30 p.m.

If you go unprepared with a picnic lunch you can pick up something from the food vans that tour these drive-on beaches. In the Ponce Inlet area, there are also some charming seafood restaurants set unpretentiously along the waterfront. Here you can sit on a shady outdoor patio by the shore and while away the heat of the day or watch the sun go down.

You'll have to head inland to get around Ponce Inlet to New Smyrna Beach and Canaveral National Seashore/Apollo Beach. If you find the Daytona Beach area a little too busy and crowded, you may want to make the trip. **New Smyrna Beach** is amazingly untouched by the high-rises and hurly-burly of Florida's population boom. Tall condominiums are coming, but they don't totally dominate the landscape yet. Much of the beach front is residential and there are even a few of those small, one-story horseshoe-shaped motels left.

New Smyrna calls itself the "World's Safest Bathing Beach." It is wide, with a long, gentle slope; the sand is firm and good for walking or shelling, especially if you get out early, before the drivers. You can also ride bicycles here or drive motorized three-wheelers. Vehicles are prohibited further south around **Bethune Beach**.

If you continue south along the coast you'll find **Apollo Beach**, the northern segment of **Canaveral National Seashore** (Cape Canaveral National Seashore Headquarters, 2532 Garden St., Titusville, FL 33090; 904-428-3384). There is nothing for miles except soft sand, sea, dunes, and palmettos. You can fish, swim, and collect shells here much as the prehistoric Indians did. Evidence of these early residents is plentiful. Turtle Mound is a 35-foot-tall pile of oyster shells assembled by the Surreque Indians sometime between 600 and 1200 A.D.

On the west of this wild and wonderful beach is Mosquito Lagoon, beautiful, and a prime fishing spot. But take your insect repellent. The lagoon is aptly named! The dunes, Mosquito Lagoon, and the marshes and woodlands preserved in the area attract a rich variety of wildlife — wading birds and marsh birds, migrating waterfowl, finfish, shellfish, reptiles, and animals.

There is a small visitor's center a mile inside the park's entrance with exhibits and an audio-visual film. If you visit Apollo on a weekend or holiday in the spring or summer plan to get there early in the day. There is limited parking and when it is full the park closes to additional visitors. Note that it is not possible to travel directly from the northern part of Canaveral National Seashore to the southern part. You have to backtrack to Route 1.

The premier spot in the Orlando Area, if you like undeveloped natural beach, is the southern end of Canaveral National Seashore (407-867-4675). **Playalinda Beach** near Titusville takes some time to reach (take the A. Max Brewer Memorial Parkway from Titusville, then SR 402), but the only thing in sight along the long miles of oceanfront are the NASA rocket installations. Don't expect to see the shuttle blast-offs from here — the whole area is closed for several days prior to and immediately after these events. If even Playalinda is too populated for you, walk north along the beach to **Klondike Beach**, midway between it and Apollo. Klondike has 16 miles of remote, undeveloped oceanfront, accessible by foot only. The nearby Merritt

Island Wildlife Preserve provides an interesting array of birds and other wildlife in the area.

Fine beaches, easily accessible to Orlando, continue near Kennedy Space Center. **Jetty Park** (400 E. Jetty Rd., Cape Canaveral, FL 32920-2499; 407-783-7222) has 35 acres with full facilities. **Cocoa Beach** has experienced enormous growth and is heavily built up. It does, however, have some of the best surf on the east coast, and spectacular sites from which to watch shuttle launches.

Beach towns — **Satellite Beach, Indian Harbour Beach, Indialantic,** and **Melbourne Beach** — string one after another down the coast, predominately residential. Beaches in this area generally have steep slopes and hard-crashing waves, and are fairly heavily built up. Temperatures move a little higher as you go south, generally ranging from an average low of 50 degrees in January to an average high of 89 degrees in July.

Below Melbourne Beach, the high-rises thin out and crowds diminish. Inland from the coast there are few roads and almost no towns. The big attraction in this part of the state is row upon row of citrus trees. This is Indian River citrus country, from which some of the state's largest, sweetest grapefruit and oranges are shipped all over the world. There are no major population centers closeby to feed hordes of beachgoers onto these sands, and it shows. If you like big expanses of ocean and beaches where you don't have to fight for your own personal grains of sand, you may want to spend some time along this part of the Atlantic coast.

The area from Sebastian Island to St. Lucia Inlet is popularly known as the Treasure Coast, because of the $14 million in gold and silver lost when eleven Spanish ships from Havana sank here during a violent hurricane in 1715. The three main communities on the coast, all county seats, are Vero Beach, Fort Pierce, and Stuart. The area has several attractive state recreation areas and frequent beach access points.

Sebastian Inlet State Recreation Area (9700 South A1A, Melbourne Beach, FL 32951; 407-984-4852) is a delight. The Gulf Stream runs close to the shore here, making this one of the premier saltwater fishing locations on Florida's east coast. In the winter, surfing is reportedly the best in the state. Campgrounds are heavily shaded and many face directly on the inlet. There are year-round interpretative programs, and the visitor center, built on the site of a Spanish treasure-salvage camp, is especially fun.

Vero Beach is an affluent, quiet community with avenues of coconut palms and a lazy, easy atmosphere. This is the northern edge of Florida's tropical zone where climate, vegetation, and ocean begin to take on that special quality of the tropics. The town has good public beaches, protected by off-shore coral reefs and accessed through four city-owned parks and numerous beach-access walkways. The rusted hulk of the S.S. *Breckenshire*, which sank in 1894, provides sanctuary for multitudes of fish, and is an interesting spot for scuba divers. Below Vero Beach are Avalon Park and Bryn Mawr, both with small beaches and beach access points.

Fort Pierce Inlet State Recreation Area/North Jetty Park, four miles east of Fort Pierce via North Causeway to Atlantic Beach Boulevard (2200 Atlantic Beach Blvd., Fort Pierce, FL 34949; 407-468-3985) has four very different day-use areas and a full range of recreational activities. Jack Island preserves 631 acres of mangrove as a bird sanctuary with nature trails. The narrow road into this area is a little hard to find, but it is worth the search. At the end of a driveway that's hard to see from the highway, a footbridge leads across the water. Across from Jack Island, Pepper Beach has fine sand, boardwalks, a bathhouse, and an especially pleasant picnic area.

The main visitor area for the park is at Fort Pierce Inlet. A small history museum displays Spanish gold salvaged offshore. Surfing is permitted outside swimming areas — beaches on the north of the inlet have the best waves because of the rock jetty. On the south side of the Inlet there is good public access to both undeveloped and guarded beaches at the northern tip of Hutchinson Island, starting with **South Jetty Park**, a small area with a fishing pier and beach directly on the ocean. Below that is **North Beach Boardwalk**, with a wide boardwalk along a narrow, stony beach and the **Surfside Beach Park** with the JacCee Park just across the road. **Hutchinson Island** is a real find if you like to get "away from it all." Once you leave Fort Pierce there isn't anything (except the St. Lucie nuclear power plant) until you get to the southern end of the island. The wide, white sandy beach runs almost uninterrupted for miles. St. Lucie County gives access to this unspoiled coastline in a series of attractive day-use beaches with guarded swimming areas. **Jan Brooks Park** and **Frederick Douglass Memorial Park** are like real beach wilderness.

Frederick Douglass is especially beautiful. Although it is just off A1A on a wide, dirt road, it seems far from modern Florida. The surf rolls in against the forested shore as far as you can see in either direction. There is not a high-rise in sight. Picnic shelters encircle a grassy area with a playground. A special feature here is a horse trail to the beach.

There are several other St. Lucie County beaches along A1A, if one keeps a sharp eye out for them. The turn-offs are all identified with signs, but they are not advertised in advance. Look for **Middle Cove, Blind**

Creek, **Walton Rocks** (which prohibits R.V. units because it is down a very narrow dirt road), **Herman's Bay**, and **Normandy Beach**. All have developed beaches in naturalistic settings with access to miles of shoreline. The high-rise world does encroach visually on the beaches toward the southern end of the island, but it is still some distance away. This is good surfing territory, by the way, and when the waves are right you can join the crowd with a board or watch the action from the shore.

Hutchinson Island has recently been discovered by real estate developers who have saturated its southern end with tall condominium resorts and "private property" signs. These and rows of trees along the northern portion of A1A block out views of the water so the route is not especially scenic. If you don't plan to explore the beaches, you might want to stay on SR 707 on the mainland and wend your way down the Indian River.

Whichever route you take, head for the ocean again at Jensen Beach or Stuart. This is beautiful shoreline and Martin County has developed a series of especially attractive areas which have lifeguards, picnic tables, restrooms, outdoor showers, and dune walkovers. Their blue identifying signs are sometimes a little hard to spot from a car until you are past the turnoff. Here, as elsewhere, you may have to do a little backtracking. Look especially for **Jensen Beach Park** at SR 707A and A1A, and **Bob Graham Beach** just south of it. **Stuart Beach** is near the southern causeway between Stuart and Hutchinson Island, right beside the Elliott Museum. In fact, if "vegging out" on beaches is affecting your brain and you feel the need for some intellectual stimulation, you have the chance here to visit a museum without even leaving the beach parking lot. **The Elliott Museum** (407-225-1961), named after American inventor Sterling Elliott, includes an old-fashioned turn-of-the-century apothecary shop, local history displays, classic automobiles, and a gallery for contemporary art. It is open 1 to 4 p.m. daily, except Monday.

At unique **Bathtub Reef**, an offshore reef forms a calm, shallow "bathtub" where snorkeling and swimming are excellent. It is especially recommended for small children. The two causeways across the Indian River are also pleasant shoreline areas. This whole area is good for bicyclists. There is a network of trails around the southern part of the island that connects several of the beaches

Hutchinson Island beaches are nesting areas for several thousand endangered Atlantic loggerhead, green, and leatherback sea turtles. The loggerhead turtle, weighing about 250 pounds, is the most frequent nester. If you want to learn more about the turtles or perhaps actually participate in the "Turtle Watch" public awareness program during June or July, stop in to inquire about reservations at the Environmental Studies Center in Jensen Beach on Indian River Drive (open Mon.-Fri. 9 a.m.-3 p.m.) or the Jensen Beach Chamber of Commerce. The evening program begins at the center with a slide show about the natural history of the sea turtle, then moves to the beach with trained staff to actually observe a nesting turtle.

Southeast Region

Southeastern Florida, referred to as the "Gold Coast," is a study in extremes. It is the site of some of the most crassly commercial development in the world and also one of the most untamed wilderness areas in America. Palm Beach on the northern end is exclusive and private. Miami in the south is a major international city, pulsating with a Latin-American flavor. Its neighbor, Miami Beach, was for years the epitome of tropical beach glitter until erosion almost destroyed its beach. Today with a newly renourished beach and lots of renovation, it is once again taking its place as a premier resort area. In the middle is Fort Lauderdale, commercial and lively, a place of special memories for a generation of college students who flocked there for spring break.

In between these well-known cities, several smaller communities express their own particular personalities. Far southwest of them all, connected by a long ribbon of road, is Key West where Florida Conchs, descendants of generations of wreckers and salvagers, continue to make their living from the sea. There is a gradual increase of tempo — an infusion of energy — as you move south from the quiet coast north of Palm Beach toward Miami. As you continue on below Miami, the atmosphere changes again as the rhythm of the keys, long isolated from the rest of the peninsula, catches and slows the traveler.

This part of Florida is crowded. There are big cities and big city problems. Miami's metropolitan area has a population of almost two million. But everywhere the blue of the ocean and sky, the white of the beaches, and the brilliance of the Florida sunshine leave their own special glow upon the landscape. You know you are in Florida. To really understand Florida, one must spend some time here. Fortunately there are lots of good beaches where you can settle in during your stay.

Jupiter Island, just above West Palm Beach, has spectacular, unspoiled beaches. Especially remote is **St. Lucie Inlet State Recreation Area** accessible only by boat via the Intracoastal Waterway (Jonathan Dickinson State Park, 16450 S.E. Federal Highway, Hobe Sound, FL 33455; 407-744-7603). It has 2.5 miles of beach, a boardwalk, and a "worm reef" offshore, popular with divers.

Hobe Sound National Wildlife Refuge off Route 1 several miles north of Jupiter, has four miles of ocean beach. This is one of the most successful sea turtle nesting areas in the country. There are restrooms, an interpretative museum, a nature trail, saltwater fishing, and ocean swimming off North Beach Road. **Hobe Sound Beach** about two miles north of Bridge Road, and **Jupiter Island Park** at Bridge Road, both give access to long stretches of beach in a relatively unpopulated area on Jupiter Island. SR 707, which winds through Australian pines past shoreline mansions, is an attractive route down the coast.

One of the special places in this area is **Blowing Rocks Preserve** (P.O. Box 3795, Tequesta, FL 33469; 407-575-2297 or 407-747-3113, donation). Just off A1A, a mile south of the Martin County line, it is the largest Anastasia limestone outcropping on the Atlantic coast. The rocks, formed by the gradual accumulation of marine sediments, are remnants of an era when the sea covered this barrier reef and rolled all the way to the mainland. As the seas subsided, thousands of years of waves exposed and carved the rock into hollows and holes. Today it runs like a long sculpture along the tideline, with a fine sand beach and dunes above it. During severe winter storms, seas breaking against the rocks force tons of water skyward through the blowholes, creating a saltwater plume visible for miles. Unless you're lucky, you probably won't see such spectacular blowing if you are just passing through, but the place is worth a stop anyway.

The preserve, maintained by the Nature Conservancy stretches more than a mile along the shore and includes land on both sides of the road. The conservancy has removed all the Australian pines that formerly lined the shore and is restoring native Florida vegetation to the beach. There are nature trails through dunes covered with over 300 different species of plants. One thing you may notice as you wander through this and other restored dune areas is the fresh herb-like smell. Healthy dunes have a wonderful fragrance!

If you are really serious about your swimming, you may want to picnic and walk in this fascinating place and then move on down to **Jupiter Beach Park**, which has a developed beach of grainy, chocolate-colored sand with rocky outcroppings near the high-water mark. Take Beach Drive off SR A1A just south of Jupiter Inlet.

Municipalities maintain many of the beaches along this section of the coast and have devised various ways to discourage nonresidents from using them. Since they cannot actually prohibit public access to the beaches, they have restricted parking. Some communities limit beach lots to cars with residence stickers. Others install parking meters that take a quarter for every 15 or 20 minutes or have a maximum of two hours. Still other beaches can only be entered through a gate after payment of a hefty day-long parking fee of $8.00 or $10.00. As a general rule, beach access becomes more limited and more expensive as you move south. Beaches — and everything else — also become more crowded.

Palm Beach County, however, has several beaches, especially in its northern parts, which are free and nicely developed. Look for **DuBois Park, Jupiter Island Park,** (not the same as the one on Hobe Sound to the north), and **Carlin Park.** Carlin has wonderful wide beaches with lifeguards and a long string of protected and shaded two-table picnic shelters. Although the tables sit on the top of the dune line, most have only limited views of the water because of the thick seagrape windbreaks. There are also larger group shelters here, which do have ocean views. Access to the shelters from the parking lot is up a steep flight of steps, but there is a paved road between them so that they are accessible to the physically challenged. Along both sides of the road, the park has a full compliment of playing fields and more picnic areas.

Just south of Carlin Beach is a long stretch of undeveloped beach with public access. Parking is along the road and narrow trails wind from the road through heavily vegetated dunes to a beach of fine, cream-colored sand. The county has recently acquired a tract of land here for a new county park, so hopefully this lovely section of shoreline will remain open to the public.

A little further down, if you are very alert, you may be able to spot **Juno Beach Park**. The turn-off is at Celestial Way beside a small lake with a path around it. There is a small amount of parking between several low apartment buildings. To the right of the parking lot is a small grassy area with a clump of Australian pines and a sign, "beach access path." The beach is long and narrow with light-colored sand, and looks like it has suffered some fairly serious erosion. Look also in this area for **Loggerhead Park** (Pegasus Park) which has an observatory tower.

John D. MacArthur Beach State Park (10900 S.R. 703 (A1A), North Palm Beach, FL 33408; 407-627-6097) is located on Singer Island 2.8 miles south of the intersection of U.S. 1 and PGA Boulevard on A1A. It has good beach and a large amount of parking. This park is on a barrier island with a unique mixture of coastal and tropical hammock and mangroves and several rare or endangered plant species. The park has swimming, fishing, shell collecting, snorkeling, and nature study.

Ocean Reef Park, also on Singer Island, is a relatively new county beach with attractive picnic areas,
well protected from the wind. One set of individual
picnic shelters circles around a delightful children's
playground. There are good restrooms, outdoor showers, and a lifeguard. Parking lots are large, which suggests that this area could get crowded on summer
weekends.

Riviera Beach Municipal Park advertises itself as
"Florida's Finest Municipal Beach." If your idea of the
perfect beach is sand, sand, and more sand, this is it.
Riviera Beach Municipal Park is the sandiest park I've
ever seen. In addition to an especially wide beach, it
has a large sandy recreation area between the beach
and the street, with a dozen or so volleyball courts and
children's play equipment. The drawback to having so
much sand is that there isn't much shade. There are a
few carefully tended palms and some picnic shelters
with palm frond roofs, but that's it. A dune restoration
project is underway which should help to give this
area more greenery in the future. The beach is conven-
iently located across the street from an attractive en-
clave of small shops and restaurants, an amenity that
contributes a nice atmosphere to the place. Parking
could be a problem here. It is limited and metered with
a two-hour maximum.

Nearby **Palm Beach Shores** is a residential community which appears to discourage transients. The
beach parking lot requires a resident sticker and there
is absolutely no parking anywhere else. If you want to
settle down on this beach, you may want to find a
place to stay in one of the community's many small
motels or vacation apartments.

Palm Beach is a wealthy town full of mansions and
estates. You may not want to spend a long time at the
beach here, but you will definitely want to stop and

look around. Be sure to travel at least a few blocks on
Ocean Boulevard. The ocean is spectacular, the mansions are beautiful, and there are few places like this in
the United States. Most Palm Beach houses are hidden
from public view, but you may be able to get a glimpse
of some of them from the Intracoastal Waterway south
of town between SR A1A and Lake Worth or along
Ocean Boulevard north of the Breakers Hotel. One
delightful way to see the Palm Beach area is by bicycle.
To get inside at least one of those magnificent mansions, visit the Henry M. Flagler Museum in Whitehall, Flagler's opulent 55-room mansion (Coconut
Row, Palm Beach; 407-833-6870, admission). You may
also want to window shop in the little vias off Worth
Avenue.

A lot of the beach around Palm Beach and the communities further south is private property but there
are some places where those without their own personal residence can enjoy the sun. This is one of the
areas, however, where beach access is free but parking
isn't. Come prepared with lots of quarters — or in
some communities, lots of dollars.

The **Palm Beach Municipal Beach** is narrow, almost
nonexistent in many places at high tide. However
there is a lot of surfing, and the paved walkway that
runs for several miles between the ocean and the high-
rise buildings along South Ocean Boulevard is very
pleasant. Parking is limited and metered. There are
some other public stretches running south of Palm
Beach. Look for **Phipps Ocean Park**, and **Richard G.
Kreusler Park** (a developed rocky beach). The **Municipal Beach** of Lake Worth has a walkway the length of
the long beach, a large freshwater pool, and a fishing
pier with Greek food in its snack bar. There is plenty of
parking (at 25 cents for 20 minutes with an 11-hour
maximum). Just below Lake Worth is **Lantana Park**

(with lots of greenery and full beach facilities), and also **Manalapan Beach, Boynton Inlet Park,** and **Ocean Ridge Hammock Park.**

Boyton Public Beach is a beautifully landscaped park high on a ridge of dunes with a boardwalk along its entire length. There are picnic areas, restrooms, and showers here. You pay for parking at a gatehouse as you enter the beach area ($5 from May to November; $10 for oversized vehicles). Parking on the upper level, close to the beach and picnic area, is for residents only.

The town of Delray Beach emphasizes simplicity and a relaxed pace. The Gulf Stream runs close to the shore here. Look for its indigo color. There are some pleasant beaches in this area — **Gulf Stream County Park,** with white sand and full facilities, and **Delray Public Beach** with a wide attractive stretch of sand that runs along the road for a long distance. Parking meters have a four-hour maximum and cost 25 cents for 20 minutes. The entrance to **Atlantic Dunes Park** is a little hard to find and there is no parking except for lifeguards, handicapped persons, and bicycles. But the place itself is delightful with shady boardwalks, restrooms, a pleasant roofed shelter, and access to long stretches of good beach. Look for the stands of Australian pines one mile south of Delray Municipal Beach across from Azalea Avenue, then find some place to park your car and walk in.

The few public beaches in the Boca Raton area are very nice and parking is very pricey. **Red Reef Park** and **Spanish River Park** offer shade, good sand, and a variety of outstanding facilities. Visitors enter both parks through attended parking gates — fees are $10 a day on weekends and $8 a day during the week, year round. If that seems a little high, try **South Beach Park,** just south of Red Reef. It has a small amount of free, one-hour-limit parking and has full facilities, including a great shelter right on the water, lifeguards, and excellent surfing. The park runs north from the entrance with dense tropical vegetation, through which narrow paths wind down to the mocha-colored, semi-coarse sand beach.

Deerfield Beach, south of Boca Raton, runs for miles along South Ocean Way (one-way going south) and has varied terrain. Part of the park is flat beach along the street. Another section is new, with a landscaped network of walkways and picnic areas on a rise above the water. The beach here is narrow with a steep slope and looks like it has suffered some serious erosion. The whole area is pleasant, with low buildings. Parking is metered, 25 cents for 15 minutes. Nearby **Quiet Waters County Park** (6601 N. Powerline Rd., Deerfield Beach; 305-421-3133) offers 427 acres of outdoor activities including a mechanically operated water-ski tow. It is two miles west from I-95 via SR 810 (Hillsboro Blvd.), then 0.25 miles south on SR 845 (Powerline Rd.), open daily 8 a.m. to 8 p.m., admission on weekends. **Pompano Beach** is known for its abundant sunshine and a wide range of recreation activities. It has approximately twenty parks, many equipped for tennis, softball, and swimming.

Although **Fort Lauderdale's** reputation as "Spring Break Capital of Florida" hangs on, the mobs of cavorting students were far greater in the past. The city's citizens concluded several years ago that the cost of rambunctious spring-breakers just wasn't worth the business. Recently they have been making a conscious effort to discourage them and attract a quieter family clientele.

If you are ready to take a break from the sand and seas, this is a good place to do some sightseeing. You can do it by train, horse, or boat. The Water Taxi, on a

daily or weekly ticket, is a great way to see Fort Lauderdale by water. Just call the dispatcher (305-565-
5507) to arrange for a pick-up at any safe dock.

Fort Lauderdale's new artificial reefs are greatly expanding its waterfront potential. Although their primary purpose was to slow beach erosion, baby fish
find shelter in them and soft and hard corals adhere
readily to the steel and grow rapidly. They have
gained great popularity with scuba divers and one in
particular, the *Mercedes I*, is now a major diving center.
Fort Lauderdale has recently undertaken some beach
restoration efforts. The results can be seen at both
Lauderdale-by-the-Sea and **Fort Lauderdale Beach**.

The **Hugh Taylor Birch State Park** (3109 East Sunrise Blvd., Ft. Lauderdale, FL 33304; 305-564-4521) extends from the Atlantic Ocean to the Intracoastal
Waterway. Birch was driven ashore here on his sailboat
in 1893 when this was one of the most remote parts of
the American frontier. He came back to live, and when
he died he bequeathed this park so that future generations might see a remnant of the Florida he had first
found and loved. The park has a miniature train that
offers a three-mile ride through the trees and along the
waterway and a 1.7 mile exercise course around the
rim of the park.

Just north of Dania is **John U. Lloyd State Recreation Area** (6503 N. Ocean Drive, Dania, FL 33304; 305-
923-2833), a day use area with nearly two miles of
beach frontage. This is part of the long coastal route
taken during the 1880s by the barefoot mailmen who
regularly walked the beach to deliver mail to remote
settlements. Today it is one of the most popular
beaches on the lower east coast of Florida. If you expect to visit this park on a weekend from March
through September, plan to get in early. It sometimes
fills and closes by 9:30 a.m.

Further south, **Dania Beach** is an attractive winter resort with numerous antique shops and a relaxed atmosphere. **Hollywood Beach** has an especially pleasant boardwalk and stretch of pale sand lined with palms. Its Municipal Bandshell in Young Circle Park and the Theater Under the Stars offer free evening entertainment. **Hollywood North Beach Park** has lots of green and vegetation and a mile-long beachfront. There is a 2.2 mile boardwalk within the park. **Hallandale Beach** is small and often very crowded.

The Miami Beach waterfront is a study in the struggle between the forces of nature and the ingenuity of humankind. A few years ago serious erosion had all but depleted most of the beach. Today, after restoration of 9.3 miles of its length, it is wide and beautiful. But the process is ongoing. Every year several hundred thousand tons of sand have to be added to keep the beach stable. Other projects — like the construction of Beachfront Park and the 1.8-mile Promenade — are contributing to this area's rejuvenation. There are many beaches along the shore here. If the atmosphere of one does not suite your taste, try another.

Cape Florida State Recreation Area/Bill Baggs (1200 S. Crandon Blvd., Key Biscayne, FL 33149; 305-361-5811), with a mile of fine white beach, lies at the historic south end of Key Biscayne, discovered by John Cabot in 1497, less than five years after Columbus first landed in the West Indies. The trees here are all Australian pine. They give shade, but kill off all other kinds of vegetation and limit wildlife as well. The Park Service is slowly attempting to replace them with native trees. Where they have already done so, you can see a greater variety of vegetation. There is a fine restored lighthouse and keeper's house here, a bicycle trail through the park, saltwater fishing on the seawall in the bay, and good swimming year round. A beach renourishment project in 1986 widened the beach at the southern end to approximately 100 feet. This is one of the most heavily used recreational spots in the Miami area, however. It frequently reaches capacity early in the morning, and you can expect traffic jams on weekends. Plan accordingly.

Everglades National Park is not recommended for swimming. It does have a few remote wilderness beaches accessible only by boat, that are primarily used by overnight campers. Information about these is available through the National Park visitors centers (305-247-6211).

The Florida Keys are small, fragile islands strung along the coast of Florida as if flung carelessly by some giant. They conjure up images of small weathered houses along the shore, colonies of writers and artists, incredible sunsets and sunrises — in sum a tropical paradise where life is so easy and so slow you can hear the birds sing and the fish jump. Unfortunately, in most parts of the keys, that reality has passed. Space and natural resources are at a premium and are rapidly being used up by large-scale and environmentally insensitive development. There is just one long, mostly two-lane, road up and down the entire 120 miles of the keys and when even a small percentage of south Florida's population decides at the same time to search for their dreams of tropical paradise in the Florida Keys, the result is a traffic jam nightmare.

Although the keys beaches are not outstanding and beachcombers can do better almost anywhere else in Florida, snorkelers and divers will be in heaven. Outstanding coral reef parks, numerous species of brightly colored tropical fish, and clear water make this a world class diving area. And, especially in Key West, there are still places where you can experience the old Florida Key lifestyle. The beaches, though small, have their own unique Keys flavor. Look for **Harry Harris County Park** with a pleasant strip of Atlantic beach in Tavernier, Key Largo; **Upper Matecumbe County Park** with a stretch of Atlantic beach on Upper Matecumbe Key; and **Long Key State Recreation Area** (P.O. Box 776, Long Key, FL 33001; 305-664-4815) which has a narrow beach on the Atlantic side with fine waters for all activities and wonderful views of the sunrise. There are campsites right on the ocean, but also very close to U.S. 1 and its trucks. Long Key is a very popular area so make reservations early. Sombrero Beach has 1,500 feet of beach located at the end of Sombrero Beach Road on Marathon Key.

Bahia Honda State Recreation Area (Rt. 1, Box 782, Big Pine Key, FL 33043; 305-872-2353) has the finest beach in the keys, a natural wide sandy beach that slopes out into waters deep enough to show their astonishing blue-green clarity. The scene early in the morning or late in the day is stunning, as slow waves break the water into moving slices of rose, orange, and blue. Bahia Honda Key is the skeleton of an ancient coral reef, now covered by beach, dunes, and mangroves. Tropical plants and rare species of birds flourish in the warm climate. The area has camping, with a concession and dive shop. If you plan to go in the summer, take insect repellent. There are periodic swarms of mosquitoes. **Little Duck Key County Park** has 1,400 feet fronting the Atlantic Ocean on Little Duck Key, and **Big Pine Key Park** is an undeveloped county park fronting Florida Bay.

There are several beaches around Key West. **George Smathers Beach** on South Roosevelt Boulevard, **Clarence Higgs Memorial Beach** off Atlantic Boulevard, and **South Beach** at the south end of Duval Street. **Fort Zachery Taylor State Historic Site** (P.O. Box 289, Key West, FL 33041; 305-292-6713) has one of the most pleasant beaches in the area, with a shaded picnic region. For a really primitive, isolated beach find someone with a boat or take a seaplane to **Fort Jefferson National Monument** on Garden Key in the Dry Tortugas.

References

American Automobile Association, *AAA Tourbook: Florida*. Heathrow, FL: AAA, 1991.

Bartram, William, *Travels*. New York: Penguin, 1988 (first published in 1791).

Beach Access Project, *An Access Guide: Florida's Sandy Beaches*. Pensacola: Univ. of West Florida Press, 1985.

Bigelow, Gordon E., *Frontier Eden: The Literary Career of Marjorie Kinnan Rawlings*. Gainesville: Univ. of Florida, 1966.

Bullen, Adelaide K., *Florida Indians of Past and Present*. Gainesville: Kendall Books, 1965.

Cerwinske, Laura, *Tropical Deco: The Architecture and Design of Old Miami Beach*. New York: Rizzoli, 1981.

Coleman, James C. and Irene S. Coleman, *Guardians on the Gulf: Pensacola Fortifications, 1689-1980*. Pensacola: Pensacola Historical Society, 1981.

Derr, Mark, *Some Kind of Paradise: A Chronicle of Man and the Land in Florida*. New York: William Morrow & Co., 1989.

Dimock, A. W. and Julian A. Dimock, *Florida Enchantments*. New York: The Outing Publishing Co., 1908.

Douglas, Marjory Stoneman. *The Everglades: River of Grass*. St. Simons Island, GA: Mockingbird Press, 1947.

Federal Writers, State of Florida. *Florida: A Guide to the Southernmost State*. New York: Oxford Univ. Press, 1939, "Archeology and Indians": 36-47.

Florida Division of Recreation and Parks, *Florida State Parks: 1990-91*. Tallahassee: Dept. of Natural Resources, 1990.

Florida Division of Tourism, *See Florida: Vacation Guide, 1990-1991*. Tallahassee: Dept. of Commerce, 1990.

Francke, Arthur E., Jr., *Steamboats of DeBary Merchants Line and Debary Baya Merchants Line*. Orange City, FL: Sun State Printers, 1987.

Gill, Joan E. and Beth R. Read (eds.), *Born of the Sun*. Hollywood, FL: Official Florida Bicentennial Commemorative Journal, Inc. of Worth International Communications Corp., 1975.

Gleasner, Bill and Diana Gleasner, *Florida: Off the Beaten Path*. Charlotte, N.C.: East Woods Press, 1985.

Grow, Gerald, *Florida Parks: A Guide to Camping in Nature*. 4th ed. Tallahassee: Longleaf Pub., 1989.

Hiller, Herbert L., *Guide to the Small and Historic Lodgings of Florida*, 2nd ed. Sarasota: Pineapple Press, 1988.

Hoffman, Carl Timothy, *The Early History of Pensacola*. Pensacola: Pensacola Historical Society, 1980.

Howard, Robert J., *The Best Small Towns Under the Sun*. McLean, VA: EPM Publications, 1989.

Hurston, Zora Neale, *Their Eyes Were Watching God*. Urbana: Univ. of Illinois Press, 1937.

Jahoda, Gloria, *Florida: A History*. New York: W. W. Norton, 1976.

Jahoda, Gloria, *The Other Florida*. Port Salerno, FL: Florida Classics Library, 1967.

Kaufelt, David A. American Tropic: A Novel of Florida. N.Y.: Pocket, 1986.

Kennedy, Stetson, *Palmetto Country*. New York: Duell, Sloan & Pearce, 1942.

Laumere, Frank, *Massacre!*. Gainesville: Univ. of Florida Press, 1968.

Leslie, Candace, *Hidden Florida Keys and Everglades*. Berkeley: Ulysses Press, 1990.

Leslie, Candace, Marty Olmstead, Stacy Ritz, Chelle Koster Walton, *Hidden Florida*. Berkeley: Ulysses Press, 1989.

Marth, Del & Martha J. Marth, *The Florida Almanac: 1986-87*. Gretna, LA: Pelican Publishing Co., 1985.

Milanich, Jerald T. and Charles H. Fairbanks, *Florida Archaeology*. Orlando: Academic Press, 1987.

Neill, Wilfred T., *Florida's Seminole Indians*. St. Petersburg: Great Outdoors Publishing Co. 1956.

Parks, Virginia, *Pensacola: Spaniards to Space-Age*. Pensacola: Pensacola Historical Society, 1986.

Parks, Virginia, Alan Rick, & Norman Simons, *Pensacola in the Civil War*. Pensacola: Pensacola Historical Society, 1978.

Pratt, Theodore, *The Barefoot Mailman*. St. Simons Island, GA: Mockingbird Press, 1943.

Puterbaugh, Parke and Alan Bisbort, *Life is a Beach: A Vacationer's Guide to the East Coast*. New York: McGraw-Hill, 1986.

Ritz, Stacy and Marty Olmstead, *Hidden Miami, Fort Lauderdale and Palm Beach: The Adventurer's Guide*.

Rosenan, Jack C., Glen L. Faulkner, Charles W. Hendry, Jr., Robert W. Hull, *Springs of Florida*. Tallahassee, U.S. Geological Survey, 1977.

Scalpone, Joan Lundquist, *Florida's Bubbling Springs*. Punta Gorda, FL: Mini-Day Trip Books, 1989.

Springer, Marylyn and Schultz, Donald, *Frommer's Florida, 1990*. New York: Simon & Schuster, 1989.

Strickland, Alice, *Ormond-on-the-Halifax*. Ormond Beach, FL: Southeast Publishing Co, 1980.

Tebeau, Charlton W. with C. S. "Ted" Smallwood, *The Story of the Chokoloskee Bay Country*. Miami: Banyan Books, 1976.

Tebeau, Charlton W., *A History of Florida*. Coral Gables, FL: Univ. of Miami Press, 1971.

Tebeau, Charlton W., *Man in the Everglades*. Miami: Univ. of Miami Press, 1968.

Waterburg, Jean Parker (ed.), *The Oldest City: St.*

Augustine, Saga of Survival. St. Augustine: The St. Augustine Historical Society, 1983.

Williams, Joy, *The Florida Keys: From Key Largo to Key West.* New York: Random House, 1987.

Wolverton, Ruthe and Walt Wolverton, *The National Seashores.* Kensington, MD: Woodbine House, 1988.

Wright, J. Lleitch, *British St. Augustine.* St. Augustine: Historic St. Augustine Preservation Board, 1975.

Zach, Paul and Fred W. Wright, Jr. (eds.) *Insight Guide: Florida.* Singapore: APA Productions, Ltd, 1987.

INDEX

accommodations, 38-50; publications on, 40-41, 45, 46, 49; *see
also* hotels; inns; motels
Afro-Americans, 86, 91, 97, 99,
113, 135, 162-165
air travel, 23, 31
Amelia Island, 86, 119, 312-313
American, expeditions, 95-96;
and Seminole Indians, 97-116;
settlements, 97-116
Amtrak, 24-25, 31-32
Apalachee Indians, 69, 71, 73
Apalachicola, 52, 118, 128, 168,
171
apartments, 40, 44
archaeological sites, 72, 73, 75,
76, 77, 80
architecture, 193, 194-196, 271
astronaut hall of fame, 201, 207,
208
Audubon, John James, 106, 243,
270
backpacking, 37, 247
Bartlett, Frederick Clay, 187
bathhouses, 295, 310, 323
Battle of Natural Bridge, 130-132
battles, 101, 108-112; Civil War,
121, 123, 129-132, 256; *see also*
Seminole Indian Wars
beaches, 37, 57, 253, 258, 261,
269, 283-288, 289-311, 312-339;
central east r., 317-325; central
west r., 300-305; driving on,

286-288, 314, 315, 316, 318,
319; ecology, 284, 285-286,
288; northeast r., 312-317;
northwest r., 289-300; southeast r., 325-338; southwest r.,
305-311; with lifeguards, 324,
332, 333
bed and breakfasts, 40, 44-46
bicycle, racks, 310; rentals, 274;
trails, 32, 255, 293, 306; travel
by, 32-33
bicycling, 255, 262, 274, 280, 303,
319, 325, 331
Big Scrub, 266-267
birdwatching, 61-62, 245, 263,
270, 272, 281
Blacks *see* Afro-Americans
boardwalks, 275, 323, 327, 332,
335; trails, 274, 281
boats, charter, 253; docks, 273;
harbors, 236; marinas, 302;
ramps, 254, 268, 295, 303;
rental, 33-34, 281; tours, 173,
229, 236, 269, 272, 279, 281,
333; travel by, 33-34
boating, 220, 231, 245, 247, 249,
262, 280, 281, 290, 295, 309,
310, 314, 317
Boca Raton, 183, 185, 195
Bok, Edward W., 192-193
botanical sites, 280-281
Bulow, John, 106, 107
burial grounds, 77, 237

343

308, 315, 320, 329
sinks and springs, central east r.,
226, 242-244; central r., 226,
239-242; central west r., 226,
236-239, 261; first magnitude
springs, 219, 227, 228, 229,
230, 231-232, 234, 236, 237,
239, 241, 242; northeast r.,
225-226, 233-236, 260;
norhtwest r., 221, 222-233, 255
snorkeling, 57-59, 127, 214, 219,
227, 230, 237, 290, 304, 325,
329, 336
southeast region, 80, 148-150,
252, 276-282, 325, 338
southwest region, 69, 79-80, 147-
148, 252, 271-276, 305-211
space exploration, 199, 204-207
Space Mirror, 205-206
Spaceport USA, 201, 204
space shuttle, 206-207, 208-209
Spain, 73, 85-87, 92, 95, 97, 243,
284-285, 316; artifacts, 93-95;
expeditions, 69-70, 71, 80-84,
162; settlements, 88
Spanish -American War, 159,
160, 167, 176, 303-304
St. Augustine, 76, 84, 85, 87-91,
119, 121, 125-126, 128, 162,
171, 177-178, 315-316
steamboats, 166-169, 232, 233,
236, 256; era of, 166-169, 173-
174
St. Marks Wildlife Refuge, 254-
255
St. Petersburg, 140, 146, 172, 183
surfing, 59-60, 305, 314, 323, 324,
331, 333
swamps, 248-249, 271, 275, 310
swimming, 57, 215, 219, 222, 223,

226, 230-231, 232, 235, 236,
237, 238, 239, 241, 242, 244,
245, 249, 253, 259, 280, 295,
301, 303, 306, 308, 309, 310,
312, 315, 316, 319, 323, 325,
327, 328, 329, 333, 335
Tallahassee, 76, 121, 130, 132,
140-144, 183-184, 191, 221
Tampa, 102, 159, 161, 172
Tarpon Springs, 144, 158-159
Teed, Cyrus Reed, 190-199
Tequesta Indians, 69, 80, 188
Timucuan Indians, 69, 71, 77, 78-
79
Titusville, 206, 207, 208
tourism, 18-19, 167, 181-185, 197
tourist information services, 20-
22, 299
tours, 87, 93, 108, 111, 127, 155-
156, 161, 187, 191, 208, 222,
233, 255-256, 263, 274, 275,
278, 308; airboat, 281; archaeological, 92; boat, 173,
220, 236, 269, 272, 279, 281,
333; bus, 204-205; canoe, 272;
carriage, 88; hiking, 272; self-
guided, 145, 195; walking, 37,
87-88, 137, 161, 173, 196, 205
trails, 65, 83, 112, 129, 247, 262,
274, 314, 325; bicycle, 32, 255,
293, 306; boardwalk, 274, 281;
canoe, 34, 35, 228, 240, 267,.
273, 282; handicapped-
accessible, 37; hiking, 37, 260,
263, 267, 271, 313; historic, 26,
249; horse, 35-36, 223, 253-
254, 267, 271, 280, 323;
interpretative, 261; nature, 37,
62, 223, 230, 231, 237, 240, 242,
249, 253, 254, 255, 258, 260,

r.= region in subheadings

DISCOVER THE COUNTRY WITH HIPPOCRENE U.S.A. GUIDES!

THE CHICAGO AREA:
NATURE AND HISTORY WITH 200 MILES
GERALD and PATRICIA GUTEK
Over 80 family outings to suit all tastes and ages.
0718 ISBN 0-87052-036-9 $14.95 paper

By the same authors:
EXPLORING THE AMERICAN WEST:
A GUIDE TO MUSEUM VILLAGES
Featuring 30 sites in California, Arizona, New Mexico, Colorado, Wyoming, Oregon, and Washington. *"A wonderful source of historical information...a gold mine for travelers"*--Library Journal
0061 ISBN 0-87052-793-2 $11.95 paper

EXPLORING MID-AMERICA:
A GUIDE TO MUSEUM VILLAGES
Featuring 22 sites in Iowa, Minnesota, Kansas, Nebraska, the Dakotas, Arkansas, Oklahoma, and Texas.
0412 ISBN 0-87052-643-X $14.95 paper

AMERICA'S HEARTLAND:
A TRAVEL GUIDE TO THE BACKROADS OF ILLINOIS, INDIANA, IOWA, KANSAS AND MISSOURI (Expanded edition)
TOM WEIL
2320 ISBN 0-87052-038-5 $16.95 paper

By the same author:
AMERICA'S SOUTH:
A TRAVEL GUIDE TO THE ELEVEN SOUTHERN STATES
The only available single-volume guide covering Virginia, the Carolinas, Georgia, Alabama, Mississippi, Louisiana, Kentucky, Tennessee, Arkansas, and Florida. *"You'll enjoy this"*--St. Louis Home
0393 ISBN 0-87052-611-1 $17.95 paper

GUIDE TO BLACK AMERICA
MARCELLA THUM
Historic homes, art and history museums, parks, monuments, landmarks of the civil rights movement, battlefields and forts, colleges and churches throughout the United States.
0722 ISBN 0-87052-045-8 $11.95 paper

THE GUIDE TO BLACK WASHINGTON:
PLACES AND EVENTS OF HISTORICAL AND CULTURAL SIGNIFICANCE IN THE NATION'S CAPITAL
SANDRA FITZPATRICK and MARIA GOODWIN
"Wonderful"--Kathryn Smith, President, Washington Historical Society
0025 ISBN 0-87052-832-7 $14.95 paper

WEST POINT AND THE HUDSON VALLEY
GALE KOHLHAGEN and ELLEN HEINBACH
Foreword by GENERAL DAVE R. PALMER, SUPERINTENDENT OF WEST POINT
An insider's guide to the stories, sites, cadet life and lore of the U.S. Military Academy; with side trips to great estates, historic sites, and wineries.
0083 ISBN 0-87052-889-0 $14.95 paper

UNCOMMON AND UNHERALDED MUSEUMS
BEVERLY NARKIEWICZ and LINCOLN S. BATES
500 regional and thematic museums across the nation.
0052 ISBN 0-87052-956-0 $14.95 paper

RV:
TRAVEL LEISURELY YEAR ROUND
ROLANDA DUMAIS MASSE
Practical, first-hand advice on living in a recreational vehicle with independence and economy.
0058 ISBN 0-87052-958-7 $14.95 paper

EXPLORING THE BERKSHIRES (Revised)
HERBERT S. WHITMAN
Illustrated by ROSEMARY FOX
"A gem of a book"--Conde Nast's *Traveler*
0925 ISBN 0-87052-979-X $9.95 paper

By the same authors:
EXPLORING NANTUCKET
"Anyone contemplating a visit to this island would benefit from this book"
Library Journal
0046 ISBN 0-87052-792-4 $11.95 paper

TO PURCHASE HIPPOCRENE'S BOOKS contact your local bookstore, or write to Hippocrene Books, 171 Madison Avenue, New York, NY 10016. Please enclose a check or money order, adding $3 shipping (UPS) for the first book, and 50 cents for each of the others.